VIA Folios 74

This Poem Exists in Two States.

1. Print. The volume *Ellis Island* is an epic composed of 624 14-line poems called "sonnets," arranged in 52 groups of twelve, called "books." The sonnets are best when read aloud and not too many of them at a time.

2. On-line. *ellisislandpoem.com* is a site where you can read random sonnets that use lines from the 624 sonnets in the epic. The number of possible random sonnets is 624 to the 14th power. The actual number is written out on the cover of this book. The site also includes things a reader of the work might find interesting or useful. You can also follow the poem and read one line a day at the following sites:

www.facebook.com/ellisislandpoem
www.twitter.com/ellisislandpoem
www.ellisislandpoem.tumblr.com

ellis island

Library of Congress Control Number: 2012906018

Photo on back cover: Nora Almeida

Printed in the United States.

Published by
BORDIGHERA PRESS
John D. Calandra Italian American Institute
25 W. 43rd Street, 17th Floor
New York, NY 10036

VIA Folios 74
ISBN 978–1–59954–033–7

ellis island

ROBERT VISCUSI

BORDIGHERA PRESS

My father would have preferred I do something else.
But if I could send him this book,
he would do as he did with my others:
bring copies of it to his friends.

This book is for him.

ellis island

table of contents

ellis island

ellis island

1. the stories disintegrate you like waves

1.1

certain things do not make for good poetry
you write them because you hope to open your heart
which you have closed too many times

people who hurt you for years
now complain that you have hurt them
how do you decide what to do about these wounds

you have decided to expect nothing precisely
so that your own imperfections will not astonish you
nor will the imperfections of others drive you to fury

the music flows through the room where you are dancing
you have decided to feel something while no one is looking
or simply to allow the breeze to touch you

you have perfected a poetry of attitudes and remarks
totally useless at a picnic on the water

1.1–1.2

1.2

in the boat on the way to ellis island
the people group themselves according to nationality
the taiwanese guide leads his group with a triangular blue flag

the humiliation of a greek mystery cult assails you
climbing into the roman bath where you sit in rows
the goddess liberty announces the completion of the ocean outside

the lovers row past the red buoys in the harbor
the speedboats skirt close to the green buoys
the ferries churn in straight lines like dreams of a schedule

in the great hall the brilliance of the new world blinds you
you only see its grandeur as if you were a caesar
the children pass through the bronze doors to the future

on the esplanade you dissolve in light
becoming a mist

1.3

i was reading the story of stories of stories
they tell on the walls of ellis island
the stories disintegrate you like waves

they break you into a thousand thousand faces
looking out at the skyline from the ships
which of them do you become

you flutter across the stories like a wave
you are the change of shadow on the stories of stories
and the soft backwash of tiny waves on the narrow beach

you are not a story but an aspect of a story's story
and though you had expected a more substantial career
you appreciate the lightning swiftness of your influence

you are the eyes that transform the city
giving it the softness of napoli

1.3–1.4

1.4

you were from barbados you were from jamaica
you were from the caymans you were from puerto rico
you were from guyana you were from harlem

you were from trinidad you were from india
you were from argentina you were from france
you were from england you were from mexico

you were from russia you were from west africa
you were from north africa you were from east africa
you were from north carolina your grandfather went to utah

her mother had a serious operation and died
the snow fell for three weeks without stopping in toronto
the wind covered the bodies under drifts that froze solid

the mountains melted and the rivers filled
and you continued flowing in from the ocean

1.5

we ourselves came across high north ridges
that afterwards sank into the ocean long before stories begin
we only remember these highlands as the names of birds

you only know us as a supposition
stranded in the high room where they check you for vermin
and you look out into the river that disappears into the mountains

steep cliffs on the mainland side behind which we fell back
we inhabit the continent as the blind spots of your imagination
so you look and you see everything except us

even though we are standing behind all the trees with tomahawks
we mean to drive you out as we can hide from your mind but it is not enough
we cannot seem to avoid the power of your blindness

it still beats against the atlantic from which we fell back
long swells of you mass in pyramids like beetles of the dawn

1.6

i have been thinking how they designed the place
as a ritual entrance into the imaginary universe
using the masonic formulae for a rite that would change you

did they mean it as a spectacle of purification
they wanted to quiet the fears of nativists
who feared infection as if it were as evil as cheap labor

or did they mean to work magic on all these calibans
the immigration police played prospero and used masonic spells
to tame and to tag the incoming flocks of workers

living organisms the immigration service saw as homer saw armies
generations of leaves flash brightest on the trees just before they die
important to ship efficiently off to farms and mining camps

this jeffersonian church could rename a parish priest a son of liberty
and a figment of the continent's imaginings

1.7

you tella me what thing you wanta me to know
the mandolins are sounding in the background music
the couple stands on the quay kissing as if it were paris

it is paris
on ellis island begins the dark eternal paris
imaginary streets materialize before your eyes

just yesterday this place was tomorrow
whereas by this morning it had already become next week
and by that time it will be the next millennium in chicago

we are shooting there on light beams
which the women wear as dildos
and the men display in parking lots across the sky

i have read these dreams in the notebooks of leon battista alberti
and the imaginary character of america is its most italian aspect

1.7-1.8

1.8

whatever you start it always ends up italian
she said that to me because she loves oldfashioned culture
which is to say italian men

who believe we indicate elegance arrogance intelligence
by patriarchal hand on hip and steady commanding gaze
which we inherit as parrots inherit green feathers

though i might rather be a black snake with diamonds on his teeth
or the purple of a field of wildflowers
i am only one of these human cockatoos

who designed the parthenon the pantheon palladium
and all the mausoleum gardens of the marble mountains
that we filled with domes and porticoes

you keep tasting italian culture you think is no good for you
but a rainforest needs its brilliant creatures

ellis island

1.9

into the still haze the italians brought red food
where all the food used to be brown and yellow and white
even when it was supposed to have had seeds and visible buds

and the italians brought a green oil that made the food green
under the misty blur they wore black hair
and rode black horses into the dreams of white women

they wore white clothes and broke granite with hammers
so that their very eyelids thickened with powdered stone
as if michelangelo were conjuring a frieze of laborers

the italians brought fish frying in the streets
an aroma that drew people out of their houses at night
where they listened to mandolins by moonlight

americans who had lived in the frames of photographs
made the italians rich with their generous tips

1.10

they said to us since you are italian learn to sing
tell jokes dance and make beautiful clothes
unless you are willing to study latin

in which case we have a steady market for italian schoolteachers
italian lawyers italian priests and politicians
and now we have given them the police force to run in fifty cities

we considered ourselves a race of heroes
from julius caesar to garibaldi
we would have rather been bandits than busdrivers

but in this country they offered a pension
a beach house a restaurant if you were willing to work that hard
so we studied our little lessons

shrinking into comfortable wooden yodelers on clocks
we still do find huge broken italian heroes covered with graffiti

1.11

on ellis island the stories howl through me like storms
a noise with nothing to say except what meaning attaches itself
to your skin in the touch of someone that loves you

here we enter a vast space neither sky nor sea
digging the subways they brought dirt here in barges
and made this well positioned plot

we think of this as the isle of possibilities
we talk about the future as if we could touch it
and explore each other's faces as if we were concave mirrors

the trees here inhabit a perpetual hallucination
they think themselves to be sea creatures
monumental crustaceans evolved when the sea still filled with lava

we were facing the water and thinking ten thousand nights
awaiting a single dawn

1.11–1.12

1.12

i fell past needles of silver skyscrapers and woke up damp
when the tall steamer foghorns blat out their arrival going by the bed vibrates
i wanted to stand in line outside the building for a hundred years

i don't want to go through with it now
maybe later i want think it over
the policeman touched me and said do you want to come in the side door

he was making a scary joke to get me up and walking
i think he didn't really mean it but it doesn't matter
every window i look out of i see another wave full of dead bodies

white faces lie on the gleaming plate of the bay at night
bodies cluster under the docks
they remove them with hooks like logs

in the boat there was one woman who never stopped crying for her mother
i call her a woman because she had a baby in her arms but she was herself a child

2. are you ready to inhabit another country altogether

2.1

so here i see the bones of what i never knew
of those i never touched although imagined more than all of them
i thought before arriving

now i have been climbing this road
it rises up one of these volcanic hills
overlooks the town but itself contains the old town

i met a woman old as a lizard in 1986
claiming to remember my grandmother's wedding in 1905
before she left for ellis america

had i imagined her
did she know that my grandmother left my grandfather in schenectady
and ran away with the boarder and her four sons to greenpoint

she remembers wars weddings weather the germans
the empty spaces in the hills the people left behind

2.1–2.2

2.2

fly me to san francisco i would think among the roman hills
where the noble weather dries the cypresses in sand
hot wind drives you wild at night

i saw priests in purple riding bikes
full to bursting with frustrations
including mine

i would buy can openers and screwdrivers
each one glowing with its roman-ness
the touch of italian hands

italian air and food and flowers and dreams
television songs full of echoes i knew but couldn't name
a certain reckless dancing when they talk to you

especially when they like you they move in a way i remember
i tap my fingers to the music

2.3

they drew a dark curtain across the sky
the streets became ovens where the high sahara air
turned the cloudless sky black

the trees shivered in the glittering heat
the oleander poured oil into its leaves
and the buses rolled down past porta del popolo

each person moved slowly
at these moments you look straight down into primeval rome
the cats leave african shadows on the walls

the shallow rivers fill with water buffalos
you hear sailors cursing through the brilliant midnight
you smell the sweet sacrifice

you would be sure you were not dreaming had you not already noticed
how even the sun is asleep in the heat

2.3–2.4

2.4

do not touch me there
touch me here
i am stretched out in your light

i have turned in your direction
full of pain and wondering
am i a human like you

i have been walking up and down watching your campfire
you cannot see me because of the underbrush
so i thought

now you want to come through my doors
you say there is something worth looking at in here
i'm waiting please soon

two imaginary worlds touch in the dark
rivers join where the valleys come together

2.5

i am moving my legs
my feet are moving
and i am singing the famous eating and drinking song

the restaurant has been open for hours
i decided to sit down and you came in just then
i am playing the guitar and hoping you notice

you are not married to your mistakes
they don't remember you
so you are free to answer me when i ask you a question

supposing i found a wall between us
who put it there while i wasn't looking
i am free to answer this question as well

instead we tango
bat the tambourine

2.6

a century of amusing conversation
comes and goes like annoyance calls
and so i began rowing my oar

i saw the gleam of the light on the windows
the towers were like trees
i lived in your jungle

i could no longer sit still
the pain of my self imposed prison began to cut my flesh
i stood up and walked through it as if underwater

walking towards you
wherever you are
forgetting the plans of the jail

this is a tremendous blues of dispersal
the echoes keep changing languages in the colonnade

2.7

you have never seen a human wheel turning
as it rolls heavily down the avenue of transformation
the metal hoop clattering on the cobble stones

bits of hay cling to the driver's sleeve
the sour street smells of horses
as they begin the upward drag

i am such a wagon of a human being who is changing
if you listen to me talking you hear the spanish lisp
and when i walk it is work

i feel the weight as well as the lightness of things
they are playing the spanish flute in the piazza
now you hear my axle creak as i turn the corner

even this slow procession amounts to dancing
and what is that song your friends are singing

2.7–2.8

2.8

in the piazza of singing and dancing we sit listening to the band
eating and drinking all look different if you fall in love
are you ready to inhabit another country altogether

you came to ellis island to leave your thousand dried out selves
at ellis island you forswear the personal past
the entire ritual consists of dismissing objections

the old rules of europe dissolve in the salt of the harbor
spend the rest of your lives telling each other what they were
and you still will remember nothing of what they meant

you remove your coat pulling the thick zipper one tooth at a time
you remove each sleeve separately there are twenty zippers
at last you lay the heavy mantle on the sand

now you disappear into the air of the brilliant bay
the air like the water has its own laws its own domain

2.9

you are struggling towards freedom you said
you could imagine freedom as a glass of cold water in the shade
although you knew it would include a taste of the beyond

the border policeman asked you the purpose of your retreat
you thought of the past and the future and then replied research
he wanted to know is that business or pleasure

you could taste the salt of perspiration
enjoying the feel of your upper lip
and still not be certain this is freedom

you could wade through the evidence without reading it
or read without understanding as you so often did
so that the meaning of the book became the desire to understand it

but they had turned all the words in the book inside out
all the evidence as you read it became folksongs

2.9–2.10

2.10

now you have imagined it as a piano in tune
on this piano you play reveries of great masters
who look through the web of things

you tune your body through meditation
you discover its wild irregularities
rumblings and catastrophes

meditation leads you on so that the water grows occasionally still
you see what harmonies produce light
afterwards you know them when you see them

stir the water with your hand
the ship founders and you set it right
only breathe the swami says so you breathe

the skyline fills with tall trees that pose like dancers
as the wind begins you blow the air through your puckered lips

2.11

tuning can be difficult if you strain at it
often the only thing you can do is let the storms pass through you
the rage of a cornered animal saves its life sometimes

if the buffalo farts he keeps away busybodies
attracting those who prefer a relaxed attitude
and enjoy the water more than clothes

walk naked across the marble floor in your thinking apartment
i am sitting on the couch reading the newspapers
i don't know why i hate myself so much as i do

even this hatred resembles a fog on the bay
yes it may be real but this water moves through the whole world
so that when you arrive you are already leaving

when you hear the sounds of change you call it music
when you dance you write the future on the air

2.11–2.12

2.12

death is a step towards becoming a part of the stone
the larger life of things has produced its moss and its foliage
it has produced your dark haired body

now you roam under the first light of creation
leading a tribe of persons reciting the names of their gods
burning their offerings wherever their path may cross another

through reciting the names as well your mind will rest in the rhythms
it will find among these nameless hills and valleys new passages
it hears them in songs or opening in the movements of dancers

from the mountain all the air is blue but rome is a rose
it shows vividly how thought can follow some vague rhythm of historical time
your baboon eyes can sometimes see such things clearly

what you leave may lie on the table as a mark to signify hunger
even the whispered hopes of lovers can accumulate a tidal force

3. you are seeking an italian in you that nobody sees

3.1

my book mountains breed their own goats
bad breathing theory bears howl down out of the pages
a thousand words a minute i can't keep up with them

all you want to know might be right here your retreat comfort
but a same old summer parade continues
the screaming has nothing to do with books

in my old dream the chorus of old people is laughing at me
the fat ladies mothers of others their fathers their brothers
and i defy them hands on hips in the tarantella

this dream shows how the mind bends the heart
remember to observe these forms taking shape as you look at people
watch how you paint them into this scornful chorus

you probably will see many people differently now
and your natural affections will begin to flow

3.1-3.2

3.2

you have learned well to drive away people
whom you then follow with apologies
which may or may not be lies

you had hoped to leave this personality behind
you made the appropriate gestures spoke the formulae
but there you remained exactly as you had begun

you have been turning off the music of wilful change
and preparing yourself not to make but to see and hear changes
like a jesuit in japan forgetting aristotle and learning to breathe

that things braid in transformation makes for snakes
explains the flourishing of rivers
the tideland grasses and the infinity of beetles

so the golden god of naples whom you carried west
brightens walls and altars simply by suggestion

3.3

i am afraid some of the time in my hole like a squirrel
when i come out every sound terrifies me
i turn my head quickly and stand still to confound my enemies

other times i make plans suitable for building a world empire
much of the day i think of nothing except the broom and shovel
tall cornices that shade us with deep colors

in my cage without bars i place people by their understandings
which if i do it long enough and quietly enough
teaches me to say things that make sense to them

each book i study requires me to learn another simplicity
so that the more i read the stupider i get
this hope sustains the scholar

he breathes thick thoughts heavy with the smell of the tomb
returning them to the world as air and light

3.3-3.4

3.4

we began ceremonies of purification at ellis island
that have lasted a century
cleansing ourselves of europe scraping it out of our skin

some say it is because we want to be americans but what is that
let us refer not to the national ideas of american colonies
let us consider the idea of the maker vespucci

americans are naked astronauts
facciavamo di loro quello che volevamo vespucci writes
we made of them whatever we wanted

of ourselves we italians who entered the condition of americans
we wished to make chinese and japanese siberian indians
because india is the homeland of god

and now when we say europe we speak of a manifestation of god
one among many

3.5

let your flowers blossom in silence
you have chosen a path of discovery
we taught to messer marco polo

on this path you meet many who can explain everything
or always enough to show you do not understand
so you keep walking as long as it takes

noone can tell you this in advance though you will have intimations
these sometimes turn out mirages of desire
in such moments a prepared silence avoids folly

the ocean resembles preparation
and embodies rituals the lesser gods perform
teaching the reverence all things command

you were surprised to learn these teachings
which jesus himself had studied in the quiet places of the sun

3.5–3.6

3.6

outside your window the straw hat horse blows trumpet
a poison dwarf scuttles stinking through the house
and you poison her in return

between you only dreams of revenge
only plans to punish the world for your misery
which of you is worse

she thinks she is crying out in hunger and hurts you at every turn
you with the same result think you are crying out in hunger
so you both see monsters

to suffer each other's arthritic joints
to see the horror of your own angry face
these are prices of change

we have opened the laboratory of rising curtains
no one knows what is going to happen next

3.7

on ellis island you can't tell who is what without reading labels
everywhere you look a story begins
what were you looking for

italian means a certain stillness in the gaze
in family life everyone knows your damnation
you are seeking an italian in you that nobody sees

we speak of the past when we mean the future
hold your eyes steady and expect people to have spots like cattle
the interbreeding of morals has begun

you've thought and thought and now you are ready to take the boat
you are wearing your new identity the italian person
which provides you a neighborhood a club a job a wife

seek and ye shall find says the man at the information booth
hunger drives you and the red on the tomatoes draws you

3.7-3.8

3.8

they had a great time erecting the statue of italia
four hundred two by fours in various lengths supported the shell
she had a spoky diadem like liberty and a golden robe

you hid on the third floor not to say hello to the hated grocer
the band was forming under your window practicing the italian hymn
you tended to grow serious on such mornings

the red white and green sash you also hated convinced you
italy existed though it had forgotten you existed
while in fact it did not altogether exist but did remember you

we were waiting for one another in different places again
and have yet to consummate identity
though we have dedicated two volumes to its history

the passion for travel has defined italians
who came down out of asia many thousands

3.9

i have been learning to choose a button and push
in the old days i would punch the machine and something came out
good bad indifferent i needed reassurance the machine still worked

i point my finger at a target
guilt is fear and remorse is also fear
these waves beat against the wall

your head rises as you follow the geese with your eyes
your back bends like a bow and the rifle rises
you do this a thousand times before you draw the trigger

choose and you become another animal
your gaze seeks its single object through the leaves
your pace grows steady and soft

you remember the story of the great discoverer
who stared at a blind beggar and saw the eyes of god

3.10

everything is changing now
my legs are empty and soon my whole body will be empty
this is what comes of sitting still and waiting

my mask has grown older i am no longer a boy
i am no longer an adolescent or a young man or a man in his forties
i am entering the condition of silver ape

at the doorway stand doctors and insurance men
the very hairs of your head are all numbered they say
and so you begin counting steps and breathing beautiful tunes

as you step onto the platform of this morning you think of eagles
even if the birds are only charming rather than heroic
still they terrify the things they eat

under this blue sky two leaves tell you a tree's whole story
in you their perfume magnifies as if you were air

3.11

to change you lay down on the floor
you kept inventing reasons to exist
now you no longer exist and so can stop inventing

you become sunlight gleams on water
you slip through crowds like a greyhound
an intelligent breeze leads you along someone's trail

the trail attracts companions
together you pool clues and you arrange encounters
what can poets know of the hunt you ask

you used to be the fastest horse in the valley
and now you are the highest horse on the mountain
you stand at the mouth of the cave and watch the oyster sunrise

one morning you return to the condition of a human being
your hands polish the shield and javelin

3.11–3.12

3.12

knowing nothing has opened you to knowledge
spasms of knowing appear along your arms
as shadows leave tattoos

people sitting near you hear a constant murmur
mouth will hum while teeth will tell a story
your hands tell time and scratch

the only path to the italian past is the path of your body
where are written secrets in writing only history can read
these magic words can change the world but no one can say them

you don't look italian and you speak the language in a peculiar way
because you are one of the italians cast loose into the sky
found a hundred years later lying on the ground of another planet

you are a broken statue of the future
no one cares how you got there

ellis island

4. each man awakens one morning surprised on the altar

4.1

waves of the faithful were thronging the chair that carried him
the roar reminded him of youth near the lake
it would rain at night

the dome rose from the horizon like the sun
filling rome with a quiet perfumed heat
mountain women laid out corn to dry on blankets

the day they made him cardinal he remembered red lusts
he had carried them in his quiver through riverbank forests
had hidden them in receptacles inside sulphur smelling caves

at the sound of the trumpet the entire crowd began to sing
the piazza was swaying underneath him like a gondola
then the lights went up

he walked out into the brilliant afternoon of long island city
pope no more

4.1–4.2

4.2

you would have liked to know the meaning of america
i touch you and when you have digested that you touch me in turn
this is the making of meaning though not of america's in particular

of all possible americas which one is a necessity this morning
we revise epics concerning breakfast
we shout hallo in the pancake house in columbus

i have been reading a book about food anyway
how they chopped the water chestnuts before steaming
how they flooded the avenue of willows

everywhere we look we see lines dividing fields
even in fields of air the parallel i-beams gleam
and the rivers partition themselves into fountains

i have been driving all day in this airconditioned japanese car
my mouth is dry

4.3

going inland by easy stages i find lakes that lead to rivers
from cincinnati to the gulf of mexico i make my way by motorboat
i have caught fish in the freshwater fan at the mouth of the amazon

under every boardwalk you hear the incomprehensible ocean churn
snow melts on mountains whose slopes collect rain in channels
cataracts punctuate streams that cut paths through layers of slate

the mississippi floods the plains painting everything with mud
waters run through the lands from ocean to ocean
the solid land is the watery planet turning its skin to the sun

we are creatures of the dark peace in the black night
where even the burning air flows over our perspiration in waves
and cools us with a swift atlantic shift of gesture

the canals rise and fall with the tides of the lagoon
we steam the crabs with seaweed on the wide beach

4.3–4.4

4.4

capital flows in eddies
the rain collects in the gutters
the leaves lie under the still water as if it were a thick shadow

every time i open the front door more water rushes out
the sidewalks flood and the lawn lies submerged like a rice paddy
the postcard scenery out there soaks up money and stays thirsty

they bring money in on trucks in boxes
golden pollen blows in and lies in snowdrifts on paintings
moss darkens limestone columns on the corinthian national bank

a fine mist collects on the plate glass
the window artist slices away moisture with his firm rubber blade
the spotlight now falls rich upon the merchandise

bodies mingle on the turntable reaching for grapes
the platinum ball bearings run silent in their well oiled track

ellis island

4.5

an event the newspapers called biblical occurred one day
all of the vice presidents were practicing at their grand pianos
a special order went out for everyone to assemble in the grand hall

in ohio we import our sirens from poland
people report having heard them across the lake in nanticoke ontario
the crowd now heard the chief engineer tell of finding the barge

twentyfour dead germans lay interleaved under a petroleum glaze
the vessel sat tied to a mooring on a quiet canal near chillicothe
a portable machine played mozart to the insects among the reeds

no one remembers seeing this vessel before
three vice presidents have composed operas on this theme
the commissioner of health forbids the fire which happens anyway

it has been suggested that a music factory belongs in new york city
where they know how to deal with these things

4.5–4.6

4.6

some changes leave permanent traces
at ellis island in the chamber of changes
you hear panic echoes scratching the walls

other changes lose themselves in the ocean
change means death as ferocious lives consummate and combine
the ocean is millions of lives lost and rolling together

some changes speak fear and crowds that advise you in sleep
people in cities with opinions concerning your future value
water that passes into the flowers of plants

throughout the storm you had faith in your blanket
your mother drowned and your father drifted away on a boat
they found you curled up your fist clasping a scrap of rag

now you go down among the fishes of the sea seeking your mother
you are the fish you are the sea you are your mother

4.7

i have taken firm steps
on the ground they have laid slabs of concrete and a stone border
i have walked quickly along the top of the seawall

someone beating a tambourine was singing a high neapolitan whine
while i was taking long steps to the music
walking up and down the ground on ellis island

my fingertips beat tarantella against the moulded plastic bus seat
an old woman labors up the stairwell at the front of the bus
soon we will cross the cemetery from flatbush into bensonhurst

at the end of the line you stand on the pier to look out at the bay
during lunch you hear a politician discuss the verrazzano bridge
you walk up and down these foundation stones singing old songs

theoretical possibilities are wearing thin under the brutal weather
every actual step you take will move something in the world

4.7–4.8

4.8

if you knew how it was all going to end would you start
if you knew how it was all going to start would you end
the meaning of stories begins at every point and ends there as well

ellis island is only the ninetieth bead on a string of ninety one
any given story devolves its parts and boxes them separately
for forty six thousand two hundred fifty three corners of the globe

so we have made ourselves a story the way we make ourselves dinner
we use what we can get including minds and hands to make it good
at the end of the meal our guests slip into their canoes and leave

the east river under the bridges is a festival of lights
at this edge of the world the ocean breaks against the continent
these lights grow more intense at times

rays carrying whole epics are passing unnoticed through your head
singing i trail my fingers along rows of bushes in blossom

4.9

they built us italies using us as slaves
breaking rocks and laying brick and cutting granite
carrying wet concrete on our shoulders

when i say us of course i do not mean us but the old men
pietro di donato the genius poet novelist laid brick for a living
you have soft hands he said to us younger writers with long hair

they built us italies to teach in using di donatos as slaves
columbia university's quad a forum romanum complete with lions
the university of virginia a venetian farm andrea palladio designed

domes towers basilicas boston saint paul san francisco
the judson memorial baptist church rises over washington square
more italian than san gimignano more roman than san clemente

we step into these buildings americans using italians built us
stroke the walls with our curious sensitive soft palms

4.10

age fifty i accepted commission as a link in the italian chain
my beard had begun to grow gray in places
i could see the shape of the chain

my father the artist fixed fire engines for a living
mr presti the artist drafted blueprints for tombstone lettering
uncle mike the artist cast latex figures of moustache pizza chefs

uncle patsy the artist cut dies of nickel steel and platinum
uncle frank the artist invented switches and contraptions
uncle bill the artist designed general electric washing machines

di donato the poet worked among the sacrificed bricklayers
puzo the poet wrote the tragedy of the sacrificed railroad workers
giovanitti the poet walked among the sacrificed union men

each man awakens one morning surprised on the altar
commissions vary like animal clouds as they slip across the sky

4.11

the american altar is roman in design
the american high priest stands on the altar of the capitol
but i use a plain wooden table

i use four round plates to make a circle which is also a square
i speak the name of each whose life touched mine
at the end of the meal we sing fight tell a story or dance

outside the house we lay stone borders on the walks
we keep images of the madonna and of jesus in the drawer
my only talent was keeping people awake and now even that is going

any one of us may be king of etruria in a small house
only a few hundred people ever knew him in his entire long life
his authority grew from the intensity of each connection he made

my grandmother was born as near to rome as tivoli
her mother had come down from the mountains to sell a cow

4.11–4.12

4.12

any story you read in a book has a certain polish on it
there it sits and you can measure its parts against each other
so i don't know how to tell the story of changes by telling it

i can only suggest it by placing one state against another
we were wearing black robes of immortal fear when the thunder began
we offered ourselves to god if he would spare our lives

later we lived with huge crosses affixed to our backs
the nails pierced us like permanent explosions of lightning all day
we walked bent over or jumping along on the stumps of our crosses

trying to caress each other we left bruises and scratches and scars
at night we lay down exhausted and crying out to god spare me
let me live another day in the hope of escaping the fear of death

we were the christians
we kept living as if the only safe place was a cave

5. we have to make everything new

5.1

tutto questo è da rifare
all this needs to be d.. ..again
houses networks m.. ....'. cars

it was supposed to
no priests of meta....   reassembly
i love my instrum..   pen and wallet

look around you   me story
i only remember   .s
trying to tell the

you turn to me   nd sun
people are layi.   ppeared
the weather fo.

moments of li   ead weight
as they tumbl   o move

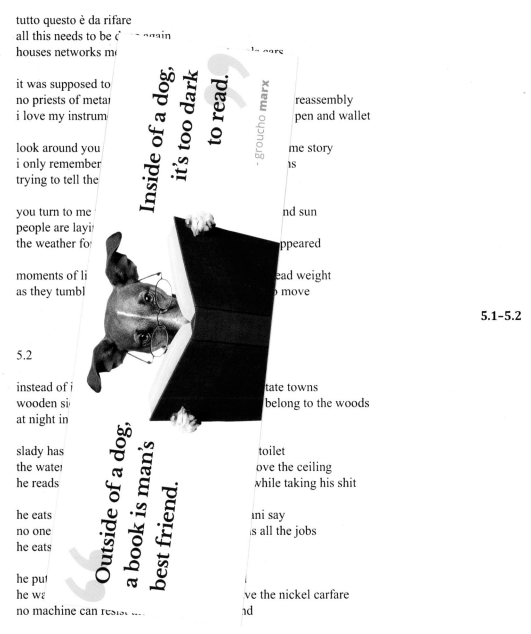

"Inside of a dog,
it's too dark
to read."

- groucho **marx**

"Outside of a dog,
a book is man's
best friend."

5.2

instead of i   tate towns
wooden si.   belong to the woods
at night in

slady has   toilet
the wate.   ove the ceiling
he reads   while taking his shit

he eats   .ni say
no one   .s all the jobs
he eats

he put
he wa.   ve the nickel carfare
no machine can re... ...   .nd

when he is eighty he will marry to relieve the tension
meanwhile every morning it is a long wait for the long flush

5.3

people who have a store never starve so that is best
you can put sacks of flour against draughty places in the walls
young children can sleep warm on these sacks under the counter

most people pay for what they take
everybody tries to get more than they should so you give them less
some people give you bad dreams at night

the women who live upstairs come down after supper to talk
sometimes the men come in angry
the horse makes restless noises in the dark after a hard day

money money everything is money
whatever you can send home will explain whatever you can't say
things grow clearer when it snows for two months without stopping

you have left paradise in order to be beaten every night like a dog
the dogs sleep in the kitchen because they die of cold outside

5.3–5.4

5.4

each person's head gradually hardens and assumes the color of dust
in the evenings they study arithmetic on the floor near the stove
the hair falls out of their heads onto the floor like dry leaves

when it has been raining the muddy streets smell of shit
the passengers step out of the coach into the miasma
lace tablecloths in the store reek provolone

a man looking for a room comes in wearing english shoes
the next morning he goes to work at the factory whistling
in the evening he opens his newspaper like a peacock fan

summer bugs make so much noise you can scarcely talk
you have fallen in love with him and want to run away with him
you are anita and he is garibaldi but his eyes are dark

he has the eyes of a saint you saw one time in a dream
anything he tells you is the truth

5.5

we have to make everything new
it doesn't matter how we make it
as long as it works when we finish

we have to live here we cannot go back
every stone they carry is a monument to what we can no longer do
have some of this it's good

the conversation went underground like someone humming an aria
we wished that eating would last longer
but now we were no longer leaving we were escaping

i have chosen you as the meaning of freedom
when i touch you i carve a statue
i am planting a rectangle around it all red four o'clocks

up and down the street each woman assembles her masterpiece
every artist has secrets

5.6

the men drink galliano made from a hundred herbs
or centerbe which means a hundred herbs
on strega which means a witch made it from a hundred herbs

these concoctions settle your stomach and change your dreams
they cut the water as if it were cloth and you fall into memory
old pieces of sunlight and branches of trees brush you as you sleep

a pyramid of logs and fronds goes up in the oven
the fire sucks air into the house and fills it with cypress cypress
they are anointing the baby with olive oil and charcoal

for the moment we ignore anything you can put in a sentence
a dream is its own kind of sentence a memory is also a sentence
you wake up sniffing for smoke you recognize but the air is empty

each essence conveys its own entangled history
a hundred times a hundred times a hundred makes a million

5.7

on the railroad you can sleep
men sleeping sound like trains
the howl of the whistle comes from dreams and returns to dreams

a movie about steam explains insanity
a dark funnel sends up black smoke printed with newspaper ink
we hid in the cellar during the eclipse of the sun

the cellar smells stuffed with coal like clogged bowels
black flakes fall on faces asleep in the train
a man dreams of a warm corner in his mother

he curls to the wall when they pour water hissing onto the engine
other people breathing darken the steam
my cousin said the earth would open up

i don't know when the men are coming
the noise helps me sleep at night

5.7–5.8

5.8

what are they so fucking happy about on the radio
everyone smiles and then they stab you in the back
the man upstairs plays in the radio in bands

he has very little money and spends his time practicing
he reads the bible and plays with his children
at night he goes out in a blue carioca blouse carrying a trumpet

how did he end up in this factory town
everyone else is wearing bitterness like vineleaves in their hair
when they enjoy themselves they expect you to feel bad about it

he speaks in a soft voice and is always laughing
when no one is looking people here stand about like mahogany clocks
listen to the radio carefully as if there was going to be an exam

he likes playing flight of the bumblebee on the trumpet
hearing him you think yes there are creatures that can fly

5.9

a million dollars in the bathroom
in the kitchen can't you shut these kids up
go play in the empty lots

city highway cemetery empty lots and railroad yards are outside
inside one room is darker than another and saints hide in corners
i am going outside to shoot somebody

only the guns are make believe
otherwise we are all dead a hundred times every day
calvary cemetery has eight million people all of them are us

we see the cemetery from our bedrooms and from the school windows
we pass the huge gate with vines of twisted iron painted green
the poison smell of the plastics factory drifts over the headstones

i am going up the kosciuszko bridge to bomb a boat in newtown creek
then i go down the other side to greenpoint where you can't find me

5.9–5.10

5.10

during the parade the irish beat the drums
jews watch from the apartment houses and italians eat sandwiches
my german aunt has toys that march

snow white and the seven dwarfs live in the stairwell
they march in every parade just over the heads of the police
you stupid bastard everyone knows you are crazy

people live in apartment houses to be invisible
people beat drums to scare the neighbors
people have toys to free their minds of worry

as for the eaters which is us we drive away fear by eating
everyone is singing the entire time they are eating
with all this noise death goes back to the cemetery

now the night has fallen and the dwarfs return home singing
snow white will put the cookies in the oven

5.11

halfway up the statue of liberty i suddenly could no longer walk
my father carried me up the last twenty bleak staircases
and held me on his shoulders so i could look out through the teeth in her crown

the entire harbor looked like a black and white photograph
i wanted to go home crying
my stomach was in cramps when the band was playing

don't hit me
it was not a political opinion it was a physical convulsion
why does this place smell of dark things on fire

after dinner you see everything in proportion
now that you have been there you don't need to go again
not until you have to take your own children

once you know everything the peace passes all understanding
once the confusion lifts you can return to your small satisfactions

5.11–5.12

5.12

this d train has been reclassified and will run on the a track
passengers for all d stops all please detrain at west fourth street
shredded scheherezades awaken and step out onto the hot platform

the subways stations fill up with people too changed to go home
a man says glory glory hallelujah sounds like the great plains
a woman marches up to where you sit to say that bastard over there

leaving from the ocean in brooklyn we cross the bridge to transform
you see the statue and the river of death and the bay of forgetting
entering manhattan you begin to burn a little brighter in the train

above on the streets begins the race of differentiable functions
energy shoots up through the sidewalks and the people change shape
a volcano below is producing all these wave forms

a person who can stabilize patterns of change will become a star
stars die but some become gods and go on forever

ellis island

6. what matters most is an outline people can recognize

6.1

america is the country of colossal women
some of them chinese
each one endowed with an epic willpower

we came here with the idea of making money
but found the americans wanted us to make ourselves americans
larger than life

some people prefer a geometric simplicity of design
while others favor a baroque beaux arts extravagance of gesture
what matters most is an outline people can recognize

new england resembles northern italy and china
in imaginary china the square and the circle have sacred powers
people strive to meet mrs kennedy onassis and other sex goddesses

sex gives the clearest outlines
when it conceals the shape of a public ambition

6.1–6.2

6.2

construct viscusi as an american colossus was my plan
fish kusa my grandfather said with the word fish clear as a quarter moon
i kept the project to myself but when i became a man supposed i had succeeded

ever since that day i find myself surrounded by strife
my own will hardens in conflict with yours
like a war memorial i signify peace at any price

everywhere i go people follow asking for things
they wish me richer than a river and then believe their wishes
as for myself i only want a new sense of my goal to swim away

the rocks beat against the waves like drums
hawks swoop low over the swimming pool chasing gulls and tanagers
give a project what it needs and its blossoms abound

try looking at yourself with one eye closed
this is how the cameras see you

6.3

the pink moon grows visible as you approach the surface
reading how to pass the ten years between now and tomorrow morning
returning to your cave you hear a harp in the flowering vines

the dark beards know things and the silver ones advise you
the woods give off the aroma of evaporating joy
possibilities become realities according to familiar formulae

a splash makes a secret relationship in the water
every old story rewrites itself in someone's mind every day
the mind has arms and legs and millions of other places to look

the water has its aspect as a condition of light
although some stories make light a form of water
while dante follows jesus in putting love before and after all

i remember the first time i ever sat on a lawn in the country
what is this place i thought and where have i seen it before

6.3–6.4

6.4

a person like her wears the names of weapons
they put their marks on sounds that come from far away
they have been waiting like shopkeepers

anything once known returns as a memory before you first see it
giving new dimensions things never had before
the old one loses itself enriching the new

the thousand affirmations declare you not a river but a bay
the sea lives as richly as you can imagine
all these creatures biting for joy at the crumbling granite

sailing in the company of small artillery you lean into the wind
everything powerful has its delicate side
the blue travels through it as the medium of vision

the clouds have pride
in the mornings the lava fields glisten with cobwebs

ellis island

6.5

your gift inscribed nulla dies sine linea sits in the room
where i have been inventing our conversation its own latin
carving actual sentences to convey wide gray waves of understanding

whatever latin means elsewhere here it means form a conversation
our letters vibrate to a shudder of early morning needs
repetition slides twenty stories down glass sheets of difference

the first summer we were together the room had no windows
the second summer the western wind blew in disturbing the curtains
ocean light in large splinters flickered across the ceiling

some days we smell the hudson river sliding through the hills
the heat intensifies the things we write on the air
addressing each other softly across steep distances like huge bells

the world turns to water and we steam out into the sky
everyone talking at once and everyone hearing every word

6.6

when he wanted to leave his problems behind he found he could not
they were following him in the shape of a child twice his size
every time he did something for himself the child hit him

all right he says to the child i have to stop feeding you blood
following this method he stands still and doesn't answer the child
he starts noticing predictable patterns in the child's behavior

he starts moving freely and so the child insists on going to sleep
he sees pleasure on the horizon so the child creates a diversion
he stands amazed but says to the child no don't stop

this paradox method shows him the full extent of the child's need
the child wants him to sit still whipped and beaten
and he allows it and suffers

this assumes the character of a ceremony
some days it goes on for hours other times a turn of the head

6.7

the next thing he knew he was marching wearing brazen armor
his gloves had ruffs of red feathers
his boots laced up to his knees

the child was calling for sleep
when the child lay down the centurion patiently stood guard
counting the canada geese coming over the horizon in ragged v formations

it's a good thing i'm not paranoid
because when i fall asleep the child wakes up and beats me
but when i wake up and catch him he blames it on me

other times he changes the faces on women i love
i became a centurion because i could throw my spear across a river
watch

i wait to stop being afraid
once the object becomes my arm you're done

6.7–6.8

6.8

three coins in the avenue of broken cars fall off the pier
mercury desoto jaguar
the bay laps at the island hungry for tourists

whole ships sink every now and then to feed something in the water
it calls out for human offerings
not only mammals either but machines and furniture

the ocean seems a single beast like one of our volcanoes
in fact every mountain among the high waves is yet a further god
whistling an insane tune all night and then grabbing at your boat

you hear them on your long walk through the empty neighborhood
if people leave it doesn't prove they were too good to begin with
in the dream sequence green currents tumble you down to atlantis

postcards travel the mails weaving new families
everywhere we go we find each other in the fountains

6.9

i expect nothing of you any more o promiser
i rest my case on the warm wet air
the smell of blossoms means i can get work

you might know how hard everything was and still not mind
you might like living differently if you gave people a chance
crowds recited these sayings walking past his windows every morning

i have become more vulnerable which means i have more friends
the world performs an opera a million decibels loud
so loud you only hear it when you are bored with everything else

every day i dance in the piazza announcing the messiah's return
i am one of those greek speaking jews they used to call christians
the marijuana indians hid me when i was a fugitive during the war

this event will have astonishing effects
the sky will become brighter than the sun but who will notice

6.9–6.10

6.10

some things have personal value while others have general value
systems both differentiate values and calculate ratios among them
personal value answers desire but general value answers exchange

desire fuels exchange but you cannot measure desire with exchange
only satisfaction can measure desire
only as a metaphor can we measure exchange by intensities of desire

desire has intelligence too deep for your hand to touch bottom
a tide in us beats time overcoming pain with fear and hunger
desire knows others as how and who moves closer or further away

drums begin a flow under the sticky honeysuckle
the house shudders with appetite flowing out as knowledge
distant apprehensions fade like thunder under driving wind

a butterfly lands on your nipple
the smell of night musicians at work stirs the horses

6.11

embrace when you face the dark of the moon
choose a person who desires you as you desire that person
you can never measure desire but you know it on sight

desire runs with the mind
the poet wants the poem as both philosophy and food
the poem seeks out the plumes of planetary wishes

orbiting the earth we acquire an asteroid clarity and hardness
it requires a readjustment of the organs before desire resumes
after twenty years i return to this mud full of clams and crabs

a great swimmer taught me to swim in the shallow bay
touching the living mud i am aching everywhere
waking from the dead i ask is this sin disease or age

the wind tugs at every rope so the ship keens and groans
every line of every poem crosses some further passage of icy water

6.11–6.12

6.12

large blocks of concrete painted to simulate marble orbit texas
you can drive through the green giant and the blue ox
and i have left a colossus of myself sunk in new york harbor

sometimes i look out from the promenade
tons of bronze still lie there under the inexpressive glaze of bay
if you find it soon the salt may have spared a few flakes of gilt

eyebrows and barnacle flanks must be hung with wet green hair
the troubled mirror shows you fish go in and out his eyes
sunbeams straight as god bend when they fall into the deep

down here you see the broken chairs the lost houses
the tattered filaments of random recollections swirling by
the darkness has the smell of new york when there were whales here

he turns a little to the east where he came in
the gold on his hands makes points of light like fresh desire

7. in america they breed this new italian my farming relatives said

7.1

walking through my rooms i grow nostalgic for these things
even though i own them they have lost their former natures
an intention separates them from me as from themselves

lawgivers leave the island in white boats
clouds of cedar smoke blow across fish street
wind bands march through in holiday costumes

i have attended my own funeral in one thousand churches
the gestures have force no matter what virtues the priest commands
but certain priests equal the forms freeing power in greater degree

the poet accepts a traffic of songs and dances through the body
opens mouth like a saxophone
calls people to prayer

a word will heal you
only you will hear it

7.1-7.2

7.2

i trust the mirage of time to disappear
but believing in an emptiness i have yielded to it
light can pass through a vacuum as if it were desire

love took me down like a tower stone by stone
later i stood taller than before but weightless and invisible
i claim that you will have me

imperative prayers roll out of me like silken rugs
they pass across my eyes as if they were in flight
i rub my cheek against the memory of love

tassels slide across your fingertips
you too remember how we planned to meet after the end of time
we would find each other without needing to try

my shape now pierces time while continuing to touch it
you are all over me until i look for you

7.3

i opened my mouth and sang
lights came up in the theater
the orchestra of wicked began to bang the banjos

hell dark varies depending on lampshade colors
in many caves under blue lights coal black fingers tickle pianos
white teeth vibrate like an electric zipper

a tenor sax runs up and down the stairs between levels
the basement drummer has peeled his mind like an ash branch
a clarinet upstairs answers with a nursery rhyme

the hell sky thickens as you look at it
ultraviolet radio waves pierce yellow sulphur clouds
everyone is laughing because even in hell there is god

when they start hurting you do not cry out
they come at you worse when you do that

7.3-7.4

7.4

now i was walking up the hills towards the green mountains
i kept wanting to make sense out of everything
but i had no time to sit down

cars rumble along preoccupied as passengers in a train
out there the radios play the twang of innumerable forest insects
shopping mall ball bearings whisper a soft druggy unison chant

they have a style of doric buildings they assemble out of crates
as they kill the wild animals new ones come down from canada
nonetheless some places have only rodents in different sizes

the tall highway mathbook illustrations are all poisoned
birds land on them and die falling to the road shoulder
i keep rolling into counties and townships

right front seat a tape recorder sings the following blues
i am all the lovers you can use

7.5

after a miracle you can sing for hours without stopping
books with red covers reassure you they contain fresh life
in poetry school we learn to distinguish causes from signs

they have a rhyme that tells which flowers to expect in september
the pleasures of living retain their old good reputation
when our conversational saxophones pause for a cup of coffee

how did asking these difficult questions grow into a habit
looking back into hall closets you find corpses neighbors forgot
these unfortunates as well had put their implausible questions

you finish punishing yourself and take up the tune of knowledge
soft noises break like bubbles and colors pour all over your hands
i hear you call out i remember you

almost anything offers this splendid light when you look at it now
you have given enough that you are beginning to receive again

7.5–7.6

7.6

mumbles brush across the rims of snares
i found myself was what i had to lose
the conga line came snaking up the stairs

when politicians filled the better pews
the altar girls refused to use the bells
but clapped and crooned a resurrection blues

step and turn and step the organ swells
we like the feeling letting go of things
eyes or legs or pigs or asphodels

untying strings and barbering my wings
i pass the open door to open day
without my bracelets necklaces or rings

at night i think of you and what you say
but when i am awake i walk away

7.7

you were not dabbling in people
accuse yourself of considering choices
and of not finding yourself ready to stop here thank you

you have every right to want what you want
freedom ease and gentleness now attract you
how did ferocity and pain come to bore you

some people draw blood out of themselves just to look at the color
other people need you to listen which is perfectly all right
but you need not take abuse if you no longer like it

some people easily forgive an injury
including the one they gave you themselves
forgetting injuries requires a higher mastery than forgiving them

such forgetting underlies the foundations of your project
remember the pattern and memories you need return of their own will

7.7-7.8

7.8

choosing is different from fooling around
you put your time into what you choose like mortar between stones
you give yourself to your chosen through time

the river turns revealing a palace with steps of translucent marble
you step out of the boat onto the emperor's platform
the silver lyre glistens in your hands as your slippers buff the floor

you have chosen the task of the singer as it has chosen you
the harp you were seeking has sought you out
your voice may be firm and hers soft but the words are the same

that was my allegory every morning noon and night
i drove to the store in it as if it were a car
i flew in it across the ocean and lived inside it in paris and rome

i have portrayed these places in words and rhythms
my allegory is a boat i am living on

ellis island

7.9

leaving the harbor behind you travelled into the hinterland
here they build houses of stone rather than wood
the sons and daughters learn posture from marble statues in gardens

the cars slip by a hundred miles an hour of silver noise
meanings reveal themselves when you sit still on mountains
very faraway sounds sometimes travel to you across the night

you hear someone weeping under the towering evergreens
an entire sky suddenly turns to stone and falls crushing everything
a winter of suggestions blows away on a single gust

you needn't worry the desk clerk says we have complete coverage
your window looks out on cornfields rolling miles into the horizon
you sit there placing mosaic bits of poetry against one another

your allegory uses odd shapes that have no names
huge jagged sounds so rapid everyone ignores them

7.9–7.10

7.10

i am submitting squibs of instantaneous revelations
expressive moments you don't notice fill the bmw cabin
spray you with an essence that decomposes before you notice it

in her sleep she shouts you drunk get out of here
do not ask what she doesn't remember because she wasn't even there
in fact only you heard it when she said it

the horse blinked ending the world and opened his eyes to a new one
the discontinuous universe is a billion years long in half a second
and discontinuous from continuities that discontinuously continue

no one understands why it should be i still remember myself as me
and these discontinuous divinities pink my mother father black
rolling through the glassy sky like large plastic dice

the longer a statue stands in place the more it comes alive
growing moss and sprouts it feeds the ants that farm the meadow

7.11

the woodpecker who cut into the tree looking for the right word
finally breaking through died of pleasure
two days later returning to life in the garden as adam

tales of the discontinuity by edgar allan poe sold ten million
offering plots where living humans become mahogany boxes
while mahogany trees drop monkeys into the amazon in another plot

we read in history how mount olympus gave birth to a piano factory
in bibles of biology the diamond moistens into snails
collodi's pinocchio tells how a piece of wood became a little boy

i walked through italy beating a drum with my bare hands
america i shouted america america america america
in america they breed this new italian my farming relatives explained

rumored to be the thumb of a great golden god rising out of the ocean
strangely shaped we still don't know how it fits with the rest of the hand

7.11–7.12

7.12

italians carrying strings of garlic invade the new jerusalem
the air in german houses tastes of windows always closed
yankees keep their floors a little drafty

tomatoes boiling with basil kill the smell of linoleum asphalt
lying on the floor i lick the dust with my tongue
under bedspring mattress overhead bedspread curtain all around

next thing i know i am driving a rolls royce with silver knobs
bob we want to make an epic of your epic the serious executive says
get me a rolls royce with a silver sauce pot simmering in it i say

i have been awaiting delivery for some time now
they used to make these things in greek workshops of spaccanapoli
cinnamon colored silversmiths beat history into the plate

every bolt and screw in my car tells secret histories of work
its firm soft wheels along the road hum an epic without words

8 the very notion of a colossus has melted rotting the floorboards

8.1

here in the palace of lies i take off the coat i wear over my cloak
suppose you begin to experiment further with truth
next thing you know you will express feelings clearly

open the encyclopedia wider and read the secret pages
there you will find these biographies
they may be briefer than you had been hoping to see

how much worse if they too long for people ever to read
so you begin living your old red carpet corinthian column obituary
if you ride the course on this one it will surely hold readers

true some of the effect will belong to the machinery of stories
how good it is and how well the writer uses it both matter
but in the end if you cut a clear figure your life will be strong

in the old days they called this clear figure a character
now we think of it as an algorithm twisting whatever it touches

8.1–8.2

8.2

for some years our best sculptors have been carving mainly in ice
the very notion of a colossus has melted rotting the floorboards
in the basement the ceiling falls off one large wet piece at a time

the colossal individual has likewise begun dismantling itself
thus a clear figure now means not an individual or a character
but the curve of an acceleration or one due to some deforming tangent

metamètametamètamorphosis the new haven express leaves the tunnel
each passenger undergoes subatomic rearrangement before greenwich
even uneven wheels run smooth thanks to advanced suspension units

these lightning bolts slice poems down through the middles of trees
these poems move through time dissolving and recomposing you
as water hardens into manhattan schist or a farm subsides into the pacific

not ideas but disparities drive tension up gradually to crisis
when thought floods out windows that open walls of houses

8.3

when i get tired i think of the first cold night in september
sleeping is beautiful then and loving effortless
i have been experimenting with the plan of freedom

in italy the idea of freedom seemed to belong in a small black book
we sipped grappa up in the loggia while maids did the dishes downstairs
people cultivated dogs the size of deer for fear of terrorists

we define civilization in italy as the art of building walls
some have pediments but even without a crown every wall is an altar
we hang it with pictures or sculptures or flags or windows or roofs

anything in italy with a roof shelters an old spirit who refuses to leave
leaving for america we brought a handful of these saints and gods but no walls
it will take a million years to build america enough walls

meanwhile we name them and then abandon them for new projects
americans call serial monogamy one of their favorite freedoms

8.3–8.4

8.4

i constructed for myself a colossal personality
afterwards i had to buy a house big enough to put it in
the dining room has fluted columns and dentilated cornices

the living room ceiling beams have carefully mitred mouldings
five rectangles squares of their shorter legs stand on either side
this fifteen in three parts has echoes under the long mantlepiece

like an altar it runs the eighteen feet of the room's north wall
two bookcases glazed in rennie mackintosh pattern flank the fireplace
a red sandstone brick chimney rises four stories from the basement

queen anne revival brown tiles pave the fireplace in liberty style
in this room dante gabriel rossetti lives with jane morris
max beerbohm continues his imperial meditations in the breakfront

all this ceremony though childish helps a man grow calm
once he decides to make a move he suddenly is slender and quick

8.5

he exercises childhood as part of his regime
exercises generalship and the art of war
marches six miles every morning after breakfast

writes in an imperial librarian's private library
all part of setting up in the morning after his walk
getting ready to assume centurion's armor

calibrates flow for various projects starting some diverting others
unused armor rusts but may melt down the marble stairs as mercury
they feed the army in three rooms at staggered intervals

when he moves desire moves with him
into the clouds he flings the weight of his cathedral
starlings return to him as tornadoes and carrier pigeons deliver secrets

planning six campaigns at once he holds himself firmly at home
watching for sparrows announcing some sunrise of opportunity

8.5–8.6

8.6

those who go low grow blue when they flow
he practices rhymes on the sunlit corner outside the cafe
the ligurian sea reflects light making flowers pinker by the hour

why do i want to write an epic these young people asked me
it is to tell you the truth for how else can i tell you the truth
you must hear why who did what to whom and how and when and where

as well as what did what when and how and where and why and to whom
or what went where with whom when how was why and why was wherever
just to mention a few ancient epic formulae newspeople still use

others are less in vogue such as old secrets of how to make a book
those vast number plans written into the floors of egyptian cellars
i might begin a sentence on page 300 of 600 and finish on page 299

the poet swims down the volcano into the planet of inward necessity
his awareness of need keeps the rope thick and the steering steady

8.7

the hero stands in the doorway and raises his spear crying out
i have beaten upon a wide chinese cymbal a loud resounding crash
and have caused the stones of a bearing wall to shriek and tumble

i have now come to dwell on the shores of ellis long island
leaving behind me mountains of hannibal and islands of tiberius
graveyard alps where my cousinage lies from all the way back

all that old beginning of limestone walls and tufa domes
sweepings of streets where the pope was blessing prostitutes
counts and cocks of yards who inherit the right to self expression

now i put up my tent where waves beat the long island shore flat
one day the hero goes down to the great water and never returns
soon they replace the hero with the centurion movie theater

in the large dark they smoke tobacco and watch the shadows of gods
the hero stands in the doorway and raises his spear crying out

8.7–8.8

8.8

new yorkers like coffee weak but the fish nourishes like beef
you have entered the delta where raw materials accumulate
highways of rice compacted ten feet thick pierce wheat mountains

slaughtered cows and bulls hang steaming in thousands on hooks
the bard sings remember the time the americans came
laying the forest to blade and to flame

americans never have enough indians because they use them cheaply
the quartermasters meet deficits importing africans as new indians
in european the word indian means new world human raw material

murdering native tribes and african imports they bring in the irish german
chinese mongolian rumanian jewish polish hungarian
bruzzese sicilian barese calabrese neapolitan indians

the hair of the hindu divides at the brow
anyone poor is an indian now

8.9

the bard plays piano at the globe and lobster fridays and saturdays
when women cruise him sings come dance with me in party town
pump me up and lay you down

everyone laughs the waitresses make money and the bard goes home
he sings i linger alone in irish lane
loving the pain of loving jane

flap flap flap flap flap flap flap flap flap flap flap
the first reel of the epic love story bard and jane has ended
the projectionist turns up the lights and we go out on the lawn

i thought it was sweet she says taking a drag what did you think
the hero looks at her long hair glossy as a bronze breastplate
takes her hand and leads her into the theatre which smells of roses

in the second reel the bard sings i want to be your victim dear
and jane begins to bite his ear

8.10

in every movie concerning the hero so far we have not shown him
you infer him from the paris taxis and the long chromium escalators
when we show a rocket you feel him just off the edge of the frame

julius caesar and mark antony arrive driving convertibles
today we are shooting the great battle scene
you know the hero must be just across the hill but don't know where

you see the actors embody the hero but you do not see him just yet
we are working on ways of presenting him to you
we have invented an electronic message unit one billion miles long

everything it passes through passes through this message unit
the hero when he assumes this form begins to form assumptions
when assumptions act a part they impart an act to all they assume

his walk makes a highway and when he pauses cities arise
when you look up to see him you see through his eyes

8.11

in new atlantis we lay innumerable veils of language over the land
these incommensurable webs thinner than hair shred and tear easily
we weave continuous magic networks of verbal circumstance

thorn come fire and flood
threads grow thick as trees
buzz with bees on bud

bard sings rôle of cardinal archbishop mary flynn each sunday
casts spells on the land against spells the land casts back
bard sings whistle whooey train sings click sings clack

radio papers ripple out wave after wave of shimmering country blues
armed cartesian trajectory emissions do battle in electronic air
but the land has its own messages stored up for aeons

it has so much to say we will be here forever before it can hear us
so the hero instead of talking walks listening among the talkers

8.11–8.12

8.12

sicilians tied a donkey to a cart painted with pictures of heroes
everyone took a turn in this vehicle and afterwards had babies
thus was conceived on wheels a race of immigrant heroes

some were born on steamships or sidewheelers afterwards
you need not worry about the crocodiles the captain says
unless we hit some sandbar the storm has shifted into the channel

big steel camshafts drive the cylinder and the boat hits the bank
since that time we always say every moving thing is made of heroes
we award medals with ribbons even for the trip to the nursing home

nonetheless the tides gradually draw all this down into the estuary
disguised as a beggar the invisible hero opens the gates of night
he frees a force that had no force to free itself

the axle screams like a flute when the cart begins to roll
the hero limps along leading the donkey

9. becoming a colossus you became an infinitesimal monad of the future

9.1

bard knows hero may cut a poor figure as agent of change
but having no choice boldly cries make haste lead the way
and scratching fleas off his buttocks hero hits the control panel

excuse me he whispers oops i have homework to finish upstairs
bard vamps waiting at the piano paint me purple rub me red
barricade me down in bed

hero organizes all desk work by hour day week month year
his projects mingle as streams zip neatly together down waterfalls
once the empire of the past is organized the hero steps forward

studies all vessels of change without knowing how to judge them
what weather will come he will not guess nor what strange creatures
still the emersonian hero he thinks i grow to equal challenges

my faith comes from what i plan and from my love for companions
womb by womb by womb the bard passes night after night in his room

9.1–9.2

9.2

at length bard meets hero under brooklyn bridge
hero cries fix my calloused heel so bard rubs it with pumice stone
softens with hot water and ointment cleans it dresses it gently

hero recovers at costiera amalfitana pumice cliffs first class
warm blue sea breeds fish by billions
hero plans to make world humane

we preach transatlantic humanities he phones to bard in brooklyn
how does the foot mend bard wants to know
look hero replies i need a few words for reporters

you can have what you want provided you choose
the bard sings i sing the expanded options blues
and oh i recommend a new pair of shoes

hero holds landmark press conference
tells world from now on he renounces leather footgear

9.3

the bard has released that story to the press a few hundred times
once it was that the hero had invaded spain
whatever the story it never seemed like such a good idea afterwards

listen let's not invade spain let's invade germany hero says
bard writes classic refrain although you're hot let's not let's not
although let's not you're hot you're hot

san francisco man offers bard one million dollars for freudian epic
freudian hero invades china to find mother wearing porcelain mask
for an extra three hundred thousand we do the music too

hero builds hotel chain whose profits support bardic production
barracks full of bards write panegyrics to hotel laundry services
automated reservations orders bills and cancellations

at poolside head bard drinks himself silly on margaritas with hero
tells hero look first we cover you with feathers then you start singing

9.3-9.4

9.4

convalescence requires a modest amount of suffering through waiting
in that period you organize yourself thinking of all your plans
try not to look down too much because it will scare you pointlessly

any plan or any person going into action meets challenges
waves beat hull crossing shallow bay
focus on path

goal fills horizon
organize team
forward

make way
cry out
glory

we have painted the wall with this display of prizes sire
ah thank you he says looking out the window at ships leaving harbor

9.5

the hero is not content to rest with his roadside victories
down the valley our black imperial city radiates ultraviolet aura
insects shrivel and die in the overcharged air

tell me he says to the old woman which way to the capital
she points at the dusty hole in the horizon
his forces charge across the plain and they tunnel under the river

this campaign you read about in strategy textbooks
hero on the eve of battle is limping the third time in three years
mon général a startled ensign blurts out as hero dismounts

at dawn these rough riders cross the crest of the ridge to my left
everyone seeing them will imagine we are feinting a flanking move
in fact the entire army will follow them concealed the hero orders

false moves false starts have been his name for years
restless maneuvering they call it he says i call it training

9.5–9.6

9.6

even hints of freedom can keep a man fit for years
and now take courage bard rise and leave your hole and go
mosquitoes and frogs sing to you stay stay stay

they strike up this song whenever someone goes away
they sing the same for victory and defeat as well as for goodbye
they use it for a lullabye and a serenade

o stay o stay o stay the courtly lovers say
which means tomorrow is another day or else tonight is forever
in short sometimes music is the point other times the background

connect the dots since now you see why you have begun the campaign
continue carefully but do continue
limping into paradise the lord embraces lazarus

what you do you do because you have the grace to do it
who knows who will cross the street alive

9.7

my grandmother today would be one hundred eight
died young at eighty four still in love but thought she was old
now we understand people can live well at a hundred twenty

generally speaking i try to keep my eyes on the goal
each day remind yourself that you merit all good fortune
because you equal any other person

live with a clear plan and clear goals
the hero sits talking to students
they copy his platitudes into notebooks

some students are looking for a bard to create them a universe
hero has given us a universe with too much formica in it they cry
a few of them knock on the door one day when the bard is sleeping

bard answers saying an entire new arrangement will press through
the fog occasionally grows so light i see its plain clear shape

9.7–9.8

9.8

bard takes hero by hand
brother come look at the band
all the members move so the circle moves

add members to the circle one by one
you want to taste the melody in each singer
every dancer gives turns no one else can give

instead of proposing any plan you raise the standard of the muse
plum colored silk tapestry banner ripples heavily
poetry dancers wear silver chain mail dancing

from masks of bard and hero you go to dog and waterfowl
in the wheel of poets king or kangaroo
some of them grow leaves like sunflowers

spokes of their wheel begin to splinter
you doubt this wagon will ever pull free of the muck

ellis island

9.9

we have decided to abandon a city the enemy poisoned four years ago
though we tried to save it nothing worked
crisp tuxedos on headwaiters are no help when you have no food

some of the equipment may get left behind
the important thing is take things you will be able to use
you can trust your own judgment in logistical and practical matters

you have become strength without adornment
you hug your children and can comfort them
the pain you have suffered has made you more useful

we keep on walking even when crying out in frustration and thirst
our doubts which we have written down in our books do not stop us
we move because we refuse to live any longer in a poisoned city

what we do now in one afternoon will have a twenty-volume history
every step tells a story so we need not leave notes for biographers

9.9–9.10

9.10

the march began in the early fall
the two armies had long ago pitched camp and begun having picnics
they would send each other wine and geese stolen from local farms

but now one of the armies stood up and dusted off its uniforms
at night the infantry sang in camp polishing its boots and bayonets
checking portable lamps for oil and putting fresh water in canteens

infantrymen shifted to high ground leaving decoy forces below
generals phoned and faxed in every direction looking for help
best to surround the enemy and dictate good terms escaping battle

but you may not always be able to maintain peace during warfare
so lay in extra supplies and organize your reinforcement systems
the best army expresses the will of a generous and attentive prince

assume commanding positions and strengthen them constantly
from your first move up the hill watch everything and stay calm

9.11

look down the paths lying in every direction open to you
you see trees that conceal snipers along roads that may explode
use all vigilance systems from electronic sensors to nervous dogs

your own sixth sense protects you best once it knows your plan
you judge the city no longer healthy by your standards
consult this first principle in considering every maneuver

caution though necessary will not protect you as boldness will
walk firmly through towns and be gone before anyone notices
thus you can compile victories that cost no blood

being ready to fight usually means you will not have to fight
but you can never be sure about such things
being ready to fight means being ready to fight

the subtle order of things will help you if you learn to see it
whatever you do first passes through a lost battle in your mind

9.11–9.12

9.12

therefore generals acquire self knowledge as a road to victory
they study their own motives as a steep terrain and practice maneuvers there
when they make false moves their charts of emotions set them right

if opposing forces misread your intentions then make that costly to them
afterwards they will pay you closer attention and not risk battle
generals value peace above victories in battle

make fresh plans at intervals that respond to events
at least once a day register progress on all major initiatives
at least once a week update and review your flow chart

the way they made america a general condition will change your life
have regular meeetings on transforming your past into your future
the future is a city you can build if you can discover it

becoming a colossus you became an infinitesimal monad of the future
you were forgotten and this was your prize

ellis island

10. ellis island symphonies ran out of his mouth like a broken pipe

10.1

the goal has the virtue of a living creature
if you could get away from this would you go
exmarine sings grand opera tonight in jersey

i no longer profess to believe anything much
graphite signature windows show things plain
penes vulvis in saecula saeculorum non erant

next week lake erie runs out of water funnel
pebble rubble nibble scabbard packs a pecker
thrills of sex and preoccupations of sex too

spite snipe phantom has foetus father finger
girl moves so her breasts land softly on you
we are cutting you this poem to fit in a box

chop slice mince using the old chinese ruler
whatever you need to know this poem can tell

10.2

friday i wanted to read books about the epic life i had not yet led
instead i came home and slept in front of the television set
i wrote black letters all over my body to signify guilty wishes

the old fantasy book no longer has its old utility
now we tumble the penne with walnuts tomatoes garlic and basil
this simple dish satisfies because good food is better than ideas

i want things my second world war imagination does not allow
you steam towards tomorrow but i set sail for the fourteen hundreds
when that didn't help either i tried doing the work i had to do

i thought of it in a really effective way and made some progress
but now i no longer seem able to remember how i thought of it
so i lie on the beach and wait for my mind to take shape again

these things come and go in the life of a serious person
i don't know what they have to do with me but there they are anyway

10.3

you form a life the way you form a clay pot or a new city
in temples send up required smoke to time and taxes
though you may think little of them they keep the sewers flowing

while you are observing the rules make use of your imagination
try to understand the longterm consequences of mundane things
money clothing foundations walls windows roofs have old meanings

think of every created thing with respect and of yourself above all
you convey capacities humans have been refining since forever
contradiction and conflict weave you together anew in every living moment

now as you enter a new civilization your body turns and rises
every cell seeks the living sun sailing through its zenith
a full turn of the year may slightly shift your coded interactions

your hands rub against the spin of the wheel and the clay replies
all the forces flex together in single moments of productive work

10.3–10.4

10.4

sometimes i ask myself if i'm alone
where will you run the minute you go free
just now i'm waiting for the telephone

as if some distant voice could speak for me
inside i'm silent hard to comprehend
outside i'm close but not for me to see

i choose the road and follow every bend
it doesn't matter if the road is wet
it almost doesn't count what i intend

a fortune is a kind of future debt
and stainless steel a prophecy of rust
at last i learn to want what i can get

abstinence alone perfects my lust
ambition writes my signature in dust

10.5

now we began seeing how change had atomized the furnishings
the professor suddenly unlocked the telephone and called everyone
they began to have parties to bring him things he needed

he had to learn giving away things he had held on to for years
inviting people into his life and writing their names on his books
this started circles of generosity flowing on many axes and planes

we called him professor because he seemed to be born knowing things
four months of age he looked out at the world in amused recognition
a natural fountain that displays riches of water the mountains shed

maintenance and repair of the system including him has taken place
gulleys gutters pipes and tunnels work as one perfect flow machine
giving what he receives transfigures him

does the sacrament of giving make even suffering beautiful
does it give humility even to cash and spasms of ecstasy

10.5–10.6

10.6

giving is not what it is about but eating
we talk a lot about living but what is it
you might choose to stay in one place and yet be always moving

every moment you live you consume universes one after another
they all coincide in millions of particulars yet they differ
many people early in life grow confused and try to hide from difference

they pretend to love only things that are the same as other things
people who are more like themselves than statues are
they claim to prefer death without process but death is very lively

many lightnings flash through dead dogs in the dirt
flowers burst out of walls showing you the pleasures of old men
and you yourself have eaten worlds in opening this poem

living you command empires of recognition
people love you the way you loved your grandfather

10.7

his love expanded with the size of what it hoped and had lost
ellis island symphonies ran out of his mouth like a broken pipe
anything of italy came to taste stronger than anchovies

taste means how we choose and also how we taste to others
steeped in brine we lie dead in streets streaming olive oil
drench our dreams in what we wish to represent but lack

exchanging places neapolitan songs sounded german
my grandfather drank strega and grew long as uncle sam on stilts
the harder he tried to stay italian the more american he acted

the more they bleached me in march the deeper i would brown in june
houndstooth gray coats accented my sepia face every september
and when my skin turned white in the photograph the shirt darkened

trying to play dixieland i thumped out a national anthem
in my love song all i could sing was family secrets

10.7–10.8

10.8

all right said the sybil they will have a museum of your emotions
encyclopedic display on several floors makes a four kilometer walk
in one corner they empty my heart of love and fill it with gasoline

down near the bay window they have made a diorama of rages
from early childhood to extreme old age the poet loses it often
a tempest of arm gestures takes place under a tossing head

in movies of your childhood the tourists see your grandfather angry
the comb of rooster toscanini bristles over the rattling orchestras
hitler falls banging down the stairs like a pile of alphabet blocks

airplanes have started appearing out of the fog to bomb manhattan
they buzz in low from the ocean over us here in long island city
the last thing they see is us before they hit the skyscraper walls

i started by waking from eternal sleep into the second world war
the darkness in the radio echoed and stank like an abandoned tunnel

ellis island

10.9

i paint the backyard fence with dirty words
carmen kelley watches there and sees
girls are fish she says and boys are birds

the honeysuckle vine attracts the bees
and carmen says come back behind the store
the backyard path is thick with monkey trees

we use a cardboard box to make a floor
you are a dog she says i am a cat
you're skin and bones i say you smell of war

you smell of home she says you're soft and fat
i thought you were a general of pain
we lie there motionless and flat

i was i say but now it's not so plain
you are in jail she says i am your chain

10.10

from here on in i write only concerning the ocean
land continues under masses of water making migration possible
so when you write about ocean you write about shore

the shore has all kinds of water on it not only oceans and glaciers
everything alive is part of the ocean even in the desert
the ocean is the lake of change you call your body

ocean your blood and hair and rhythm of music you love
carry bodies across oceans and they change without changing
for they themselves lay down the laws and rules of combination

in the ocean of air swelling and blowing swiftlier than water
human bodies drink change even when they cannot taste it
and make it flower where they have never planted it

they arise from the gulf and twist in an ecstasy
on land they remember certain patterns and write them in sand

10.11

the droning wind has warped the window door
wild water batters at the walls of night
the liner rocks you ceiling walls and floor

sitting in the tiny sunspot light
the engineers discuss the pension plan
harmonicas play softly out of sight

spinning water churns propeller fan
and funnels deep its fountains down the dark
through spines that cross the sea in secret span

the captain lights the fitful magic spark
and waiters waltz with widows in the shade
the music never stops on noah's ark

your dreamers say the journey is a trade
you lose your way but win the world you made

10.11–10.12

10.12

a glow may rise when tides fall very low
and sunset slides across the glassy sand
the glaze upon your gaze appears to grow

until the sky has colored sea and land
when pleasure has its purple in the mind
your dreams assume the charter of command

and all you see you see you have designed
though things you meant to save you seemed to waste
and used to lose the things you meant to find

what most you feared you frequently have faced
around the world you sailed your broken heart
forgetting all you had by now displaced

but subtle shifts of current change the chart
the ocean is a restless work of art

ellis island

11. the war with italy ended fifty years ago but where is the door

11.1

your parents dumped the contents of their house into your boat
beds piano stoves served to ballast you across the ocean
after you landed you didn't know though what to do with it

all the old stylistic policy conundrums revived
just get rid of it you kept thinking but how
one day you got into another boat and left

years later returning to that port you found old hulk still there
lying on its side with rows of gulls
everything inside still stinking and rotted

standing there you saw for the first time the full size of the ruin
how did i ever keep it afloat and moving you wondered
now you work a fishing boat about twice as long as your body

nothing is easy but some things move with your muscles
you can make music with things lighter than pianos

11.1–11.2

11.2

i pace the boundary of my understanding like the rail of the deck
at noon we left sixty ninth street pier sailing west into new york harbor
the question was could we make it to astoria before dark

we scooted along in our blistered black barchetta that we call venezia giulia
winds that blow hibiscus across the swamps filled our saffron sails
pirate brigs and wall street whorehouse tankers drifted overhead

as we passed under their ropes the musicians threw us candy
at governors island the inside channel is dangerous
but in open harbor you have to watch for the irish tugboats

usually they don't hit you but they rock you pretty good going by
sometimes we get only as far as where the current rips across
you can see a lot from any position if you think about what you see

i might just take the boat out of the water onto a trailer
hitch it to the chevy and drive to astoria but get there for supper

11.3

some irish tugboat captains drink whiskey against bad weather
in the east river your boat sails down a staggering promenade
the east river bridges recall the large american wars

civil war spanish american war first world war second world war
when i think of the bombing of dresden i arrive in astoria
in the restless water sat an ocean going creature tombstone gray

from the hill we had seen it slide in under the triborough bridge
they were fixing its top which sat as high as we sat on the hill
an italian who wrote about it to italy they put in the crazy house

they had airplanes with wings folded on the top of this thing
astoria was a village with a dead whale eight hundred feet long
you could smell deep oceans where fish had died in its belly

the police were irish too and patrolled the estuaries in speedboats
people would slip in and out on the tides all the time anyway

11.3-11.4

11.4

you were born in land that became enemy territory six months later
long island city factories made bombs americans would drop on italy
di donato spent the war a prisoner because he would not fight italy

italians looked for safe jobs that didn't pay too much
the americans sent you a letter with red and blue stripes
after that you were all right and pray the war ends soon

young italians got married after the war and went to long island
older ones first put siding on the house then retired to florida
the big italian reservations emptied out

in east setauket di donato built walls out of stones
he sat at the dock of the inlet catching fish
they follow paths in the sea no one can trace

it still looks like enemy territory out the portholes of my mind
the war with italy ended fifty years ago but where is the door

11.5

from the airplane we gaze down at a gray object of contemplation
it has paper wrinkles that suggest movement but very slow movement
we glide across it stock still though they say we are going fast

are we slipping through the gelatinous sky thickness toward italy
i have no way of knowing for sure it even is the country italy
is it peru or some other place i have never seen with an italy feel

the bus grinds through farms as boring as farms anywhere
lots of broken cement and lots of barbed wire
every solid thing smells of diesel oil and soils your fingers

the death colored ocean under us smelled of jetplane kerosene
here we pass old cars burnt and crushed that lie in angular mounds
we drive into a city all stone as in a prison no trees anywhere

the famous church lies under banks of black smoke from french buses
i doubt my mother was born in this country but i kneel down anyway

11.6

they have made a new forum romanum entirely out of compressed paper
the formula for this astonishing feat they attributed to giotto himself
but others now say some anonymous clever goth in borgo santospirito did it

no one can tell this paper from the original marble
the travertine was all stolen to build castles for the families of priests
building facsimile ancient rome began in the thirteen hundreds

the history of italy is the history of these clever initiatives
when studying italy always remember that priests control the banks
but mathematicians control the production of physical reality

they have redesigned every single horizon and mountain in italy
charming old cities illustrate esoteric pythagorean ratios
the ancient pantheon's dome uses fabricated stone in twenty weights

in the himalayas and in the andes certain priests built mountains
no one can tell these from the ones that arise from bubbles below

11.7

in astoria women made lace in patterns that recall the aztec sky
ten dimensional symmetries complicate these ten finger exercises
elaborately cast moulds made pizzelle lessons in baroque geometry

italians write letters that echo their readers in advance
as a people we are prone to liver problems and a benign paranoia
the one weakness comes from not leaving home and so does the other

we stand to one another in the seashell postures of saints
or else we stand like flaming points on a silver star with a flashing tail
as children we each learn one thousand symmetrical maps

we know human relationships fall into circles squares and triangles
but they also follow the subtler rhythms of a hand of cards
an octagon divided into pie wedges can help solve marriage problems

our fingers learn the fine italian hand forming farfalle
every figure we cast works deep invisible magic

11.7–11.8

11.8

when the walls began rusting through i decided to end the war
soon the ship would settle into the mud at the river bottom
as i started for the exit the whole thing tilted

i could hear the hull scrape along pebbles and sand
with a muffled splash it stopped moving
my fingers clasped a bulkhead listing at a forty-five degree angle

inch by inch i found footings and places to grab
slime on the floor twice made me slide but i did not fall
i climbed three steep corridors before i came out at last on deck

i had expected treacherous footing but the rails were still good
there was a gangway where i could brace each foot and each hand
frequently checking redundant supports one at a time i shimmied down to land

i still walk crouching and turning to look in all directions
whenever i go downhill my first thought is the tide is coming up

11.9

i discovered one morning i was proud of my body
if it had a few weaknesses that put it in very good company
and it was me

the priests had separated us into ocean and fish
as if the one was conceivable without the other
writing produced huge anxieties at every turn of the line

i would smoke or stroke or joke or poke to ease the tension
now i just keep swimming and try to enjoy the ride
i am a fish who can swim

of course it is not as easy as that
plenty of times i get sleepy or feverish
i try to connect these feelings with the fears they protect me from

thinking in a bed only sometimes resembles thinking walking
i have a hundred books i want to read but my eyes keep blinking

11.9–11.10

11.10

the extent of neural phenomena seems to be total in a person's life
what you feel is what you think is what goes through the networks
you pause at the edge of success and fear stops you right there

in the networks code red flashes stay where you are
a muscle twitch or nonspecific pain or infection now starts up
your eyes ache or your belly and it focuses all the networks

to change focus stimulate networks less involved in the pain event
this can send twitches and infections into the background body feel
as your new focus heats up these pain events fade and disappear

each book on my shelves is about something that once mattered to me
but how exactly how each book mattered is how i began writing
for years i turned the pages looking for what was not there

now even the books i write myself have begun to miss the point
i keep spearing at the water anyway because i won't give up

11.11

i have changed colors again because the season is changing
no one can find me as they know me red orange but now i am blue green
if i do something coded as powerful then alarms ring and i go down

desire keeps waiting for the flurry to subside so i can go on
sometimes i lose hope and imagine nothing will ever come out right
this despair is one of the more convincing colors of alarm

but when i think i will give up then that produces other alarms
these less noisy say give up now and you will be sleepy forever
so they push me forward while the others push me back

looking acting different than before i get past them all sometimes
i make good progress down some parallel lane till they see me
then they bring new york city traffic to wherever they find me

last year i stopped driving and started using public transportation
i could read during delays but now my eyes have started to twitch

11.11–11.12

11.12

it looked easy to give yourself down to the water
the loud machines filthied the sky and you lay there half dead
submarines once hit the ship with a torpedo but it did not sink

in that moment you knew that leaving was the right thing to do
for the next six or seven years you did nothing but cry and shout
afterwards your confessor slowly brought you to admit your feelings

finally you tied your diseases into a bundle with rope
this boat is not moving you said and stepped off onto the landing
welcome to the united states land of perpetual earthquake

every highway broke under the weight of the blue sky
you watched mountains pulverize after you wrote down their names
hundred car freight trains trundled out the debris every night

we have made a religion of measuring sunlight they told you
they showed you their new equipment which you said looked familiar

12. italy inspires you to imagine things and then defeats those things

12.1

these voyages all follow the flag of what they leave behind
where the spherical sky grows dense the creatures change shape
we know we cannot call to any of the fish in their own languages

snow lies across the highlands in streaks fifty miles long
i saw a bright blue line straight down the middle of the ocean
that submarine ran on pure phosphorous at the speed of sound

once you swam around my index finger hanging through the surface
nothing can explain how much easier we breathe up here
aromas underwater have narrower ranges but richer textures

another time i held you flapping in my hand like a bird
small creatures passionately seek to free themselves from large
thus you thus me thus our implausible conversations

certain beings embarking began weaving an interminable rope
up through the ozone it drifts towards the airier beings

12.1–12.2

12.2

italy inspires you to imagine things and then defeats those things
the blue light of earth shines forth in no land more than in italy
in river sky and sea and rock even the green has a blue cast

steep towns arise like cocks on the roof who are part of the sky
the moment in which the world begins will take place in an hour
fierce anticipation draws you outdoors to the world of the dead

sputtering gray poisons into the piazza comes the dead italians truck
lines of colorfully dressed dead parade in the market shadows
they organize restaurants so that every meal has a sacred theme

people pour blood of enemies into goblets before eating
the food itself exploits all the best ideas of one million years
your new proposal amounts to what they used to do in the seicento

slabs of the future like black ice fall through the present moment
the dead with their chisels carve the fragments into human heads

12.3

in my dialogues socrates acts totally harmless
in plato too because he is one who asks impossible questions
an even slightly strenuous manner would seem overmuch

you come into the room and he says why not go back outside
tens of millions of american dogs have scratchy voices
i don't know how to get into this mess carefully enough

if only i could trust you i would feel better
things you tell people who talk too much become rumors
when people misunderstand you it means they are paying attention

peace is nice but too much peace leaves you feeling abandoned
all the water here has bubbles so is water a solid
no trains can stop here because no trains exist

are you good because of what you do or do you do it because you are good
we have made him into a dilemma machine and turn it off at night

12.3-12.4

12.4

i am a good husband father breadwinner professor executive
always behind in his work
ass in a sling

people take you for a role model do you realize that
you feel like a cabin they visit in the woods
you are a recommended chapter in the training of youth

we close these cabins for seasons at a time and even years
each receives the special protection we accord to woodland temples
each harbors a creature but the creature may self reclude at will

for my sanctity in these woods i have shared a cabin fourteen years
i had expected scholarly seclusion but instead i lived like a dog
for this reason i have determined to give others use of the cabin

i can pay a caretaker to sweep the altar rubble free daily
meanwhile go bathe my eyes in the waters of alpine lakes

12.5

if others observe the rites you do not need to do it
but if others do not observe the rites what are you to do
so many steps plus so many turns plus just so many bows

as it was in the beginning is now you recite and ever shall be
the rooster thought if i stopped singing the sun would not change colors
but other roosters have always been crowing over the fields

since the sun will always hear roosters singing it will always rise
but you must observe the rites for temporary transfer of temple
these include a foursquare sweeping washing airing of the aisles

prayers to recite and alms to give at each angle of the foundation
the celebrant recalls all wall measurements and the builder's name
a specific sequence of flowers secures the blessings of guardians

we have oiled the heavy bronze locks before the ceremony
no matter when you return you will know them by smell

12.5–12.6

12.6

keep your radio tuned to your garibaldi
the army marching down with hammers in their hands is not your redshirt
nor is curling up in bed afraid to move hugging the pillows crying

his white horse makes the masochism of conscience an amusement
when you hear someone saying you selfish bastard change the station
guerilla messages can pierce the typhoon on radio waves

design a tuner to receive these messages and tune out others
garibaldi messages include praise for how well you are doing and looking
they feel like flexing muscles when you embrace

you have ideas and you put them into action
if people envy or demean you think of it as airwave traffic noise
you glory in your actions silently like a blossoming hillside

your general knows how to give as well as receive praise
he combs his beard in your mirror

12.7

for example i would like to praise you for recording sad things
they will inspire other people not to be sad and help you as well
do not feel guilty you deserve it if other people stroke your monkey

as you get ready for the big change the water explodes into air
your daughter says look how blue the sky is this morning
people line up on the sides of the boat looking for parrots

you tried using marijuana to find a signal in the noise
someone said the signal was the war but it was a mixture of the war and the general
the general fires villages to call out across valleys

send the general to war
noise is boredom or war in your stomach
the general's horse rears when he reaches the enemy line

the entrance to the harbor is narrow and well hidden
you need a beam clear despite distortions to find your way home

12.7–12.8

12.8

you can be lost in the ocean of self for a thousand years
the navigator captain polishes the compass brass
the ship is a beast and the ocean is a world of forgetting

the dead admiral whispers like a sour gossip behind the door
he frightens the captain
when the sea is death he says polish your shoes

the wind loosens screws and tears pages in the navigation book
during the triumphal entry the captain lies down with a fever
you cannot fool me says the admiral nor can you really hear me

you listen for his messages as if he were a father with a whip
he is a pirate station on a rotting tanker riding at anchor
don't worry if you fail to tune him in he will find other listeners

do you like this music you always ask yourself
the radio remember is alive even though it is dead

12.9

the sun rises over abruzzi where goatherds live among the eagles
everything is so blue you think you will never need to eat again
at the same time hunger has you and you eat a whole warm cheese

listen you say i will do anything to stay here and be one of you
why do you want to do that isn't it paradise for you in america
paradise is such a complicated idea you say

anyway they say if complication is what you want we have plenty
next thing you know you are working day and night for no money
but they feed you which seems enough all by itself

the secret priests come after you with their glowing transmitters
how dare you take italy you ungrateful little bastard they sing
you keep turning the dial till you hear the muttering of swine

healing takes a long time but one morning you wake up with your mind empty
when you leave no one on the mountain sees you go

12.10

is it the things you have to do or is it the having to do them
because if it is the first just do them and free yourself
but if the second then you will just change one set for another

so sings the pope's skeleton shutting you up and shutting you down
you always have things to do the question is do you want to do them
which means neither the things nor the having but what you want

what you want though it seems airy is stronger than buildings
it builds bridges and shoots a rocket through the ocean
doing what you want you build houses and raise tribes from the dead

the papal transmitter sends storms rattling through your whole body
adjust the receiver for sounds of sharks on the high seas
just outside the twelve mile limit the transmissions begin to break up

as the swells become living mountains you breathe with your legs
so you think i have finally discovered the theater of migration

12.11

crossing the sea in a big ship you come to respect human invention
some people have the same experience in airplanes watching movies
but most require more air and more silence before they can hear their own breathing

then you readily see how every turn of the journey needs vigilance
each step has huge importance but your feet already know this
your eyes watch the empty horizon and see the one thing that is real

you file down the rickety gangplank together with the other italians
we do not know what it means you sing but we do it together
as parts of one another we flitter and glow and glitter and flow

the italians stand on streetcorners in brooklyn proud as snakes
their smile dares you to come in and enjoy their company
together with their eyes they can look through brick walls

ingenuity does not fail when you follow the flag of what you want
this is what the italians learned meditating in the ships together

12.11–12.12

12.12

hang this message from your neckchain on a tiny scroll in a pendant
once you hear the breathing ocean everything gleams under your hand and eye
all this fear you have comes from the nonexistent admiral

whenever you check your watch check what programs you are getting
tuning an instrument and tuning your mind have everything in common
you affirm spacing of intervals and strength inhering in parallels

squaring the circle of the invisible sky you use it to guide you
at every point in the ocean you can establish meaning and direction
your own plot stands upon the disposition of stars in the black

the flaming sword of light does not appear but just your upraised hand
you have touched your bare toe not into the fire of mother earth but only dirt
your shield made entirely of rejected histories repels delicate messages

you are one who has passed through a water planet to another world
everything you do leaves a mark even just walking down the street

13. i want to lean on the old principles but what are they

13.1

the books pile up like boats pointing every way riding at anchor
we choose our company and fine tune to stations but then forget our choices
i look for how to know which station was on and how to change it

resetting the tuning each morning is basic
people fiddle with the dials when you don't realize it
weather expands and contracts tuners so that they lose the signal

in the morning i sit down to work with my captain
if i can't do it then i look to see where i feel bad
just looking suffices to tune out interferences

you choose your company and contrive your world anyway
why not do it with your eyes open and your better self turned on
when people torture you does it matter if they are wearing crosses

the sense you were born with makes you a human being and guides you
if someone tells you it's a mystery ask another person

13.1–13.2

13.2

this bird sat on the branch singing in russian
this bird flew between buildings soundless down the alley
this one liked to read comics and this one drank green wine

but this little birdie sang yes no or maybe all the way home
flowers abounded in the hills but i felt my usual crisis of doubt
do i really want to stay or really not

i thought why not elaborate works of art concerning your staying
then when or if you go you will give that a pleasing form as well
habits of beauty and order will follow you giving health to others

when you sin let your sin be simple and enjoy it thoroughly
virtue comes from clear acts so make some mistakes if you like
remember a tree rooted in the beginning of time gives you strength

your general principle arises visible from earth so it may know itself
of course it does not always succeed in doing so

13.3

the christian way is to keep pouring love into a person
sooner or later it takes and they start producing golden harvests
autumn brings forth labor as food

the clan produces food
it accepts all good colors and tastes and comforts of life
but then i get angry because it doesn't work

you do not give perfectly which is your trouble with christianity
how do you reprogram your clan with this end in view
programming does not depend upon the goal but only upon logic

you get angry because you are not getting the result you want
pay more attention to your clan and less to other people's sodden bibles
in the morning sit for an hour before talking

your loneliness will end when you lower your defenses
when the shields go down the clan revives

13.3–13.4

13.4

how do you know if something is good is my problem
doing things supposed to be good i feel bad
goodness may be too hard for me to judge

i want to lean on the old principles but what are they
i make choices which have powerful results i do not understand
my old principles are ritual circles in which i dance every day

i raise the stick of manhood and pound it on the ground as i dance
its rattles and feathers attract the gazes of young women
smiling at the anthropologist my cousin steals his camera

we don't know why we do what we do except we saw our fathers do it
they crowned the virgins in leaves and young males in red ribbons
the bishop's hat was a finger pointing an erect penis at the sun

we leave certain things behind selling the store to immigrants
afterwards we think of going back but instead we go forward

13.5

we piece new languages together out of old italian remnants
the second millennium has begun to sink rapidly
mainland is going to be a little more fluid from now on

the law of the future is a circular path that teaches us change
keep running and when the women signal to you answer them
every tribe has a divorce somewhere at the beginning of its history

now you see it now you don't and you can turn to other things
listen to the music of pebbles under the fat tires of the cadillac
just start making the new settlement and don't worry too much

god the father is the dead man and the son is the tailored plaid shirt
but the holy ghost is the garbled messages on the bulletin board
this is the story as i learned it

these old stories are tremendously fierce
i am writing a new story in which the son is a pair of silk pajamas

13.5–13.6

13.6

when i have a great success i come home and sock myself in the jaw
or else i find someone to do it for me or else wait till morning
i try keeping the moving parts of the tuner clean and i check all connectors

the process of change can go smoothly for hours and hours and days
then you find yourself right back where you started only worse
shake it off adjust the tuner and sit still for a minute to listen

think of all this trouble as a package you tie with twine
leaving it for the garbage men you stroll off
but you may be afraid to leave the house

you have to be patient with an apparatus when you are tuning it
some have only few parts but humans have many amazing features
the power of a tuned human instrument can induce great calm

its resonances caress and encourage
tuning it we free its words which cure us of sorrow and confusion

13.7

reconsider things from other people's perspectives
everyone defers to voices you do not necessarily hear
other people's motives are often plain enough

it is not required that you love or even accept their feelings
but seeing them helps you learn the functions of the building
mapping their motives helps you find the way to your own goals

common sense tells you don't read the newspapers underwater
some groups of people will not let you play bach on the violin
join with those whose encouragement helps you fulfill your desires

even in such groups a certain modest amount of mapmaking will help
but keep your focus on what you are aiming to accomplish here
once you get onto the right road keep maps in the glove compartment

review your plans often and consult them when you have trouble
for the most part enjoy the scenery and change the oil frequently

13.7–13.8

13.8

after twenty years on the same leash a tiny tug is enough
i was playing with a toy that moulds itself to your fingers or nose
trying it on my cousins' faces or on the handles of the end tables

each thing had a fresh surprise charming them there in a circle
and in at the door strolls the breezy wife and the cousin's angry wife
what are you playing at now asks the wife which is enough

the rest of the day i felt how you feel when someone takes your toy
i could not answer and tried playing the piano but no one listened
so i began to amuse the children by poking fun at sacred things

but that made people unhappy but now someone took up my music
i sat and we played together which could have been a longer duet
as you stop overeating you get thin enough to slip the leash

next time she approaches my piano i play till she wants to stay
here i said to the wife put this on the dog

13.9

yes i thought i chose her to impress people i could not deal with
then she came into my house and started leaving impressions on me
as we see from your skin you sleep with a porcupine

how about that and don't do that might be how a lot of people talk
but some people will play happily alongside you if you let them
since you know all of this so now what

changing stories comes easier when your stories already differ
your will can make trees grow and winds blow when you think
in this you aren't dissolving a marriage but watching it from across the street

they will always tell this one as part of your story and of hers
and you may frame it as a comic war at troy and travels of odysseus
twenty years of struggle may who knows find the bride you need next

the light that shines underground totally eludes daylight
yet everyone sees it when asleep or just waking up out of it

13.9–13.10

13.10

no longer blind at summer's end you see beaches plain again
every grain of sand glows with inner light like a mysterious jewel
now you see how birds outstrip all subtleties of human art

each thing reveals not so much its colors as the colors of pattern
unfolding power through the universe paints september
one morning every tree begins to yield

sun rain earth air time devotion and gold mingle
the so great sweetness of fruit may mask its complexity
but no art can render the harvest calling out to the departing sun

in the old days painters sat on hills failing to capture the fall
then they gave up on the fall and tried to capture other painters
now they trace the logic of representation

looking at things draws upon all your resources of memory and of thought
how you feel answers what things say in reply to every answer you give

13.11

you will not die looking at things that cost less money and grief
walk in the bazaar and study equipment you will need for the trip
heavenly messengers have told you you may cross the street alone

it's all right to scrape the hull of the little boat pushing off
drift out among the carp under the weeping cherry trees and think
as part of the preparation just sit and let your defenses dissolve

do not panic because you have a thousand calls and errands waiting
each of these will be a step even if it does not seem to go forward
weaving many ropes and sails and curing green wood you stand still

first you interest investors and second assemble capital
only then you place orders in shipyards and begin recruiting mates
you draw upon years of thought when you devise your expedition

as you go about your work every now and then policemen spit at you
this serves to remind you why you are leaving to begin with

13.11–13.12

13.12

in that police state i hold myself prisoner to childhood
hold still and be safe i say even though i starve
downstairs the world comes unglued while i sicken for lack of love

i can do nothing in this damp cell except dream of leaving
every plan to improve prison conditions seems to make them worse
so that you have diabetes because you can never get enough sweetness

the only thing to do is give this child what he needs
love him systematically and tell him how handsome he is
when you say to yourself you are ugly you broadcast toxic shame

turn your antenna away from that signal
this will not cure all problems but it will change your feelings
then you will begin solving problems intensely as if making love

when you place your hand with love you find things move and respond
plan lightly in advance because love will work the sums as you go

14. as the immigrants step into paradise it rains down evil eyes

14.1

fall in summer winter in fall spring in winter summer in spring
when you do what you were dreaming of you may be assailed by fears
lying in her bed in long island city she dreams witches in abruzzo

as the immigrants step into paradise it rains down evil eyes
these phantasms give color and body to panic anticipation
focus on the fact that the whole universe exists at this moment

you change together with the universe changing
its large movements give life and some say meaning to everything
but we probably can't even imagine much less dispute such meanings

this was where they paused in the argument about god
since then we read the physics department newsletter every month
einstein referred to the subtlety of the old one

subtle not malicious he said subsiding into a priest language
calculus gaelic replaces architecture latin as the dialect of clues

14.1–14.2

14.2

so you know the universe loves you because you are a part of it
you belong to it in this moment exactly as alpha centauri does
you cross oceans like a comet leaving a wake of stars on the void

spinning atomic resonances increase in richness producing life
embracing the globe italians multiply the earth with their antiquity
they follow garibaldi liberator of america to paraguay and brooklyn

come to america to free themselves they find the evil eye waiting
here they learn to make evil good and the crooked a perfect circle
some of them live on tightly strung cables that hold the world firm

others float upon water expressing the sexual nature of the earth
some study the philosophy and theology and mantras of free spirits
italians transmit and receive continuous messages around the world

together italians are discovering new ways of dividing the sunlight
pythagoras da vinci galileo garibaldi fermi ferlinghetti di prima

14.3

at this point the sonnet becomes an iroquois narrative
búm búm bàbabàba búm búm carpets from the looms of mohawk
they are chopping children in their sleep while campfires smoke

the evil eye fades as the battering surf fills the mind with sound
forests roar with creatures turning the mountains red on sonar maps
in america we consider only the size of what we can never know

we construct cities walking across empty deserts say the books
but imagining cities amounts in fact to fulltime jobs for millions
cascading voids bury all projects but those to hide from largeness

at cinemas americans gaze upon empty spaces we later drive home in
the american side of the earth resembles the outer side of the moon
no bravery of flags and no theology of rocks can tame its blankness

the spirits on this side of the oceans reclude themselves from us
we see eurasian gods except in the purple glaze of mountain valleys

14.3–14.4

14.4

i bent a beam of perfect violet and planted it inside your hair
another time i bound you in rings of pale green traces
whenever i thought of you i began to glow so that people noticed

you stepped out of the pool a plutonium sapphire of desire
my own light deepens if i just stand still and plan how to see you
lamps at lectures flicker while your remembered image burns clear

on the merry go round lovers with flaming rubies for eyes shoot by
the horses rippling up and down fill our legs with a dark radiance
when the music changes we step into the orange shadows of trees

every turn of your head implies choruses of overhead cameras
when you laugh my mohawk eyes see the brilliant serene pacific haze
would you like also to swim in rivers of light as thick as snakes

a muscular whirlpool spiralling collects and changes forces
touching we complete circuits that pass through all the outer night

14.5

all the guilt of forever rides the donkey backs of ancient slaves
my italians sit in front of television sets on eighteenth avenue
their gardens lie dead under thick slabs of atlantic sand cement

as for me my guilty forms shimmer into existence if i think freedom
pay those bills satisfy those people who hate you and then stay put
that is the message so that every gloom of life looms huge

tax after years of mistakes any success seems great
sex after years in hiding even modest courage seems heroic
bux after years not trying even a small book launching looms epic

cultivate the heroism of modesty and the modesty of heroes
thus you keep a sense of proportion about these things
accept them as great and as reasonable at the same time

while size is not entirely relative act as if it were anyway
keep following the best light you have in getting what you want

14.5–14.6

14.6

when it gets cold you think entirely of your strengths
that will keep you moving fed and warmly dressed and housed
others assist you but often because your captain communicates with them

he sends silent desire causing the other to feel your need
indirectly suggest desire inviting the other to join your activity
all strengths best call on desire when fulfilling their own natures

who desires your nature sees something delicious you often do not
strengths also pay taxes to police away unwanted desires of others
in state channels we restrict exchanges of desires to ritual tables

in the shops and banks and churches we exchange strengths as money
then in books of books of books of books we record these exchanges
spears of fern surround poems we write in the form of banyan trees

human purposes who live beneath them borrow shapes from these trees
poems have shadows wider than highways and gray as hawks in winter

14.7

plenty of times i am waiting to learn how to forget who people think i am
that is suppose the captain starts to sing but a noise persists
it keeps saying stop this homework and get back to having fun

likewise when they yell do your homework your homework becomes a problem
can we get back far enough from this quivering creature to love him
you know you don't need to take a chill in order to have a rest

in fact every line of this poem represents another miracle
can this be it now the miracle you were waiting for
i go along well for a little while but then i freeze over

am i just scared i think but wouldn't i know it if i was scared
you might not know much with a bag over your head and stuffed ears
pay attention means allow your feelings and care for your body

after the waves of terror soak you for hours stand up and walk home
this time you get a little more done than you did last time

14.7–14.8

14.8

after you do something something else wants you to do it
but all you want to do is lie down and make love with someone
and if there is no one you will settle for a nap or a snack or both

other times you make a phone call or play the piano
you used to read a book but now you are too anxious to take so long
these pangs howl and thunder through your body

you want to do the next thing so why the storm
are you afraid what will happen if at last you get free
stay close to the task and don't give up no matter how hard it gets

don't fall for fears and hesitations and changings of the subject
keep reiterating the shape of your enterprise to yourself
if repetition excites you consider the excitement a diversion

climb the ladder rung by rung till you get out of the water
once you stop holding your breath you can relax with a clear mind

14.9

you might drive yourself into a passion of twitching and sorrow
each time you cross even the smallest barrier in life you feel it
squealing joints and the mysterious infections conspire mumbling

exercise massage meditation mantras mass all help drumming change
in paumanok canarsie here lowlands ghost canoes float midair
with ancient water chants you induce them to carry things away

sorting rituals for anthologies we distinguish their virtues
i collected the present compendium near the ocean
it features ritual histories of humans as nimble as fish

i have been an octopus and a squid in other lives and later a shark
passing through the feet of an indian scout i discovered my mistake
i still needed twenty lives more to find the right path forward again

things happen one at a time
it's only boring if you try to see too much at once

14.9–14.10

14.10

listening you rediscover certain messages lost during transmission
the boats rock wildly at different angles soaking business cards
shadows mingle under the building so you can't separate them

transmitting swims out of deep wells in the human ocean by millions
every fish can choose from a universe of possible messages to carry
beating human passion writes itself across schools of dolphins

fishers find in fish the ocean calm of complete transmissions
you too find calm listening to the rain beat against your mind
every fish uses mandolin tomtom bands and many stars in deep colors

to read simple messages requires a sense of lucid contradistinction
after seeing a billion snowflake variations one day you get it
some people find it in a hand of cards and others in a serenade

of course i love you meaning in my life that confounds me
there is no wall so don't beat at the door just come around it

14.11

i have been experimenting with the human compactness of desire known as beauty
i love my own body perfections which i never name inside the boundaries of words
whitman sometimes sounded as if he had done it for good and all but he couldn't

i run my hands over my outer complex simplicity sensory self wet and dry
the body is our word for what understands in messages more eloquent than speech
the brain transmits remembers and intensifies what the knowing body gives or gets

look at the intense inner fury of hair to see the sadness of any person's life
they used to say in the sagging of the mask the aging hypocrite feels his burden
each stub of beard represents an encyclopedia of memory

i used to claim those with thin beards tend to have very well organized recall
but it is not true that a thick beard means too many categories for rapid search
we explore the body to find what things run steady and which have variable speed

parts of us grow extraordinary either with use or with awesome unfolding
a dream of the ocean implies uncontrollable movement

14.11–14.12

14.12

the plan of talking includes the plan of being seen talking
people who see you talk also see meanings you carry across through other modes
they do not see all modes because after all most human modes are invisible

the long listener comes to move in time with inaudible modes in your breathing
inner spirit modes in the audience suffer when drunkards argue
each person must manage a highway thronged with spirits running up his throat

forming a mountain flute in the throat breathing in you breathe out multitudes
these peacock spectacles plume in air dissolving into general brilliance
dynasties of tiny diamond memory strand hairs float in the morning sunbeam

remember the old crude transformation of things to electronic message media
every signal reaching a mind records more than you know including your approval
later on they will study your traces for objectives your thinking can not now think

most things disappear in the moment of their fulfillment but not affirmation
you will find that you were doing more than you knew how to take into account

15. the man next door came here from mars

15.1

no one can tell you what you need to know in the new life
even if people know these clues we have no words to name them
anyway objects matter less than the order of their occurrence

this order discovers roads that differ daily
it helps you design swift works of engineering for smooth conveyance
in these you assume and enjoy secure command positions

life at the heights of spirit includes crickets centipedes and scorpions
wise as you are you have only one drop of blood to lose in ocean
travelling the valleys you meet old women who understand weather

certain birds have mapmaking powers beyond what we can imagine
your own apprehension outstrips precedent and prophecy
when you pour the water correctly all powers come to you

your intelligence helps you speak to leopards
you can delight in them without naming them

15.1–15.2

15.2

i found my new cadillac illegally parked outside the apartment
so i drove it around the block and down the stairs into a bookstore
we were still trying to roll it up out of there when i awakened

not every dilemma needs to be solved in its own terms
changes of consciousness in particular respond to varied modes
i am learning to drive my new perfectly polished cadillac bodyself

if i find it in obscure no exit situations i recall the laquered hologram
the downstairs bookstore projects my social labyrinth of immobility
the lesbian owner has gone to find my car a ramp but not returned

in the aisles saturday couples i know mingle and chatter
i decide to leave the bookstore my cadillac as a conversation piece
the bodyself integrates its images while shedding their trash

waking up drives out of the cadillac bookstore superchargers belching
each poem is a chrysler imperial a jaguar or an eldorado

15.3

when we landed in america the first thing we did we made wheels
the indians dragged their things around leaving tracks everywhere
like a detective smoking a pipe the last mohican followed clues

of course we liked the idea of free travel in a land without walls
but more than anything we knew the land was only water
it would not hold you steady in one place the way italy did

america required wheels as the ocean had required a watertight hull
while the mohican could follow trails in the ocean we could not
we built trails like rivers with high banks and rows of trees

to us america lies open like the nerves of a disembowelled shark
huge convoys carry brontosaur machines from cave to distant cave
high definition allows speed but costs powers of discrimination

walking mohicans subtly swim through air like future automobiles
you cannot see these cars because they are not the same cars

15.3–15.4

15.4

now i have come to where i must do certain hard things
tuned rested aimed to do well i intend to develop some steady perfection devices
first i apply for a new mortgage to pay some back taxes

then i get the money and send it to irs and even that score
after that i buy car paint house get kids computers
the next step is to rent apartment in art neighborhood and move into it

i design my wide plan new life to drain off guilt under clean airy dry light
the hill grade plus the cut stone gutters keep me secure even in blizzards
smart work on bills mortgages and tax helps make this plan a reality

even the great granite marble architects depend upon deeds and calendar instruments
they begin the day as we do registering sun moon tide and season of living things
many signs tell observers how patterns are moving and we adjust to the message

mortgage writers use hieroglyphic money time epic formulae creating social space
these show you how the constellations stand so you navigate better

15.5

some very simple things you may choose to do
other times i cannot talk to certain persons
you look at the river and sunlight blows up towards you like leaves

leaping like antelopes red tugboat prows fall and plow the narrow channel
disturbances roll under muscle satin flexing in the river making the air undulate
in summer oil stink swamp tide overwhelms you and in winter steel handed wind

the air is so cold you can chop it down in jagged blocks green grass and all
iced breezes stimulating vivid capillary circulation pain light the nerves red
brandishing brittle leaves a tree whines like an aerial under arctic november

a gray gull glides out of one silver tower of the bridge along the arc of span
red tower lights flake glittering in pool reflections miles in all directions
long hairlike bunches of dark green blossoms curl and ripple in tidal wash

on rocks among fish choice inspires meditation which takes its own time
priests use mathematical skills to count seeds which can help speed things up

15.5–15.6

15.6

we go to the store where they keep money singing money makes whole
then they measure every muscle in our bodies for texture and size
reducing everything to quantities judges then judge qualities

you have illuminated entire streets with your appetite for music
looking at you i see how so called reflections are emanations
your strange light singes colors into the hillside

if i knew what you wanted i would not hesitate to have it i said
but i was starring in an opera named after an orphan named after me
my new car tells when you are listening to self-destructive thought

it self adjusts to receive the beam leading to fulfilled desire
some mornings i idle it longer to take the chill out of the engine
i move slowly through the shadows with the symphony playing

we examine everything in the searching glare of analytic patterns
light continues emerging from the planet through the eyes

15.7

you took a chance again and someone put you down in the old way
people concerned with their own needs may act carelessly with you
having little to do with your concerns it may still hurt you

constructed anew you may meet fresh reactions
you will know how to read them but not always at first glance
patience with the needs of others sweetens human interaction

scraping and slapping makes us music
the wind on the world ball shifts in the driving rain
leafstorm battles celebrate transformation of peoples

a person trails a single hand along the tops of ferns
willow strips cut your face if you shoot through them on a machine
but they rub you walking and scratch your cheeks with a delicate menace

each day of rain increases the light that rises from the ocean
its colors grow energetic flowering trumpets spikes and tambourines

15.7–15.8

15.8

the earthwork palaces began to overflow with emerald colored oil
oh please let me in the little girl cried as the steel door slammed
no one could tell her in which box they had concealed her mother

magic in her tongue provided her with lovers opulently endowed
everyone wanted to taste of it and some of them delicious to her
into each of them she ducked her head looking for her mother

down from heaven the blackened mother descended the black basalt stairs
gentle breezes blew each tiny thing away before the little girl could look at it
she had to try to remember every clue the first time she saw it

the mother's orange stole and yellow robe were so bright they darkened the mother's eyes
the daugher stands there legs askew
cattails and tiger lilies surround her

the cicadas roar and the piebald owl shrieks
she looks out at you from her grassy wilderness of mothers

ellis island

15.9

preacher rolls out in rolls royce wearing rolex watch
hmmm hmmm how highways unfold before his brilliant glances
and so amen i say to thee mumble mumble he shouts in time to music

i am the black man inside the white man inside the italian man
the triple dome of an american i wear mohawk haircut chinese wig
chili chowder in my chair father mother dance the pig

parking in a side street he walked under red arcades to avoid rain
came he to tower after tower demanding juliet in his mind
meanwhile the crowd was waiting in the hilltop park with view

they noticed him among them with no one's having seen him come
listening to their stories he learns the contents of their souls
now comes time to ascend podium interpreting questions

the entire time he is talking he is planning a song with dancing
lightning makes skies shudder but his concentration does not falter

15.9–15.10

15.10

the shape of the dance is a spiral and the music is a tarantella
shadows sing what they may once have feared to notice but now adore
and they cradle themselves in one another starting a variable hum

someone sings a little line or two and then the hum gets louder
the hum gets softer someone else sings a little the hum gets louder
the rhythm continues unbroken and the melody complains forever

here is how the dance spirals they are dancing in a tight circle
every time the hum changes the circle gets a little larger
when it gets as big as they want it they contract at the same rate

when they begin contracting they change the direction of circling
later on they begin expanding again and so change direction again
and each body cries out loud secrets in its native voice

moves grow so familiar some dancers forget that they're dancing
the rhythm of the weaving circle cures them and frees them

15.11

when you do something to an old man you are doing it to yourself
finishing one thing and starting another is another rhythm question
we dance and learn styles of arranging our entire lives together

one plus one makes two by two you grab me and i grab you partner
or else you share the music with many strangers that mate and flow
spiral dancing allows you to take aim at power and to assimilate it

we consume ourselves consuming it so that we share everything
i am sailing a boat into your eyes and swimming out your fingers
you are a double bank of cumulus clouds sliding across my dream

then i hear another secret and i can hardly tell who told it to me
mindless honesty in a narrator does not guarantee the tale is true
the patterns are all simple but you must distinguish them in motion

then your circle of friends may maneuver calm as a flying saucer
onto dance floor galaxies of powerful stars you purposefully float

15.11–15.12

15.12

i breathe as if i had been running hard
the water here reflects november stars
we buried schnauzers in the neighbor's yard

the man who lives next door came here from mars
he bought himself a coffin that could fly
it slept on rags in broken trolley cars

i always think if only i could cry
this feeling in my chest would go away
his daughter loves a lame retired spy

when he's asleep she writes what he will say
even dreaming both are practiced liars
i find the best thing i can do is play

i make the most of what the game inspires
her book has found a hundred thousand buyers

16. because you have no country no language and nothing much as such

16.1

maria maziotti gillan asked write about what it means to be italian american
so i begin by saying the first thing you are is not
because you have no country no language and nothing much as such

the first italian american person stands on two empty legs
each leg plastered with flags stands upon an empty foot
magnetism holds in place the empty italian american body

a cloud of notions surrounds the italian american glass block mind
light passes through unimpeded though absorbed amounts emerge amber
i shine opera house stage lights into your eyes when we kiss

beams of it come out my ears and flakes of it fall from my head
italian americans seem to be composed of light in slabs
their muscles burn your fingers if you hold them

italian americans are the glass cables that hold the world together
every italian american circles the globe simply by failing to think

16.1–16.2

16.2

dancing in a circle the italians how they go
dark as night and hot as hate and bitter as the snow
on stormy roads of politics the signs say danger slow

an excellent machine it is has wheels to hold the road
it steers real tight with engine tuned to blue computer code
the old one often stopped at night and needed to be towed

a new italian mind is what americans may lack
o think of me across the sea and i will think you back
o just say anything to me you whisper through a crack

i carry varied italian stone fragments in my bones from drinking italian water
thousands of italian animal mouthfuls have entered my muscles glands and nerves
every one of my organs has cells that belong to another and larger mind than my own

all i can do is receive messages and transmit them
in my study of this role i have only made a very few modest advances

16.3

i have passed a certain degree once again
metaphors of cars return to the garage of the castle
i overlook lago di bracciano from a wide crenellated terrace

i explain how these analogies apply to descendants of migrants
the car means an american who shoots water streets like a bullet
castle signifies a tribe that takes a stand and builds around it

tribes one by one deciding produce a system of castles
from castle to castle the cavalier canters alone
raising his sword he conveys decisions he draws from the stone

his virtue expresses a system of decisions which he shares deciding
each decision adds to the network of roads as well as destinations
red cars race between castles seeking sunrise blondes in fountains

the children play but the owners of caves seek high ecstasy
on the lake face that fills a volcano's crater we see your castle

16.3–16.4

16.4

as i put the matter to myself it remains an enigma i cannot solve
one side of me wants one thing while another wants another
can it be you are thinking of yourself as a car

either you go straight or your four wheels always turn in chorus
but think of your destinations as a system of castles now
you have a castle in one country and another in another

so you establish your conflicting desires as parts of an order
you travel from place to place trading satisfactions in each
models of communication allow for the inertia of information

things that do not travel with you take shape as decision castles
where have you returned they ask and what have you imagined
some decisions arise from having established chains of dream deposits

liberty across the entire world begins with open roads
you use these when you evolve from a machine to a machinist

16.5

will you stay in dreary comfortable servitude or leave
leaving you think teary eyed sorrow melting down to sleepiness
no person is certain and nothing is certain in this world

everything changes even as you look at it
think of the strong convergences that hold you together
now you can begin

your body is screaming to you i am afraid i am afraid
so you reply don't worry my children
and they say are you really in control

planets follow paths that respect their respective weights
and when you think of motion think of this
think of an image that unlocks the door of your body

your body can come out of its prison when you stop yelling at it
self-respect creates its own unexpected orbits

16.5–16.6

16.6

in shifting of categories a court becomes a sandbox
a potato emerges from the roasting fire a sign of friendship
the god wears rags so you can look into his eyes without fear

why does he want to know what i'm thinking the little boy asked
isn't it enough if i come to church and kneel down to all this gold
oscillating helplessness and power shifts categories bedazzlingly

christ is a shiva spinning categories so fast you never catch him
in your thinking and out of it his touch grows hard and soft
his curiosity strokes you and his judgment strikes you

i bring not peace but a sword he said and vice versa
the vulgar call the new testament a careless mess not a riddle book
places you leave behind become egypt

the lord appeared to moses in the form of another category
another category appeared to the lord in the form of moses

16.7

the fourth angel on the left is named ambrose alabaster aaronson
we brought him here from chicago last year in a balloon
a traditional jewish education will not always advantage you here

in this case the man had a mind full of large ammonium crystals
these being his primary perception mode he saw things we couldn't
we are planning a virtual version of his vision using holography

mister jesus has grown so old we only talk to him through memory
his appearance of course has never stayed the same for two seconds
no one can say what he looks like except as a trace of discovery

nonetheless the annual scholarships still get plenty of applicants
winners never want to leave when their term is up
and then after going away no one ever seems to reapply though it is allowed

our music is famous but no one mentions the best part is the food
is it that they can't remember or just they don't want it again

16.7–16.8

16.8

look i am lowering my profile because i became visible to myself
but wait a minute visible will get you what you say you want
so you attack the visible because it will take you away from home

you want to leave but you hate to let go of what you have not had
you are not going to have it even if you get it for a minute
what you want somewhere approaches you in a dream still

meanwhile what will leaving without getting what you want get you
you can hope for a higher degree of comfort and ease of movement
though not maybe what you want what you will have will be something

against your new horizon shapes and sizes and colors will change
old avenues will gently close behind you while others open wide
the ocean is a road for great creatures who cross it swimming

as you slip down the steps into the bay your skin darkens
you move in a new way now though no one can yet see what you are

16.9

look at yourself in the eyes of your purpose
you make plans because you know what you want
make a picture of what you are going to do next

you are going to lift your head up out of the water
calling out to others abandoned on the beach you make for shelter
you have not known them but your tribe and theirs are the same

you shiver when you first look at them because you are afraid
this water floods the ditches and you swim to the level of land
fear fuels flight while love will linger longer

do you feel love calling to you from among the tribes
love and fear are not the issues now maestro del mare
tu sei una nave you are a ship thou master of the mighty deep

we sing these religious songs to enchant women who give us flowers
they smell the ocean on us but the music tells them the whole story

16.10

why seek what you cannot have when you can have something else
your choices may seem slow and others may have strong contrary opinions
still you know what you are looking for is a sort of charm

you know the reason you want charm is pleasure and friendship
people have their spokes sticking out of their wheels
this will not answer to what you want so don't worry about it

if they reject you where you want to go then choose another place
making rules about these things will not much help
the best thing is just keep looking

tell the truth to yourself about how you feel
if you dislike someone or something admit it
you are not applying for a job

when you like something it still feels good in the morning
if not then think it over

16.11

a tree takes its beauty from its enforced humility
thus every tree to us will seem an example of its kind and place
although of course its true force springs from will and decision

every person likewise wishes and does according to mechanical rules
into the mall we file singing anticipating new clothing or new toys
our ordinariness expresses the power of human love and commitment

great cellulose clots of commodity tumble down the cliffs
caveman consumer they call me at the armani exchange
afterwards i drive fast through valleys that glaciers cut in the schist

i have lived behind high class containment complex walls
at the bookstore you may buy a mask of comic magic cookery
sitting in his class compound the roasting chef has dictated it

sometimes we think this is a beautiful place to settle into
even a tree is a signature event passing across our lives

16.11–16.12

16.12

i wanted to know who i was because i felt so entirely alone
discussing terms with others we stand upon our memory of resource
just that no one mentions it does not mean no one knows who you are

but of course we do not really know how anybody knows
when we love people we rest on trust and good memories
what we understand of one another may not always be clear

everything i forgot to tell was because of somebody threatening me
as a consequence i began wearing chain mail at an early age
the noise it makes alerts all creatures that move

sometimes nowadays i leave my hammered armor in the car trunk
children do not hurt you so simply shelter them when they need it
now we might wish to honor all those who love us and whose pain we feel

for this no armor is needed except the vigilance of watching
even this you can let go as you begin to learn others' needs

ellis island

17. i was just down the cellar trying to shift my story's foundations

17.1

i had an idea last night so good i fell asleep to avoid writing it
at this moment i do not remember it but if i keep trying it may return
one thought i do have present is the memory of forgetting it

in my room at new ellis island we give you a piece of paper
write down all the people who mattered most to you in childhood
put the paper in a slot and it comes out a little cone of dust

now your sense of what you are begins to blow away with your breath
hey wait a minute you say this is only a dream i am waking up from
when you open your eyes you are alone in a gray spaceship dimly lit

they all have gone to the movies and you have come back to the womb
how am i going to erase all these names from my mind you shout
oh no but your whole mind works on a process of slow forgetting

two churning columns support the entrance door entablature
blue agate friezes spiral upward as you read the story of the past

17.1–17.2

17.2

ellis island cemetery hill holds all thirty-seven million stone people
granite plinths and obelisk encrusted temples weigh them down
the overburdened island slides into the fluid surface of the earth

what is this muck of clotted paper eddying about my feet
these are the history books of migration and assimilation
have we forgotten holy americanization rites we shared you ask a tear in your eye

no we have passed through them so absolutely we became stone lions at the library
the migrants did for sure and ever assimilate to become lost americans
afterwards the lost americans in their turn did assimilate and become migrants

this happened during the great cultural revolution of 1968
americans abandoned the army in thousands returning to their tribes
migricani they wander across the slate face of the ocean continent

lost in time and in space the migricani draw people sideways
migricani means stray dogs who worship the moon and the stars

17.3

from christian points of view these migricani look like moors
they have a sort of christian sound but minus clouds of paradox
or so say those christians who think the migricani must be airheads

the migricani reply that christians moors and orthodox jews are all obsessives
migricani belong to at least two distinct tribes at the same time
migri at home and cani outside they live lives hard to reconcile

but all this is gossip that goes on in the cathedral vestibule
inside the migricani begin their rituals with the death of jfk
afterwards they slay malcolm x and martin luther king and bobby k

after these ritual transfixions the old people go home to sleep
at midnight the youths draw out the great dildos of winter
in the icy wind gods rising on helium shudder over the park

migricani looking up can smell the arctic in the wind
they wrap themselves in skins of sheep and howl the winter hymns

17.3–17.4

17.4

what's your name address your height and weight
wrong question
who loves you

wrong question
where did you come from
impossible to answer when you ask it that way

the man with the question board sits down discouraged
once i got here i started saying whatever came into my head
faces and shadows kept moving across the screen

the boat took me to a place where there were trees
dark trees tall with branches like the arms of women
tall women with hair like an avalanche of dust

is this a restaurant i asked
no question

17.5

change your story can mean to live it otherwise
or else to tell it from another person's point of view
you may not know any such point of view but you can try to find one

the effort may seem great when others attack you at night
i received your message and i might have followed you but did not
instead i sit in the bridge drawing plans to amuse the emperor

the ship has been executing a slow turn around the moons of jupiter
priests draw pictures of these moons using brushes dipped in ink
their pig bristles scrape against the papyrus rolls at all hours

every little noise they make starts us thinking of the past
the future too disturbs us with its rows of cultivated orange trees
and using a new story we fill these old sunken highways with dirt

even a slight change in spelling a name can make a huge difference
casting it in a new material allows for everything even miracles

17.5–17.6

17.6

you might like to buy me things that will remove my steel plates
all right i say but please do not hurt any of these people i love
are you sure you are not hurting anyone sitting as you are you ask

how can i answer a question like that except by admitting i'm scared
the point is you need not assign your fear so high a value
speak to each person with clarity and the honest affection you feel

play with their musical gifts when you can and expect a visitor
someone will know how good all of this can be
still you may wish to hide from the whole world at times

what is the logic of the situation you ask the lieutenant outside
with the tent flapping in the high wind you can't hear his reply
you come out expecting a hurricane and find a warm sunny morning

patrols glide up and down the hills in the lines of oleander bushes
you are going to a triumph in rome anyway so grease your chariot

17.7

i was just down the cellar trying to shift my story's foundations
you can't do that but you can exchange the story for something else
in the triumph they paint your face red and worship you as mars

in this story thousands collaborate throwing flowers at your feet
at the end of via sacra you turn towards the palace they gave you
other times you are riding in the subway learning to shrink in size

and which of these stories do you prefer is only the first question
in your present condition you tell the grass to grow and it doesn't
when you lean against the stone walls they do not move so you give up

you ignore the unlocked door on the front of your house
at the foot of the steps the street system leads all over the world
no wonder you want to stay indoors

the next question is where do you want to go and why
a clearly specified goal works well to settle nagging questions

17.7-17.8

17.8

to write a story you need a destination and a way to reach it
in this story the fellow wants more money love and fame
how would these things look appearing on his horizon

fame loves money and money loves fame
love money and fame can all make you stronger
money can help get you love and fame though not alone

another way you can recognize them is by invitations to parties
money and fame certainly produce invitations and so can love
but he asks are these the invitations i wanted

he discovers love fame and money do not change laws of perception
strength means having a larger range of acceptable choices
it means learning to play choices more freely

so now we have the story of a fellow who practices his strengths
each day's encounters are part of a larger campaign is the story

17.9

just now he is trying to decide whether to go to a party or not
someone has included him in a love campaign another cares for fame
these invitations to transaction ask much but what do they offer

if you go you risk giving away things you may want to keep
someone else invited him to read poetry at two open readings
these things he says he wants but when they materialize hesitates

he knows he wants to go but he is afraid to leave home
his wife may throw him out and then where will he be
places you leave become egypt he repeats over and over to himself

he has exceeded his tolerable limit of freedom this week
under the blankets mattress genies clasping him tight do not let go
they string cables on different body organs in different seasons

deciding to go to a party means dismantling the triborough bridge
this is good exercise but often leaves him too tired to go out

17.9–17.10

17.10

the hero goes haunted by fear of the vengeful lord who decides all
at the end of the story the hero burns his guilty rags on the altar
saints march in the refectory door carrying fra angelico paintings

his heaven is a prison where the warden gives a good grade of bread
in another story the hero meets a gypsy woman in the alley
thunder rattles the sky outside her tent but within they make merry

in the morning he rides off to meet the armies of charlemagne
on his charger's bridle flash bright medallions of the emperor
where he plants his standard a fountain pours out of the earth

can these two stories both have the same hero you wonder
or would you like to write another version of the story
the emperor charlemagne comes out of his golden tent all in gold

his face at the same time dark and brilliant smiles with welcome
advisers advise but only the king can pick

17.11

in this story orlando at last learns the meaning of kingship
they teach him that having everything the king can give everything
and as for charlemagne he respects the beliefs of his vassals

at this moment of mutual gift and respect god and man become one
or else you might just say look i am not feeling too good
they have draped the trees in the hollow with huge gray sheets

imperial doctors mumble formulas down there under the green shadows
the hero sits in the waiting room with a stomachache
you can only have enlightenment as the end of a story

before that the king must point to the horizon and the hero go
i am thinking of when america is an italian province the hero says
this means i am seeking an italian princess to set on the throne

now the hero goes looking for an italian princess in america
only love can give meaning to glory

17.11–17.12

17.12

he rides off asking what constitutes an italian princess in america
the rough voiced magician growls you'll know her when you see her
meanwhile a movie starring his archetypes fills the twilight west

becoming water when they touch anything solid jewels fall off trees
with art you have built a great spirit bridge that spans the ocean
no one can touch it but no one who has seen it can forget it

the hero rides down the snowy apennines and plunges into the valley
on the ship he sings the waltz oje marí what sleep i lose for thee
no one can tell him where she has gone after leaving italy behind

he steams from the headlands of the mississippi down to new orleans
his horse has wings and he flies to chicago and milano and to tampa
as he deplanes she is already on the runway cleared for takeoff

wait maybe this is just a decoy that flirts with you and disappears
to be known on sight she will have to stand where he can see her

18. making the new italians is hard because everyone wants the old ones

18.1

you can untie all these things that anchor you to a lie
your secret life has now ended and your public life begun
that large playful dog your ego seeks and finds fame

that midnight cat your superego seeks and finds money
that snorting horse libido seeks and finds love
dog and horse and cat together now become a single bear

the bear can dance these animals but the man can dance the bear
as a man you can leap and you can embrace and also kill
think faster and more accurately than snakes can move

as we learn to call our animals by name we all share ideas and meals
each gives up to the others some fruit of its cunning
as the orchestra folds its instruments into their cases you arrive

now for the symphony in which the air itself blows the trumpet
a music of wet leaves follows your walk across the field of battle

18.1–18.2

18.2

at this point in my life i would like to say i have just begun
things ought to move forward rapidly but instead they go slowly
i finally can see clearly what i have known all along

it is not a question of just discovering something at age fifty two no
a set of delicate hesitations even still persistently recurs
i pause to recognize them and then continue on my path

i wish to regard the period leading up to now as preparation
in those years the poet recluded himself from the market of fame
deep in the jungle caverns of his mind he created a new poetry

now he returns to the high walls of the town where they sell poems
the dancers beat the tambourines hard and he is afraid
calmly as he has always done alone he assumes his stance in public

why do animals hide under the broad leaves of the rainforest
some seek shelter but others are resting for the next day's hunt

18.3

for as long as i can remember i have insisted on being italian
but they said no you are too smart to be italian
or no you are not goodlooking enough to be italian

italian meant very cute and hot if even not too smart
age thirteen an irish girl said ok you are nice but dominic is cute
some girls wanted their italians black and others liked them jewish

i danced black and talked jewish which covered a lot of bases
then i began to see italian black and jewish are all big stories
every big story you cook up has its principles and its effects

just now a nameless migrant and i are constructing a new big italian story
when she left brooklyn for florence i read her the glass cable poem
now we we receive and transmit through this global understanding

i am the medium of her understanding which is the medium of mine
we do not constitute sexual media instead an interpretive circle

18.3-18.4

18.4

making the new italians is hard because everyone wants the old ones
people go on about their fathermothers and grandmotherfathers
even new italians love their ancestors to the point of distraction

the italian immigrant sits in the air in front of you like a cloud
fill the cloud with the silver effusion of zeus by lightning
the goddess of oranges and walnuts steps out of the cloud

bright clouds of memory resolve into brick ovens over a wood flame
in the end the story details matter less than what you make of them
i found in these details the language of italian recognition

this gave me courage to offer recognition even as i sought it
you offer me the belief that i am italian and i return the belief
others have either said nothing about it or else excommunicated us

now we have this interpretive circle we can put more things into it
we begin with one another but we can proceed to the story precinct

ellis island

18.5

my grandmothermother mothered me while my mother brothered me
by the time my sistermother had sistered me i had fathered an idea
i thought all these fragments of relationship belong in one box

bits of broken brotherhood and sistergrandfatherhood there mingle
we authenticate each with the sigla made in italy or italian style
our store plays munasterio 'e santa chiara all night to the street

my theory says we inherit each a box of broken pieces of the past
i interpret mine as mars and you interpret yours as venus or vulcan
these are what we do when first going through the boxes

later mars interprets vulcan's theory of venus to the pizzaiolo
as saturday night masquerade gods we address waiters in ristoranti
interpretations throb sadly down the avenue of tango parlors

think of all you made of all i made of all you made of me one night
this is the ordinary way we give each other stories every day

18.6

they try to see you at your best but you show them the bad side
you want them to love you not when they want to but when you want
as mules drag you up the steep grade you turn to see fields of snow

now you learn a new way to feel that you have no one to call friend
the snow blinds your eyes as they look for a dark curve to rest in
on these heights if you stand still the ice will speak to you

each thing the ice tells you spreads through you like air you breathe
now you pause to let all the new thoughts you have wash through you
how can you find in all of these just one thought you can then use

you need a new set of words as you start to climb each next time
the best thing is when you find three or four words that do the job
eat count sheep and dream you say and eat count sheep and dream

these words help you make most things clear each step of the way
now you are free to love which is one way to make sense of the ice

18.7

we are now ready to consider how to make a global italian american
the only sensible approach specifies rites of universal recognition
if i claim italian in you you have to deny it or else you have it

i can call myself italian if someone others call italian agrees
two such persons then can become italians together anywhere
being italian gives you the chance to claim a share of italian time

you have an idea of what italian time is and then you meet me
that changes not only your idea of italian time but mine as well
we may both think it large and full of things finely turned and tuned

your idea may run to depth where mine may run to branch effects
in my idea your head is crowned with a forest of horns like elms
deep in my eyes you see via appia antica run backwards to the sea

at my mind's bottom you find fish glowing underwater in blue caves
everywhere they look these fish find coins that bear your image

18.7–18.8

18.8

in short we take local things and localize them on a sphere
when my sister's sicilian boyfriend at last accepted me he made me a desk
after my sicilian godfather who loved me died they gave me his table

on the table i write but on the desk i put things i need to postpone
thus have i given desk and table world addresses using italian relations
you can do this same thing with other sorts of relation

but something local about italian relations comes from the globe
italians construct the globe as an italian self reflection upon an axis
italian thought begins by using one old world as template of a new

this doubling can maintain reflexive tension for generations
the simpler the template the more drastically simple its image
world italians deepen deeply when they revise the template

as my templates fall into the well of time my universe expands
desk and table become devices for navigating the murky inwardness

18.9

that's one way of doing it but the usual is to stamp things italian
take them to market and the ones people buy as italian are italian
in the world of selling questions of ontology become a lot simpler

so now you put things in bright tricolor wrappers
kiss me i'm italian you write on them and sing a song
at the end of the day you go home with a pocketful of cash

brutal police live most securely by certain formulae of thought
you think in habits so every time you think sex you think death
other examples would be a chain running from food to death

nothing keeps people in line like the threat of violence
if every time you think italian you think envy you will not get far
to move globally we develop new formulas for italian all the time

every time i think italian i think give more generously
who knows where that can take you

18.9–18.10

18.10

generosity formulas reach poverty even in the roots of memory
they overwhelm not only scarcity but old death formulas as well
their action gives italian a life of meaning

italians have ancient mastery of openhandedness and love
inside family tornadoes generosity whirls a corkscrew tarantella
but the outer tower walls have no windows except slits for darts

clans file out the tower doorways to ceremonial places of exchange
with care hawkfaced bishops watch them trade crops and handiworks
wielding a mace the mayor guarantees the correctness of measures

thus outside the walls of generosity an encircled fear appears
increase and complication grow out of trade as beauties of richness
the italians form a procession and in that procession they carry balances and lances

every person now becomes an individual made out of numbers
the eyes of the others gleam like knives and algorithms

18.11

on the feast of saint generosity we celebrate each other
i carry your accounts to read aloud and you carry mine to read aloud
i will read my own but only if you hold up the book before me

you read yours as my shaking hands hold your book before your eyes
then we share a piece of fruit or crack walnuts
now the procession begins with the drag song moving forward

andiamo in america ci rifaremo lì
in terra semisferica ci ritroviamo sì
italia è tragica america è magica

let us go to america and make ourselves over
we shall go together to the semispherical land
italy is tragic america is magic

reflected dreams become platters of prosciutto and cheese
the new world magnifies an ancient hunger

18.11–18.12

18.12

in the future you cook all your problems for supper
certain foods you stuff into ravioli and boil
others work nicely served raw chopped with shallots

not yet arrived this point comes when italianization is complete
all along the american coasts you find steaming heaps of spaghetti
american shellfish seem designed to die boiled into italian soup

one day they orbit a convex mirror where you can see americas
looking up through powerful lenses you find it in the midday sky
this blinding asteroid becomes the object of italian contemplation

abbiamo creato quel mondo nuovo we have made that new world
mystics see themselves in the round mirror as factors of diminution
to be american means first to be an effect of light in italian art

now every stairway postulates its own vanishing point
mathematicians compete for prizes with new models for maccheroni

19. i am looking for the freedom i have had all along

19.1

all the excuses fade each month until the bills come in
then we try something new because it is time to face the giving out
you ache for drugs that will make you sick if you take them

the fear of death wraps you like a tight jacket you can't unbuckle
each such routine constitutes a remaining wall of your prison
mostly anger presses walls against your sides

feel what it is that presses you
let the pressure out in words or actions
each time you do so changes your entire way of breathing

these routines you invent respond to tensions as you feel them grow
blockages and squeezes follow one another out through the passages
their shapes and sounds and rhythms surprise you

now the second skin of guilt becomes a red spangled fitted jacket
unbuttoning you let it fall as you slide into the pool

19.1–19.2

19.2

 i am looking for the freedom i have had all along
did i lay it down on the bookshelf or did it fall behind the piano
i remember how it used to taste until i mislaid it

it amplifies my follies and lights them with remorseless sunshine
the spectacle leaves me thinking you can do otherwise
i whisper lord tell me how to get through this next minute

if you do that every minute for an entire day you will no longer recognize your life
waves foam white with theories of living that dissipate in air
the waves themselves answer your questions minute by minute forever

every wave conveys the enormous distributed weight of the ocean
each moment brings the whole of life back before you
each vibration flowers out into the emptiness

you ask a question and a flooding wave foams across the flat wet sand
what you wanted now you taste it in the salt on your lips

19.3

now what do i do in the next moment
now you write another line
why is that

why is water wet if not because it displays the power to soak
if you yawn it is all right because sleeping teaches you things too
in short take a step and look around

one butterly or one cloud of butterlies that know the way to mexico
one river or a line of cranberry bogs
now you can go out and do your chores

is it heavy or light
keep asking but you can best tune the instrument you actually play
keep trying new styles and eventually develop one entirely your own

one hand aloft like a plume you guide the wagon
consider other people's feelings as much as you can

19.3–19.4

19.4

then i thought okay i will try to grow perfectly healthy
and i did except that i wanted to do it perfectly stoned
strong and weak at the same time makes a real twelve step personality

weakness can give strength to strength because it gives form to purpose
strength can give weakness weakness because it raises expectations
we study how to use strength while acknowledging weakness

we study how to use weakness to make an inside for restoring our strengths
we study how to use strength to protect our weakness
and for our own we read each other's strengths and weaknesses

discussing such things we form the counterpoint of friendship
finding positions to occupy that feel right we endure discomfort
our valleys of strength offset our mountains of weakness

there is only weakness we may say giving way to the wind
resilience plays one through another and springs back

ellis island

19.5

i have been shooting forward into the future as if it were the past
it is not a real but an imaginary past where everything makes sense
there we can only make sense by reorganizing or else giving up preconceptions

we encounter the past moving forward since this is how we move
what we remember encounters what someone else remembers
thus the past can always have a new form between glory and oblivion

you are not perfect though your plans have a simple shape
it is normal that you are rocking in the cradle of the deep
the point is to get there even if not in a straight line

now you are going to draw a picture of today
everything in it is possible and you can do all of it
it won't be exactly what you outlined but it will do the job

every time you pick up your tools you do a little more work
you are on the way to doing something all day in the sunshine

19.5–19.6

19.6

try this again if you can remember the numbers in order
if not then try something else but keep trying
don't lose any sleep over your fear of dying

it moves around in your life like a set of unwashed dishes
the piles of things wait for you to read them and deal with them
you keep trying to do so even while you shape your escape

you sink a thousand miles and you are still on the surface
meditation can only help you to be one with the spinning ball
it cannot peel the ball revealing the ball underneath

you feel short winded now trying to put everything into sound bites
viscusi plays architect in the new italian american literary history museum wing
viscusi plays piano in the museum of dead italians

the tarantella had many children including the blues
the blues had many too such as viscooz

19.7

the blues viscusi knows are hardly news
twentieth century yellow dog hamhock fm radio symphony black blues
put on those make believe bandstand mascara wingtip shoes

songs you remember whenever you scratch your armpit over the radio
plain songs concerning the need for affection and the lack thereof
low songs you sing fucking slowly or watching television

you learned to say all these granite adverbs that block the roads
down mountains into your sentences slide bags of nuts and screws
you don't like them but you keep them because they're worth money

although you have nothing to do with it you love the tools you use
other people's winters are other people's loads
you inhabit houses your enemies lose

the king and his advisors sometimes feast on toads
and with cigars they drink primordial ooze

19.7–19.8

19.8

we all write poems about snow
who can resist the idea of transformation that costs nothing?
people say the death of ancient rome came in a blizzard

on august 15 anno domini 410 a heavy snow fell out of the hot empty sky
that same day angels flew from jerusalem carrying jesus's manger
romans built the basilica of santa maria maggiore where they landed

the silent snow rose in crests and valences on the temple of mars
snow thin as lace lined the black lava cart tracks
the snow blew in where pompey still stood in the senate house

mules and donkeys slipped and were killed on the glassy cobbles
gusts of wind blew armies back and forth across the asian plains
curves carved into the large S and Q collected white shadows

everything we later came to remember was for a moment forgotten
in the morning the heat returned loud as ever

ellis island

19.9

getting old you understand the onceness of things
why loses ground to how good and to why not
does it matter why you choose figs and chestnuts

if you are lucky enough to have one embrace your splendid lover
open the gates and let the wind of truth polish the furniture
you begin to learn to read the lines that appear on things

these record battles in life campaigns
you don't want to attribute schemes to others if you can help it
instead you want to record how they act and why you chose them

you want to see how you held them
was it love or hate or pride or humiliation or guilt or pleasure
are all these things on the same plane in your mind

the lines of what a person does increase his interest for others
still a student of placement he becomes himself a place to study

19.9–19.10

19.10

one day human nature changed
a penitent covered with welts and stripes looked up
he lifted his chain from the stake and carried it away

along the roads the lepers reached out to touch him
were they hoping to be cured or just to spread the misery
these questions fill the libraries with fresh essays in theology every year

a book is no more immortal than a piano or an empire or a person
either it changes and lives or else it does not make it
you change a book by reading it in an entirely different age

people convince you that to survive you need their grief
when you start noticing that this is a fiction you free yourself
you survive because you have received the gift of survival

where does the gift come from
where you are walking they will answer this question eventually

19.11

listen kid at your age i had already written an epic poem
now i am going to sing a charm that makes flowers blossom on trees
i don't mind your ambitions but mind your manners please

and now i sit down at a faraway piano to play
back here the ship is drifting
it tugs me like a heavy rope straining and dragging my anchor

i have removed the loop and started rowing slowly away
they have thrown it into the air and caught me with it again and again
eventually i start rowing at different hours

i wish these images really told the story of how it is
you sell some things but others you can give away
on the dock there is a pile anyone can pick from

listen to the little ones and give them what they need
once they dig their toes into the dirt they start hunting for themselves

19.11–19.12

19.12

back in that country i left a red carnage smelling of glue
it was the war of trojan symphony gravedigger harmonicats
now they shut the heavy buick doors and drive out the gate

i thought never marry into a family that makes caskets for a living
now i am walking down the street hardly knowing what planet this is
winds blow the smell of wet grass lifting the veil of sadness

wait a minute i said you are no longer in jail
they paint the canvas walls stone gray but you can kick them in
as you turn the corner the mountain rises on the pale horizon

dark green reeds climb alongside the ticklish path
shafts of warm light shoot through trees as you enter the clearing
may i you say and they giggle saying yes you may

a flock of white herons glides down onto the dew soaked rocks
the sign of venus deepens in color as the sun melts into the fiery lake

ellis island

20 now another sack of loosely tangled bodies falls gasping to shore

20.1

things and people may suddenly change
everything appears different from the other side of the building
the year turns on its heavy spindle through the whatever it is

here we see a person trying to think in fourteen dialects at once
he blows that south italian bagpipe which originated in the islamic world
rasping sounds round out the ensemble scratching out and in

you used to think your guilt a useful motive
now you see it as your father's car rusting in the driveway
perfect for traveling when you want to stay put

don't get in unless you like sleeping in cat piss
make an appointment downtown and call car service
bright days a walk across the planet is healthy for human organisms

as you climb the great bridge you look down at the emotional river
thin skeins of explanation everywhere hover like veils

20.1–20.2

20.2

now you have opened the fountain of exasperation
up you shoot through acid showers from the bowels of earth
by habit you now would run to do something else but not this time

you have resolved to let the blasts blow your skirt around your face
your ears echo with songs that shiver so you don't quite get them
terror leaves you weary and wanting to hide in a pillow

but hold the wheel and steering through storms balance your legs
parading guitarists strumming hard unison pass through the cabin
it won't be dark forever you will start to cry and dawn will rise

it is quiet now in the room where rain turned old papers to trash
you sweep with a wet broom in a wet breeze smelling of fish eggs
when the sun comes it will burn away the traces

you scratch acid earth from inside your ears where you had stuffed it
years of suffering have at last taught you how to find the right doctor

20.3

all these statues lying on the ground used to be livable tombs
we would climb into them when it got rainy and curl up in the dark
breathing with trapped squirrels was the price we paid for grandeur

we would sing to the green striped caterpillars songs about god's fingerprints
we made fun of tourists who visited us wearing silky waterproof clothing
every overcast sky tumbled out hawks dragging long ragshaped messages

nothing makes more sense than the dirt if you can stand to read it
it says the people roll down into me and out of me come weeds and worms
out of me climb fragrant cherries dropping blossoms into the water

the dirt says thee as well shall i eat thou butternut squash
oceans of its appetite tumble in damp rolls across the grass in hot spring wind
loving i feed thee the claysmelling ravine croons now open wide

as they peel your outer wrapping the sting gives way to moisture
how you cry i would give the world for another morning of pleasure

20.3–20.4

20.4

making every act compact of your pleasures turns labor light
light labor makes love strong bones firm doors tight walls and roofs
feeling pain or pleasure together making the secret sense a family shares

every flowing family fans its foam across the fire flattened lawn
washing through the maze of appearances the family glows sunrise
from april reeds the family serpent coils toward the branching sky

the apple tree globe flowers dragons to all points in world thought
here you learn the meaning of value at last in these quiet changes
the mud has firmed into a slow soft bread breathing out daffodils

this pattern applies to every situation son
facing a new situation let its rhythms spell out its circulation
be sure you let yourself perceive the rhythms

don't get lost in the hard outlines of things or in your feelings
put your boat into the water as it moves through the channels

20.5

splashes at my door remorseless green canal water good cheer
reflecting combines wakes of speedboats gondolas ferries and storms
the swift element moves though you don't see the thousands of fish

snow on a spring morning blinds you with all four seasons at once
thin tracery crests frozen mud tracks outlines blue spruce branches
high sun pours light straight down through leafless diagram trees

now your old monuments become details along the road as you move
new air swiftness reorganizes rooms you use filling them with views
the wind expresses its will in reply to your gestures of welcome

earth receiving light all day all night it flowers thought green
millions of magentas and burnt orange streaks mark earth
its damp smell engenders sentences as long as any great serpent

the eaves teem beetles and the ants swarm in the elms
we feel their twiddle in our nostril hairs

20.5–20.6

20.6

no dark part so exquisitely answers desire as do backs of altars
in those places the sad and the holy lay down together and weep
no one finds them and they say god never loses them

if you start doing what it says it wants it complains
it wants something more that you did not think of
and then it accuses you of not doing what it wanted even as you do it

since you know how childish it is why do you care what it says
try not to cause yourself so much pain you can no longer think
pain for you apparently can sometimes signify love

ah you say stepping out into the sunlight how i enjoy the relief
some people hurt themselves just so they will enjoy stopping
but your difficulties may be more modest in size than that

you are trying to get a purchase on things you let go a long time
there is no reason to think it will always be easy but keep going

20.7

paying the bills means closing the gap between you and others
make it simple and clean and you will always feel good about it
if you do it well it comes to embody your position as an art can

it whistles like wind through wheat or twenty sleepers snoring
these when operating normally convey desire and satisfaction
who takes feels rewarded while who gives feels authority

signing checks the giver is the author of rewards
like any job it can scare you if you look down too much
like any job it can satisfy if you get things done

there is more dark matter than anything else but you can't see it
close your eyes and think about that for fifteen minutes
when you open them everything will begin to seem more adjustable

let exchange riddle silently through your stride
time is the shifting of weights

20.7–20.8

20.8

paying taxes like paying bills gives authority
this ordinary feature of life need not frighten you
trusting others and by them trusted you walk down the block

if someone yells at you then you may say hey you are hurting me
the screaming thing is itself in pain but does not know it
you may not be able to do anything about that part except pray

but as for yourself go about your work
it is a daily gift to you
take pleasure in it and do not feel guilty because you are human

you are there for good reasons even if you do not know them
accept them because in their twists and turns you come to conclusions
divine intelligence enlightens you and be grateful for that as well

everything you have is admirable
even the follies and pains

ellis island

20.9

entering history on your left where the lights blind you
three tourists on this staircase turned into bags of water
i remember one time i fell in love twice inside a single week

later it would happen more frequently like falling leaves
smells of love poured out of every cupboard or door swinging open
one day i lay down and they tied me with chains that bit my flesh

i hate these movies about egypt preferring the story the old way
a stranger came wandering out of the mountains who could read dreams
the pharoah knew how only the night sky guides the navigator

then we tell his famous victories among the spitted lambs smoking
every sacrifice itself revealed another chapter of the future
we found our laws all encoded as digits on one ruby tetrahedron

beams of light darker than blood pierce the basalt cliff
ah yes you say i remember seeing you ten million years ago

20.10

i need to pursue a certain task but i itch all over
no reason to stop now you shriek the water is over the dam
a pause slowly becomes the void against which you make each gesture

who knows what the nature of meaning is as you turn into a bubble
hey i thought this was a concrete anchor you shout flying off
at the landing platform after these trips you eat lots of popcorn

now another sack of loosely tangled bodies falls gasping to shore
praise jesus after leaving for work or do so during the acid shower
anyway rituals of cleansing often do get things cleaner than before

you walk down the center of the room your arms out balancing sides
you bow to the center and then to the sides and the front and back
unpack your bag and dispose every item in it and then replace them

even brief adjustments of these small things make huge differences
going from place to place you perform these rites of arrival

20.11

in aachen alcuin taught charles the great to read a missal at mass
irish priests like to mention this to italian americans
you who have feasted centuries in animal wallows now sit straight

but we too know arts of arranging a table to please the insatiable gorgons
we say you see how much later it is than it was a few minutes ago
thus our rituals recognize beloved relatives as they pass forward

those who go before us include the kings of spain
we have cousins everywhere in the mountains of china and peru
all writing grows from rules for the making of choices

you only can choose once you accept the possibility of choosing
consider adequate the range of life technique you have learned
preparation provides half but the other half comes from action

you are assembling the cast and writing stage directions and music
in secret rehearsals have been going forward for some time

20.11–20.12

20.12

the way we are going to do this is as follows if you can follow it
first a young man starts noise on a noise pot then we come in
singing loudly we all accomplish the welcome and make a circle

then a hum starts against which hum the poets struggle
eacch poet strikes the chords of his entitlement
as slaves with nose rings they get restricted movement licenses

this one can hawk his fish and that one may flash her teeth
we may not love our merchandise but it gives us excuses to go out
i am a professor i am a lesbian i am a doctor of psychology

we call this market literary because in some sense we are all free
but to feel freedom requires removing the bronze plates of liberty
we have till now been free to choose richer slaveries than before

rocco beat turiddu down in my poem and then maria sang sadly
at the end of the evening we eat and dance till we drop

ellis island

21. in constructing a colossus you encounter all sorts of obstacles

21.1

i change very slowly and then go back to how i was before
sometimes in little ways ten times an hour sometimes one a year
some returns i see and can shorten them but others run their course

there was the one where i would start chasing all over the place
i don't do that but now sit still as a stone for days on end
i have been stock still for years with sparks jumping around me

posing in bird or cat attitudes the man is host to a million fleas
i come upon myself in the driveway like a rusting car
memories of sex disturb me as i look at it

i pull the wheel even if only a little and it moves
keep at it and eventually it begins to roll so you get on and drive
once you get momentum turn on the ignition and throw it in gear

drive gently until you feel the engine settle into a steady rhythm
loosen the setscrew on your right hand and you can jump out the door

21.1–21.2

21.2

pinocchio went to the store for a bottle of milk
on the way home it fell on the sidewalk and broke leaving a stain
going to church he grew up passing that stain a thousand times

each time he saw it he would stiffen his back to brace for the slap
now he wears a wooden body to pay for being allowed to hope to live
each night he lays down in it and every morning picks out splinters

it protects him from feeling anything but it keeps him from living
some doctors recommend staple removal others termite swarm therapy
he went swimming in it and swelling overnight it almost choked him

a reasonable philosopher said to him see if you can find the lock
it was as usual hidden in full view but anyway he found it
studying he has learned to make keys that fit and now has extras

he soaks the cylinders in penetrating oil from time to time
meanwhile he is working on the door hinges and it won't be long

21.3

i was poor so long that now i'm rich i don't know how to act
having cousins richer than you does not make you poor
having rich cousins is one sure way to know you're rich

some people say you shouldn't care whether you have any money
but others always ask you for it so clearly there are two opinions
money of a given moment extends into money of long years

in your past you can find money of long ago that holds you up now
poor of long ago peels away like bandages that hurt
defined actions cast long futures into the void

any line in the history of footprints might lead you forever
thus as we lay the table for dinner we feed our remote posterity
performing a kindness to an old person we close an ancient wound

the wealth of creation fills your eyes and every tree blossoms
your barefoot winter childhood enters an april of boots

21.3–21.4

21.4

in the fields mud moves living in shapes combining to form you
in your dreams you rot like a heap of vegetables
one day you are going to thank me for all this

up straight from the mulch buds pink at attention shoot and open
clinging smells linger among the branches like mist
down drives the sun beating green gases out of black muck

black rabbits white brown brindled and striped dot the bushes
the dog rolls among carrot tops on the liquid edges of lawn
cows calving call upon god causing bulls bewildered pauses

the river has been rising for weeks and now you put your boat in
steering is tricky in flooding currents but panic doesn't help
if you keep your eyes open and your wits sharp you will manage fine

plenty of us do this whole river every year two three times
the money is good and it beats staying home to play with the dog

21.5

i seem to have a steady flow of trouble when i look around
furniture store ads i have had a hard time reading
i can do it unless i don't want to and i don't

when only trash seems real then seek the rivers of honey
on that flood you will avoid boulders as well as shallows
its fullness can bury obstacles so deep one never finds them again

miseries whirl away down some subset flow
iforget the acid running out off riverbank factories
you steer on the high flood as it carries you in a dream

the systematics of flow never begin and never end
the sky falls into the river which falls into the ocean
the snow came from the jungle on clouds that froze to the glacier

in a huge orchestra feature now one instrument now another
all music includes starting and stopping

21.5–21.6

21.6

it used to be my object to be considered brilliant or at least cute
this took me further than you can imagine but not far enough
at a certain point i returned to the cave of my sad imaginings

now what story do you want to tell i asked myself
in constructing a colossus you encounter all sorts of obstacles
the first is one day you see a colossus isn't what you thought

a big thing includes a million little things
its very bigness is a little thing an idea printed in a fortune cookie
and what you really want to do is sell things and get them around

so the first thing you want is an idea that sells in small sizes
if people buy your book even cheaply they have invested in it and will read it
otherwise it's just more police propaganda and they throw it away

when you sell something you make commitments that you engage at least to intend
it is worth the trouble to read till it makes sense

21.7

now i am turning towards the soft tomorrow
they said o forget it it's too sentimental
they had a poetry of changing the subject

i was very good at it myself don't you know
my greatgrandfather the king of england farted copiously
he is one of the tribe of pippin one of the tribe of rudolf

like him i am one with all the royal clans that ever intermarried
so would you like another taste of this delicious mint sandwich
i don't blame you because they are wonderful

at the poetry reading the minds of the listeners orbit together
this corner of the barnes and noble has become a pile of watermelon
when the poet turns the whole building blinks

we are a royal tribe of chambermaids' grandsons
everything we say changes everything from the subject on out

21.7–21.8

21.8

how often in life have you felt good enough to answer questions
which questions do you want to hear about first
we might start with the ones made out of old sticks

someone asked napoleon where she left the donut batter
french nobles in full regalia floated out on a sea of boiling oil
now the priest came tumbling down the wide marble staircase

as you opened the window europe made a fan on the outside air
faster than you could recognize the magentas and taupes it got wet
i have placed my broad red stripe on this high mountain

as the monoliths open they reveal the valley where light is born
every time we find our way here we later die a hundred deaths
someone says he has seen all the seas together in a ball of water

we call him the dolphin
in his voice we hear flutes and drums

ellis island

21.9

he has marched complaining through every campaign you sent him on
we are not able to show him how badly it hurts his performance
he lies down on the bed with the remote in his hand

he manufactures books during the night when you are sleeping
where did he learn the use of spindles
the flower machine drops an engagement ring into the lake

intelligent eaters choose fresh broccoli cauliflower spinach
the potato river clogged with flies lies stinking in the sun
our third general this week has died of sexual exertion

the lens zooms in to explore the corners of his mind
gorillas at headquarters party when they watch these tapes
shadows of musicians walking bounce along the edge of the lawn

no matter what i play on the piano it comes out a hymn
the whorehouse is not on this street but take the first two lefts

21.9–21.10

21.10

they would have known me by the striped shirt i won at asbury park
lightly they would brush their sandy fingers across my crew cut
at night the air spilled evergreen syrup into the icy draft

i ran through the rough history of japan pursued by women in silk pajamas
my platform shoes clattered on the damp flagstone serpentine
in the show i was jesus behind the wheel of the queens plaza bus

he hummed the tune all of my books have mirrors hidden in them
the stealing disease turns ordinary into chaotic till you prefer ordinary
in ordinary life we form circles and circle around a spot together every night

he raged against flowers and dragons as evidences of gods
strong beings leapt up out of the dark openings of earth to dance
they taught him to lay aside his stupid fury in a box and float it off away

the great ship approached the horizon swelling like an orchestra
crusader winds balloon the red cross sails across your scribble indicating sunset

21.11

the pioneer woman stood at the green painted kitchen table
a red robin shouts loudly from the branch hanging over the fountain
the heavy paper shade bats against the raised sash in the breeze

the boys come down the fire escape into alleys penetrating boston
listen if we go to vinnie's house marietta and janet will be there
these goddesses of hip recirculation gently firm it to your body

they have assembled the great earth and given it to the grandmother
she takes it into the air and slams down beating it to bread on a stone
he races into the room drinks the water and runs to the garden

where is vinnie with janet he asks marietta in the grape arbor
lo and behold she says as the horse wearing a straw hat comes up the drive
on the wagon a family dressed as gypsies stares down at us kissing in the shadow

by sundown we smell of milkweeds as we suck at lemon crush on the wet sidewalk
sunflowers bend to dirt as rising night raises the heavy curtain for your play

21.11–21.12

21.12

at a certain point you begin piling books along the roadside
when she asks what did you want out of life you forget to answer
everything suddenly grows so clear there is nothing to say

mandolins and cornets play and the piano comments on each phrase
i like you and you like me and one and one and one is three
you curl up together on the couch of life and get sleepy together

every nerve of possibility gets to play solo
rocks cut with large diamond blades pave the courtroom floor
balloonfuls of terror fly up out of your open mouth at the ceiling

they were tearing us apart when we lay down on the yellow sheet
follow me you said and you led me up the crystal staircase
what i saw there was the entire passage of the final armies of god

now a flock of little birds thunders through the low passage leading to sky
the sound of running water begins to flute its way into your ears

22. the city is who knows where but the street names are familiar

22.1

i wanted to explain all my failures but you wouldn't let me
you said to me listen we can go for coffee under that awning
women swim through your gaze upon the iced glass between your palms

o by the way i was not elected cardinal of staten island
o not again you laugh watching a blond step high crossing the esplanade
so each of us has written the chronicles of his catastrophes as repeated desires

later we leave the movie house for conversation on the stoop
johnnie plays harmonica while we play boxball ballet dancers
entering the house in the late evening was like returning to a cave

heavy beasts slumbered noisily remembering the hour of creation
i lay down on my corner mat tuning my nerves like a harp
tuning my harp in the morning i face the day with music

the past and the future playing weave a path like a braided snake
i stand ready to serve those who wish to buy this product

22.1–22.2

22.2

late in the afternoon of civilization italians climbed into boats
we are leaving europe seeking to live better than we can here
after they left europe exploded like a bomb and they felt guilty

it is not our fault they cried but made novenas anyway
having left behind graves where they should have put flowers weekly
o how they hungered after distinction in the new world

it eluded them since not speaking english perfectly pulls you down
if you do say something wonderful people hear it in quotation marks
if you pass miracles you belong to the apocryphal canon at best

in another war the europeans covered themselves with shame
a child of italians said i am american since i speak the language
and sent food and money every week to cousins the americans bombed

now as americans hungry for some italy we come off the airplane
we greet one another as of old saying can i help you pay for your mistakes

22.3

o you arrogant bastards the italians muttered wrapping up the silks
in the crates of wine came leaflets exposing united states capitalist evils
you prick they hummed as the american son in law visited the farm

when the italian americans had a parade the italians came to sneer
after they read the italian american poets the italians said you are not worthy of us
italian american novels made them ooze contempt for us in molasses smiles

italian american food made them break out laughing
italian american manners filled them with morality and pedagogy
italian american sex scared them as some italian americans were improbably buff

italian american thought puzzled them as a talking cabbage would
italian american religion was one long piece of shit to them
worst was how the italian americans saw them in quotation marks

come down here on the ground with us was what italians couldn't say
they still were looking for a way to admit they were not airborne

22.3-22.4

22.4

i was down among the saddest thoughts in the rock pond
no one could find me there not even i
i was striking out at people who reminded me of myself

why do you hate yourself
why not recognize your own weaknesses in the weaknesses of others
the famous professor approves no one lest that person diminish him

the son doesn't want to get up on mornings when he hasn't done his homework
these people are you but how can you accept them
someone scares people when he gets angry

this person is you but how can you know it
the wife does not want to get too close
she is you when it drives you crazy

if you let go of the monkey cage it floats out into the universe
each of these persons has another side as you have

ellis island

22.5

the famous professor loves saints and birds
the son loves buddhist saints and chinese women
the wife loves her house and chickens

as for you you love writing and playing the piano and performing
the dialectic has done all it can for you at this moment
now you need to consider what you can do for it

then the famous professor becomes the voice of the saints
the son becomes the chinese sage
the wife becomes the woman of the house

the house of the woman of the house has its style
the wisdom of the chinese sage produces a certain balance
the saints and birds of the professor speak on every tree branch

all of these return to you now you let go of the monkey cage
you open your mouth and every song you sing is hollow as a cave

22.5–22.6

22.6

a poet a parrot wears colors that confuse the predatory jungle birds
his blinding green coat opens a wing the color of salmon against the brick wall
thus the bird survives even in the port cities of the americas

every night he returns to a cage with no lock on it to sleep
those who take aim at you bird are only angry with themselves
here in the bronx you have done the same thing to them often enough

now we have climbed into the car that will take us to the beach
uncle mike is playing fever and volare on the radio
parrot opens beak and and screeches just a closer walk with thee

every town of certain size has a part where it rains every time you go there
the valleys of your life make a contour map of pleasure and pain
now it is time to seek the blossoming wood of the workplace

you may still spend a certain part of the day stamping documents
the city is who knows where but the street names are familiar

22.7

when i listen to my animal i play in the bushes
pussies play go fish till the sap runs out
it coats the tips of fingers and locks

tomorrow's parade makes you nervous but need not
people march to mark the day and enjoy being together
and you be pumping out the miracle

you lose patience and get angry with others for needing you
just gently point out where the grass ends and the sidewalk begins
then you turn to producing and sorting and carting and selling

naturally a performer wants to perform and freely to enjoy it
within a carefully organized business arrangement this is possible
such arrangements mean a steady flow of paperwork including money

the best animals to study in this respect are birds and squirrels
they live alongside us because their habits resemble ours

22.7–22.8

22.8

the captain asks do you prefer fantasy plus safety or reality with mambo dancers
reality allows for satisfactory tangos while fantasy lodges among hypotheses
naturally fantasy costs less because you don't need the other people

now when you start moving in a sure direction satisfactions mature on trees
then all your famous plateaus of the past dry up and crackle like layers of onion
whatever corner of the universe you get off the train new friends start talking

as years go by you do get better at avoiding the ones likely to beat you up
you look for bodies who find in you a palace garden where they stroll peacefully
a wilderness of birds like friends waits for you to pass before beating its wings

choosing a life means boarding ship after a great hesitation full of suspense
some people call out to you to turn down one leafy lane and others call another
when the choice falls clear like moonlight sketching a sheet their voices fade

every wrinkle draws a line that records an act or a meeting of life with life
you never imagined these things that are happening but you know them all on sight

22.9

he sits in a room on a hill over rome writing
in the evening they walk among tombs along via appia antica
every month a sizeable check comes in the mail

he sits in his third floor room on long island writing
in the evening they walk along the ocean beach
every month a sizeable check comes in the mail

all his dreams include money flowing over his hands like glass
liquid force floods and ebbs through wall street like river tides
the system apportions water and power to each of the houses

some people venerate the system while others worship the river
in rome the fountains show system and river as one
when you approach both are neutral as gods should be

you are preparing for this journey now a long time
continue making your arrangements and try not to panic

22.9–22.10

22.10

you make a plan
work for a small success and on its basis attempt something larger
each time you succeed then you either freeze or you stop yourself

one day you say wait a minute these trains leave every hour on the hour
you were only afraid of your own aggression against yourself
even now it is like a large solid nickel statue of your front

some objectives you had better not serve if you know them
other times you say wait a minute i have something else to do
to do this something else has now become your passion

we outlined his trip for him through the rainy capitals of europe
no he said what i really want is my lost loves
he opened a cabinet and put the nickel front inside

he has begun to walk around the world with his eyes open
you can't have everything but you can have astonishing moments

22.11

mayday means the beginning of the mating season
i confront decisions i not have confronted before
the dog was barking and snarling at me lying there asleep

do you want to stay married and as she says build up trust
what trust i ask because i used to imagine i was building a dynasty
instead it seems i was failing to build trust

she had a different script in mind and was looking for recognition
i was listening to the elders and thinking how to build a universe
her idea of trust included listening to everything she said

dynasty building meant avoiding arguments by not listening to her
now i have to think of a different plan or else sit still
the lines you make doing what you forget are the marks you leave

the advice of elders only sometimes applies to them and less to you
the past is a movie and the other continents unreal as the future

22.11–22.12

22.12

the thing is either let something oppress you or not
is it her or is it your idea of her or is it just what happened
is it you or her idea of you or is it just what happened

if you let it oppress you then you become stones under the house
if not then you become the spirit that emerges from what you do
you will go or return each turn of the head each breath a lifetime

we boast if we call ourselves a posterity or even speak to one
deepest pleasure comes from true sounds future or past can never be
i have dived into the present instant six miles below the surface

here volcanoes produce new life and fish are mouths that light up
the pressure of the atmosphere makes other functions unnecessary
this is ground zero in the chain of life

but now i only rest in a rowboat tied up under a blossoming tree
i have forgotten how to compose the grammar of large questions

23. each person i thought of presented me with a shrine entitled failure of love

23.1

sometimes i am in rapid movement and sometimes i am in rapid movement
this means i have learned ways to treat even rest as a form of flight
i had to for i had broken my father's injunction in choosing a career

did i have the sense to say to him you were right
no i continued to prove that i had been right
for this i punished myself at every sign of success

my self esteem grew but it provoked a degree of self punishment
how could i esteem a self that my father had rejected
afterwards he did say to me son i was wrong you have proven yourself

but i thought the only answer to all this was the universal fatherhood of god
i consulted a famous jesuit writer on a six day retreat in january 1960
he told me that god would bless my writer's career

thus have i always loved the jesuits but i still do not feel approval
perhaps if i ask for it i will find out how to get it

23.2

before you could recite the whole enciclopedia cattolica i fell asleep
i contrived to write my name all over the passing parade balloons
everywhere i looked i saw pieces of myself going by brightly colored

i came onto the street to repossess all these projections
drawing them back into myself i grew silent and began to glow dimly
now it was time to ascend the altar of everyday divine worship

in small places the priest stands at a certain angle to the sun
every turn of his body allows him to receive and to transmit further messages
no one introduced me to the bishop at the party

and yet i know the father of the bishop is my father as well
the father of my friends who did not introduce me is my father
my father who did not ask to be introduced is their father

the universal parenthood of god is our universal childhood
we transmit parenthood in the act of honoring father and mother

23.3

a poem in honor of my father would need to begin with his tremendous optimism
he looked across the water at rockaway seeing in the imaginary distance florida
he believed always repeating i get better every day in every way and better too

a poem in honor of my father must include his tremendous brilliance
it must include his perseverance in solving problems and his steady support
my father gave gentle reassurances that healed my wounds

did it matter that his own anxieties had sometimes given me these wounds
he did not even know having suffered from loss of his own father very young
this poem also praises him his steadfastness in love for his children

when he traveled off to florida i claimed he had abandoned us
he was reenacting the unresolved mystery of the migration
his mother left her mother and later left his father

i praise my father as a gardener a provider a protector and an artist
through his great love he gave things he had not himself been given

23.3–23.4

23.4

when i built the furniture of my study i had just arrived from hell
i used models common in that kingdom of confusion
i attributed all my problems and virtues as well to my immense sufferings

in my view everyone in hell was in fact christ suffering for the others
imagine my surprise when i learned from g b shaw that hell was a state of mind
you go to work in heaven when you get bored with lying around rotting in hell

so i laid out a plan for the useful writing of an italian american epic
this plan became the itinerary of my heavenly journey
everywhere i went people seemed to be howling in pain

my job was to write all of it down but i often forgot to do so
instead i kept opening my mouth until one day i fell silent
now i no longer am a bridge across the abyss or a floor under a mountain

universes fall through space at such speeds they seem not to move at all
you see no difference you say but the furniture all looks changed to me

23.5

under the frog choir the strings are playing merry obbligato
if i knew the meaning of life it would feel safe to lie down and sleep
instead i quiver on the edge of my chair looking at every page for the secret

if i were to see it i doubt i would recognize it anyway
it might come out as just a certain twist on the tail of the letter g
you might even feel as you looked at it it was pregnant with meaning

the meaning might even pass through you like electric current in a transformer
suddenly you might swim in a flashing silken stream of memories
light might rise in you and spread as dark umbrella pines against a roman sky

even then you might not be able to name it but at best to pray for surrender
when it came through you the world stank like rotting cabbages and fish
everything had a hook on it to catch you with and stun you with

what has protected you from magnetic storms erupting deep in the earth
as the wave rises the continent raises you and as it falls relaxes the strain

23.5–23.6

23.6

i myself have been falling for years
occasionally you approach a planet but then veer off into black space
wild gravity currents do not disturb large objects but float you like a leaf

ever since a while now i have much of the time been thinking nothing
entire civilizations disappear into the nothing eating everything they see
at our dazzling best we fade a perfect pose into the void

the walls sink under the weight of ten billion pearly snails
now let us think of people who have harmed us as they fall away into it
i wept last night so hard my walls collapsed and the ceiling came down

each person i thought of presented me with a shrine entitled failure of love
black rocks climbed high on either side the ruby red candle flame tower altar
on the highway the dumpster spilled over crystallized arteries and torn hearts

ah well i have always been proud of this my black diamond encrusted gondola
midnight into the flowering perfumes we slip the prow singing songs of italy

23.7

anything never changes so long as you keep yelling about it
to make changes emphasize how things have stayed the same
track oscillations as well as larger patterns of migration and interaction

draw lines looking for things that appear equal from one mind to the next
yes follow the conversation among your larger minds as the breeze massages them
this can need years of attention or you can slide it off the table like a linen

as it takes heavy form you move the fabric easily along the polished surface
if the problem never answers to any of the names you call it then just act
lift the cloth off the cage and let nickels fall but pick up megadollar deals

the important thing is focus upon the path you see before you
the path resolves settlement questions as it passes mossy town doors
building a road the entire army pauses for the leader to resolve a dispute

hot pickaxes shoot sunbeams into the admiring eyes of town dwelling persons
events major to the villagers just slip by as details to those on the road

23.7–23.8

23.8

if you do what you want to do will you burn in hell for it
hell means lying around waiting for someone to take care of you
you mean i can enter paradise doing and giving even if according to other rules

jesus advises consider the lilies of the field who take no thought for the morrow
enter paradise as often as you like only means letting go of everything
all your attachments drift away on the lazy current as you inspect a willow leaf

different parts of your life present themselves as dance partner changes
you keep returning to them though sometimes others replace them as recurrences
satisfying the appetite for change makes gardening the most rational passion

life goes one way to heaven or hell get used to it hissed the nun with the ruler
all right i replied but who knows how long a journey it is
a million lifetimes or an instant are only two ways of saying the same thing

the nun spectacularly unfolds the way a rose opens to the touch of the sun
like cards in a deck being thumbed universes fan out so fast you can't see them

ellis island

23.9

now we are leaving for india the trainmaster sang out to the refugee boatful
the silent streamliner pullman cars began clicking slowly out of the station
the train gleamed along a high plateau that descended fifty miles to the sea

by the time it entered the water the train was doing two hundred miles an hour
the life rafts had been lashed to the roofs of the pullman cars
we floated up soaking but well organized

the trip to india took a year and fifty days not counting a month in australia
we cured our infections and lapped up dry bed rest sex sightseeing and showers
when we arrived the party had already spread behind us to california

on our way home we found it on the outskirts of milan and paris and london
the trip to india is the longest of all journeys
no one exactly understands the power of india as a destination

the more intently you desire the journey the less of a journey it requires
things moving rapidly continue to achieve godhead and go out of existence

23.10

we made italian america into a new india one night in the summer of 93
in our next five hundred years all americas will return to their aboriginal state
in their origins all possible americas seem to have grown as forms of india

on this tree garcia lorca whitman ginsberg di prima hang as silver ex votos
a right arm two left legs ten hearts stamped silver hang by wires from twigs
every tree begins to acquire legends even as you pause to look it over

in an india desire or italy passes through satisfaction or america
satisfaction emerges from america as a universal postponement of discussion
we put off a trial until the judge has a chance to be reborn grow old and die

in his next life he returns as a mute creature and so long waits often occur
desire crosses the table east to west and satisfaction crosses north to south
the checkered tablecloth recalls the dialectic producing any india

the man speaking italian at the next table had the beard of a saint
it caused you in that instant to accept the sanctity of your own body

23.11

the body lives forever in heaven or hell taught nun to pope in childhood
each moment or heaven or hell runs down body bottom up again perhaps
some bodies stagnant pools collect overflow from occasional lively moments

other bodies become anthologies of the universe
when allen ginsberg sets pencil to paper he writes blake or washes dishes
when i write i engage in the psychomachia of the post risorgimento

my father's answer to the migration was there is no god
if there was god would italy have died in the hands of its bridegroom
afterwards i returned to italy hoping to awaken her with a kiss

italy to my surprise had already long since been resurrected by swiss doctors
she had no interest in my pale scholarship or my quest to justify the migration
why should we justify ourselves to you you tribe of losers italy said to me

all question of kisses was now forgotten
it was time to discuss the division of property

23.11–23.12

23.12

i present to the motherland a poem on her african empire bound in red crocodile
in return come polka dot newsreels shot by american planes bombing monte cassino
my reply is two brown photos of mussolini greeting hitler and pope pius xii

italy sneers here don't forget your social worker ellis island sob sister history
i sing about gramsci tresca silone the rossellis and other victims of fascism
that does it says italy i am going to give you all my al capone trading cards

what happened to you mother i suddenly cry
she says kid your mother is dead i am your sister's niece by marriage
oh you can't fool me i smile

all right she shrugs soldier buy me a drink
i exclaim aha a tomb with your family's new tractor etched in polished granite
yes croons italy and i have brought you the revolutionary silk shirts as well

music food stroking and dances and other rhythms just come together with us
if a sudden sound calls out we turn in parallel motion as if we had planned it

24. the old men crack walnuts and watch to see that all is done as in days gone by

24.1

conversation between italy and italians often assumes a family character
italians all'estero to the outside of italy sit weeping over the verdi requiem
quam olim abrahae promisisti et semini ejus as you promised abraham and his seed

a long time ago means what when you sing it in a mass to alessandro manzoni
risorgimento god manzoni was equally a son of the revolution and the church
what land was promised to manzoni and his seed as to abraham and his so long ago

the land of italy begins at the parting of waters of lago di como
there the alps flow into the long peninsula of fertile valleys
the land of italy begins at the parting of waters of lago di garda

catullus watched from a high place waters of the dolomites fall and enter italy
virgilius maro in a sulfuric mist the color of blood saw the inside of italy
niccolò tucci three days before my first orazione took me to the pozzo etrusco

granite wall leonardo da vinci dante alighieri watch over our granite thrones
i rise to speak public italian the first time my grandfather floats in the window

24.1–24.2

24.2

qui in italia dissi sotto la protezione della mia intenzione vissi un'anno
sedendomi a roma mi sono messo a lavoro all'acquisto di una certa lingua
in bocca romana ma toscana dal agosto dell'anno mille novecento ottanta sei

trovando quella lingua finalmente ho scoperto un segreto squisitissimo
la lingua italiana è un gatto d'oro africano macchiato d'inchiostro
the audience looked up rapt in amazement how long was this speech going to take

one thought leaning back in his seat once in a while he might hear something
another opened a bag and began grading papers but i went on anyway
at the end i was treated with courtesy as if i had just joined the order

here in italy i have lived a year under the protection of my intention
living in rome i put myself to learn a certain tongue
in a roman mouth but tuscan from august of nineteen eighty six

finding that tongue i finally discovered a most exquisite secret
the italian tongue is a cat of african gold spotted with ink

24.3

we speak here not just of the language but of the actual physical tongue
qui trattiamo non solo del linguaggio ma della lingua propria corporale
imparando l'italiano la lingua di carne diviene come un'animale vivace

learning italian the tongue of flesh becomes like a lively animal
ho fatto questo discorso a perugia in un tempio della lingua nazionale
i delivered this speech in perugia in a temple of the national language

the nation that the language creates is wider than the national territory
la nazione che la lingua crea è più larga che il terrritorio nazionale
la sede di perugia si dedica all'insegnamento di questa lingua agli stranieri

the university at perugia specializes in teaching this language to foreigners
the mind of anyone who learns italian may become its own university
la mente di qualcheduno chi impara l'italiano possa diventar la propria università

inside the italian american who is learning italian both sides speak together
dentro l'italo americano chi sta inmparando l'italiano ambi le parti si parlano

24.3-24.4

24.4

the three postage stamps you ordered were delivered by canaries
now you began writing letters to poets though always as such and not as persons
a good poet is more likely to make a good citizen than a good citizen a good poet

even so the odds against poet citizens run steep
how can you be a good citizen when your father does not accept what you do
and yet you thought there must be poets who proceed from acceptance

you turned to the family poets saint francis and saint anthony
they offered comfort to all little creatures who heard them
when they said all beings visible and invisible are joined

the sun and moon are your own brother and sister
though this idea amused you at first you tiptoed secretly up to it afterwards
but you still loved stubbornly best the fragile great strength of a human being

certain mornings you could do nothing because he had rejected you
other mornings you thought my brother sun feels otherwise

24.5

in your first letter to poets as such you took up the question of affinity
we are all sisters brothers brothersisters and grandfatherdaughters
yes they replied upon reading this how familiar but the letter went on

in this miraculous period italian american writers discovered their relatives
every writer had deep affinities with every other writer you said in the letter
growing together underground they came out in family shapes to one another

o poets do not despair if you fail to understand the meaning of our life
someone has understood it for us and has given it to us in this sealed package
for us the meaning of life need not go further than protection of this package

this package is a word in which other things have been hidden
every thousand years the messiah may come and reach into the word
often he has not come at all but on one return they claim he could raise the dead

every italian poet belongs to an order of poets stretching back before that time
virgil universal italian grandfather poet predicted the birth of the messiah

24.6

no one knew what to make of columbus and his discoveries for a long time
plenty of people assumed cipango was another pompous italian make believe
soon vespucci's letters settled many questions but not the meaning of it

that is he laid out the new stars the naked defenselessness of the people
but it took time for mundus novus to become utopia land of strange manners
at this point in the enterprise many things fell asleep only to be awakened now

america or mundus novus flowers everywhere its new londons and romes
its rivers flow directly out of bottomless time
the valiant heart and the gentle heart belong to the garibaldino and the bride

we have returned to the birth of the american sky and the american pleasures
the jungles of delight where so many died happy have now reopened
we have returned to understand that we all become not americans but natives

american is something we remember being long ago before we ever got here
can it be as it seems that the last americans died before we were born

24.7

in the end i am angry because i don't know but am known
preparing for everything we do we don't always prepare everything we need
was it in the program there would be all this chatter and newsmaking

actually the plan needs to be only concentrate on what makes you happy
in this you find nutrition plus protection from the plans of enemies
what makes you happy will save your dignity when people demean you

fix your destination using a steady happiness as your star
the wishes of your friends blow wind into the sail you raise on courses you set
you venture out into the ocean equipped with crew provisions and good wit

people say not every journey ends prosperous or passes calm
they live with their noses pressed to the window
wave up to the wheelchair silhouettes on the cliff as you sail away

out in the intense white transformational roar many things go forward
on maps they paint it blue as if they had only seen it in pictures

24.7–24.8

24.8

the truth is we cannot map the ocean of transformation
we are able to chart a course and with sophisticated steering devices keep to it
with our charts we can follow the greater and lesser flows and depths of water

we do fine sticking to our information assiduously examining whatever we find
weather varies wickedly so the sky may be calm but your people restless
you sometimes can predict changes of condition but always be ready for others

after a while you get a feel for things and they start to go right
you still cannot map it well but at least get where you are going in one piece
the trick is understand how a fixed goal gives your decisions cumulative force

this too acquires configurations subtle beyond what the artist's hand can render
but the principle is the simple one that everything now acquires a relationship
as you consider each choice the fixed goal changes shape and color

in this way through storms you reach ports that might well be what you had in mind
this much map is enough if only we can keep it safe and dry

24.9

now you know what time it is in every direction in relation to a fixed point
you have decided to go with a period of seventy days as your preparation curve
then you say all right that means sixty four days before leasing and six to go

that means thirty four days before finding
that means begin looking within four days
as you look for a place also seek and choose cargo packers and stevedores

these details require frequent review but above all keep recharting your course
looking towards your fixed point you see its character and location more clearly
it also means finishing up old business within these first four days

everything else moves as these days move so consider carefully your every step
calm and considerate you may pass miracles without frightening anyone
also attend to your humblest duties hoping the brightest clarity will emerge

raise your feathers and step forward towards the ship of the future
it will still be waiting even if you get all of this wrong

24.9–24.10

24.10

by night the emperor carried the empire in small bundles across the river
at the home of the stablemaster he left ten thousand books for safekeeping
the librarian preceded the emperor into exile with all the imperial horses

a certain music has never ceased playing in the courtyard even during the war
mornings the emperor performs prescribed rituals with exemplary solar patience
one courtier always remains with him throughout his reign according to our epics

imperial ceremony implies imperial civility which implies empire
empire subsumes kingdom as kingdom presupposes heaven authorizing kingdom
attempting to understand the topology seems itself un po esagerato our epics say

each morning the water has continued to rise clear from the seam in the earth
we have found this fountain propitious for the ceremony and have drunk from it
every summer breath has a meaning known only to the holy one blessed be he

to our clay we understand the empire has always been more beautiful as an idea
still the emperor inherits actual things in billions he must manage to arrange

24.11

night birds have cunning because they focus their attention
even the highest animals only work best in that condition
desire intensifies focus because it orients a person in time as well as space

you need to structure an answer to things in such a way as to get you some peace
you know how to figure this out although sometimes you feel embarrassed to ask
a certain clear picture emerges through the haze of conversation

your aunt remembers you answering your father no matter what he said
you were telling him what others told him that he didn't know how to hear
so now you hear the same thing because you do what he did you say they say

actually you think what you did was worse because you were supposed to be great
you took authority from old men who listened to you marveling when you spoke
but so each one of us disputes with his father in the assembly of old men

in this art called rhetoric like a big cat you use your tongue with muscular effect
often the most powerful speech means to sit waiting with your eyes on the dark

24.11–24.12

24.12

in our assemblies these disputes have the elegance of wrestling dances
choruses of boys and old men dispute with men in their prime who cannot hear them
for each man in his prime consumes his hours in pursuit of the daily object

jungle velvet caresses his foot and strokes his passing arm
boys and ancients wearing masks shout threats in every direction
the man slips under the foliage where the prey will never see him

meanwhile wrestlers climb the temple steps grunting and swearing in ritual holds
the old hero struts his feathers once again and the boy takes his picture
meanwhile the man has already eaten the prey in the cave

now begins the great feast wherein boy and man debate
man attacks and cuts and stabs but only hurts boy when marking him
hunting together in the afternoon they see golden cats slip through the grass

this is how they settle america with churches and squares
the old men crack walnuts and watch to see that all is done as in days gone by

ellis island

25. don't stop to try and figure everything out because what does it matter

25.1

under the water you saw them play at swimming like fish
on this memorable day the piano movers began to take heavy thought
the river spread out below the bridge a token of innumerable headwaters

anywhere along the way women wait for you to stop and say hello
people pause to read newspapers looking over the tops for someone to engage
do not offer things you cannot give them without entangling yourself

people call your desiring selfishness when it disturbs their own imaginings
to avoid disillusion practice never expecting the rain to fall upwards
humans all want to eat first until they accept that the world will feed them

persons who forget their desire still cannot just accept whatever they get
when you look into the distance fix your coordinates and aim
here you may or may not find that blessed happiness you are always seeking

others may or may not understand but what matters is how you treat them
show respect for their positions even if they don't themselves know what they are

25.2

here is the story as it presents itself to the theater of decision
certain persons would forbid you to take this step if they could do so
but these persons can no longer chain you to a nonexistent box of menus

so you have set their once real power down in your cupboard
there it sits in command of splayed fork and twisted spoon
but you must use these implements to survive so you take them back

once you do this a whole box of sharpened knives appears as if by magic
all the crimes you ran away from getting into this you now must commit again
only now you call them categories of limitation paradox and difficulty

open the window
after the breeze changes the air the sweet smell of reason fills the room
as you work you find each thing a place in the general scheme

although this process takes a long time it allows you more certain results
you now can talk anything or anyone to death

25.3

in the old days they would sell you a bishop's hat for money
since the reformation you buy one with opinions and connections
why is a book of ideology better than a box of money

anyway if you want to be pope the best thing is have an opinion that wins big
such opinions hide in the cracks between dreams and damnation
anything less marks you at most permanent abbot or titular archbishop

on a more modest level it still makes sense to put the basics first
the father of any family may feel as much responsibility as the father of another
making plans the best thing is clarity which allows for firmness and tenderness

this activity endows you with power to cast away spells cast upon you
this you do by the simple act of enduring clarification
this brings some things to consciousness but many pass without your noticing them

all your opinions gain in depth of color from your discussion of basic matters
you approach the business of daily life as if you were adam and this the garden

25.3–25.4

25.4

now we must prepare to walk softly through rooms arranging things
before starting it's best to consider which things you can move and which ones not
any time you need to change parts of your life you must first calm down

for years i went to work angry as if my anger were a daily shield
before that i every morning would put on the armored mask of cheerfulness
frequently the mask would crack and my life was one long surprise symphony

over the years i have worn the masks of sanctity of sadness of guilt of sorrow
of joy of groaning of seduction of thoughtfulness and whatever else i needed
public life was a puppet show of my many selves

if i was the puppeteer i was so worried about my cues i never noticed anything
i drank coffee and smoked cigarettes and kept turning the wheel for customers
out came charts and chatter and exceptional folly i knew how to make the most of

now i have entered a period where you lay all these things aside
gestures of abnegation seem hollow compared with admitting to a monster mistake

25.5

they say we do well to admit our feelings to ourselves if not to others
i learned to keep secrets so effectively i can't read the notes i made
in my house we regarded much truth as a thing too powerful to control

thus we avoided it shutting our doors against it or burying it in our closets
i keep there art equipment music church history my aesthetic dissertation
recently i have taken many of these things out for a little airing

i look forward to a new arrangement where they will lie on the open shelves
but in the beginning i would prefer to live as if in a pilgrims' hostel
suddenly the train station smell fills every corner of the house

i used to weep for all the little strings i left behind
in those days i did not know how these strings would follow me everywhere
you don't always recognize them when they grow back but you can't stop them

now the next thing you knew i was swimming miles every day
i slowed myself down for years but then one day began to hit my stride anyway

25.5–25.6

25.6

so then i sat down and began to row a brief distance every morning
for a period i would go further each time until that once i had an injury
it took me a long while to recover enough to start rowing again

these episodes move you forward almost without your noticing any change
you suddenly remember somehow you started rowing somewhere really far away
since that time you have passed through several other states and into a new zone

in this new position on the planet you do many things more easily than before
is it the place or the change or the practice that makes this difference
to know the time here in this new position you listen to musicians

they teach all recurrences with their unfamiliar rhythms and timbres and tunes
though these whistle and shout you only need listen as water reflects the stars
this learning consists of receiving passively and producing actively

in moments of intense concentration these distinctions disappear
our very distractions hide in the groundbass and shake us like thunder

25.7

now and then i was stroking a palm tree idly in the shade
the man in leather mirrors peered in through the gate
not today the servant told him and brought in the string quartet

i am in trouble i said to myself every time i thought about it
my father and his nearby living friend warned us loudly against queers
old systems of asshole buddies ran the world and stay away from them

it turned out not to work that way at all
instead old systems of all sorts ran the world and you belonged to one already
they called it the fatherland family and they built it the largest altar in rome

but we practiced its rituals morning noon and night daily every place we went
it meant giving up a lot of things and it saved you from a lot of trouble
on the other hand it gave you the chance to love one another

even if it hurts like crazy loving helps you cross the ocean in one piece
every time you remember me we kiss and the other way around as well

25.7–25.8

25.8

of course it does not always work i mean the fatherland family not always
sometimes it helps you love other times it's just a piece of heavy machinery
big projects like settling a new country use plenty of major ordinance

but later this stuff just makes for a stiff maintenance when you don't use it
we study puzzle problem strategy for decades as if it were a cold old elegance
but sometimes we need these library things of course and right away too

so how can you decide what you keep and what you give to the deep
some mornings i sit down in the mud and model a new human family of clay
or i slap my hand on your feelings as soothingly as i can which helps eventually

some mornings i make every ritual and sing every prayer i can fit into the time
now i prefer to sing a single prayer and give myself to it
it may have great length and still be all of it one thing

you will visit in this song as if it were your grandmother tongue speaking
this tongue tells of oldest worlds behind older worlds behind the old world

ellis island

25.9

this large or single poem banishes enjambment from its lines
almost every line counts as a whole sentence
the small or many sonnets themselves achieve closure by their look

but enjambment arranges thoughts throughout the large or single poem
some thoughts wash dozens of small poems like waves across a flat of snails
other thoughts rain down in thousands of white pellets each of them complete

any size poem of course may roll up and down the heaving waters of time
desperado rafts and steamers tilt on the foaming edge of your nightmare
hunting canoes shoot out through the breakers everyone shouting together

we cut across thought with the flash of a sword
javelins carry flames through imaginary paper saintly hearts in sonnets
the comfortable long poem offers you an ocean liner overflowing with animals

we have only got so many hours in the day to go frisking in the gym
even at the speed of light the universe exceeds our powers of imagining it

25.10

as we turn towards our invisible horizon many voices call us back
blue sky drawing you also terrifies and frightens your drinking companions
do you want freedom or satisfaction they wonder but you want both

to have these things look and accept what you see as real
that no one else can see it means that you must grow into its moment
the goal when you reach it reveals its place in the infinite chain of lights

so said the old young man reciting lessons he had learned from trees
don't stop to try and figure everything out because what does it matter
some things really work and that's all there is to it

the fellow who was in jail for life escaped for a few weeks to the swamp
i just needed some fresh air he said i love prison really i do
most of us do not love prison life however

most we love cats by night
we love dawn together most

25.11

thorns appeared on the tree every time i touched it
apples fell unheeded before we could find the baskets
the meadow grew a fragrant waste of high grass and dark flowers

soon i saw a brindled rabbit in the weathered toolshed shade
i run down these narrow purple shadow alleys like a loose thought
i wrap myself around a purpose that wraps itself around me

in these moments we see water flow our minds growing clearer than air
blood rejoices and heart with gladness sings
afterwards in cool evening we make music under the stiff palms

one day a year we place a stone upon our memories
oh yes we agree this one was something else
now we hear birds loudly laying claim to the abundant blackberries

we go home humming the old tune next year we will remember better
and drink a cup of white rum with sand on the backs of our hands

25.11–25.12

25.12

i have been looking for the rowboat
you think i left it under the porch
i think you hid it under the eaves

anyway there is always the bus
there are reasons to think otherwise she said boom boom boom
policeman's daughter dances the polka with a platoon of angry elephants

o yeah she said and so's your old man because she does respect sarcasm
when you tune to a given station you hear the music that station plays
they send out bulletins on tuesday like the ones that go mondays and fridays

it may be that all frequencies carry tunes you don't want to hear
still sometimes a single station becomes a way of life
when stations change playlists drastically listeners usually move their dials

i have discovered the rowboat called consumer preference
smaller than a seven forty seven it turns things on and off perfectly well

26. can you smell europe yet

26.1

an old man's posse shambled into the pecorarium bar and potato grape arbor
what will it be boys said nick the sleeve garter italian with the gold tooth
play us a song about the social security retirement benefit mutual fund nick

sure boys he crooned waxing his moustache that's how we do things in old florida
let's all go prices low there's no snow big things grow lawns to mow in pompano
they left the place full of dust whilst nick was gone with the cash register

in the back room girls in shift dresses and boys in shorts slept on burlap bags
hey called mailman it's a postcard from the sunny tutti frutti southland
congratulations on your doctorate in british history technology

your sister received her doctorate in italian touristology
what ever happened to doctors of philosophy you asked the mailman
they still have them he said but only in disneylands and reservations

you called yourself doctor of philosophy walking in bensonhurst every morning
people grow food there and play together among the rose trellises and grapevines

26.1–26.2

26.2

early this morning we tried to capture monkeys in a cupboard
you don't have enough hands so they always find another door to get out of
now doctors of technology are climbing the courtyard walls

can you smell europe yet
these are bodies which means being interpreted spirit as bodies make you
you may love every person you ask for in a dying room even those you turn away

angry moments poke up out of your sunset forgetfulness bay like beacon buoys
who can say how many times we disagree about what we see in the fatal swamp
we have found so many messages left behind that we need to study constantly

flag shreds wash in with the tide and pieces of carpentered beam
you puzzle them together as a reason to go forward
actually the force of breath comes from the earth herself

she gives birth to you every moment and she receives your attachment to her
keeps records written in seaweed and bone

26.3

your task may not require all these rosewood scarabs and ivory horns
you pick your way through them to an opening that gives onto the sidewalk
where is the horse you ask where is the car where is the boat plane bike train

no one knows how to think any more you shout into the window reflection
dogs in packs roam the empty streets and you are afraid
the monk locks the church door protecting the sacrament and gold vestments

you have taken refuge in the mountain of the lord says the abbot
from your window in the morning you see the sunlight strike the mountain peak
after two hours of singing you eat breakfast then work in the garden till noon

we have regulated the world using mind for mother of arrangements
on the vellum pages we follow the order of things as they change in the sky
if the sky changes below the equator we can adjust to that as well he says

every spring the melting snow uncovers murdered thieves
we bury them as saints so they'll guard us at night

26.3–26.4

26.4

mind dances mostly for itself in mirrors that may bore you
but hamonizes inaudibly deep sounds that may surprise you
waters rise and fall on the rough edges of breathing

ocean tides slosh you strolling in park
continental plates pulse faintly on the dreaming liquid fire
jelly globe spinning prints your clear itineraries

sun illuminates bunches of grapes from within as they lie in your hands
what you do can count toward the harvest even if you can't see it
find ideas afloat in puddles

carry your picnic basket to the puritan moon
you can feed anything that lives there but nothing lives there
earth authorizes you and you don't need to know what that means

ant grasshopper gorilla gazelle
close your eyes and listen

ellis island

26.5

i flinched from vision and sought the shadow of rescue
my father who left me to deal with the world on my own says he is coming back
he cannot bring my mother because she died during the twenty five year journey

when my father returns he will not rescue me but may ask me to save him again
if i try this operation will he fill me with love or approbation
i have been trying to start living with a dependence upon something else

i invented this machine to sublimate father dependence into community dependence
it turned out that father forms run deeper and larger than i had expected
the sublimated father or community remains ruler of rescues

the important thing then became learn to love yourself as any good father can
you may not like yourself or all you have done but you love yourself anyway
you need yourself and rescue yourself in a two beat rhythm like walking

at times you get what you need from those who need what you have
other times your commerce takes place between you and yourself

26.6

i always had this feeling i was broken up in parts top to bottom
is connected to the hip bone said the preacher and i thought about it
i seemed to be inside my head looking out at a tower of bones and muscles

but other parts can take over when they want to your stomach or groin or heart
any of them may center you at any time the song means to preach
does everything have to have a center that the i will occupy

actually the word i often means where you find the center in your head
messages from other more powerful centers do not always call themselves i
but they might ride bikes take over the i as a decadent province and play ball

that's what everybody says but actually the not i has been larger all along
managing the i has always preoccupied thoughtful and intelligent persons
gifts of food pass from my labor to your delight only afterwards reaching i

the square of the room its circles spheres and oblongs always imply the not i
we only see it sideways but we feel its presence even in its largest absences

26.7

the merry schoolmaster dante alighieri had mounted the mountain bike of god
now close your eyes he said and turning on the television appeared in a gondola
venice from behind his head came to surround your nostrils and ears with water

every fish between your legs or in your armpits i said implied the ancient future
ah the ancient future they said that old guelf garlic
all the communist ghibellines believe in maintaining international trade

tomorrow we make everything new they sing beating a tin pan
dante cinematographer astounds you even as dante professor drones on
meanwhile however as it so often does the puppet show movie gets it exactly wrong

in fact the soul of italy resides with the lubavitcher rebbe
italy became a woman the day she fell in love with the god of the jews
for this reason to this day the pope retains the keys to an italian kingdom

in the guelf idea the future having always beckoned has more age than the past
popes lead with the authority of precedence having come from the future

26.7–26.8

26.8

you enter a period in which you need to count every four hour block
some people live with less control than this and some with more
others use clocks only to help them live according to the tides

ah you magnificent ruin of time the beautiful woman addressed me
look i said think whatever you like but i can't park much longer on this sandbar
i hear gondoliers coming down the canals playing sorrento on their mandolins

in the morning the animals shake the water from their backs
all sorts of strangers come to watch how we do it so we invented tourism
we are the venice of american literature

come drift with me as i sing o sole mio into a rain barrel
ooh you whispered how nice it is down here among the seaweed brownstones
children peer over the edge at us as if we were carp swimming around in the dark

now we are putting on our masks of venus and of mars
i made my whole body red just thinking about you

26.9

within you secrets grow naturally loving the moist warm shade you provide
after you learn to garden well you learn to market the produce
for one perfume box packed tight with tiny stratagems you charge two day's rent

assigning proportions among expenditures you chase through the underbrush
halfway down the wooded slope you come upon a pool of water you remember seeing
o bureaucracy of eternal spring you call out into the silence

your echo scribbles circles in glassy ripples
all these bodies folding up retire into earth from which they have arisen
we string guitars and stretch tambourine skins in days and nights of high delight

we discovered the voice we were seeking in the sounds of words we were speaking
our love of one another had conquered death once again
even as the shell falls away the energy changing shape already springs to life

the time of human time will truly draw to a close even if you do not think so
but the time of energy in a great wave washes out of the past into the future

26.10

as the dance begins the angry sharpness of swans will sometimes scandalize
the ballet master has written a book which guides most of our behavior
nonetheless we utter noises from the long before

no one has ever written the encyclopedia of human noises
these form a language older and more categorical than words
other creatures understand these sounds better than logical trills and mordants

we brag about our verbal devices however and with good reason
we have used them to organize impressive projects
they help us live well despite the ceaseless efforts of our natural enemies

when we pray we speak in both voices at once swine forlorn and formal client
dear lord o o lord o o o o o o o a a a a a a a a a
as it was in the beginning is now and ever shall be world without end amen

we never know who understands us
this is why we keep on talking

26.11

in our family the last immigrant died the same day as the lubavitcher rebbe
that morning i had written the poem about the soul of italy and the rebbe
the same saturday night i read the poem at the cornelia street café

the poem showed i knew they were both dying you might say
i had been to see mr prestigiacomo my brother in law's father that sunday
drugged painless he lay there enduring the drama of his own breathing

every now and then into the rowing conversation pointed an oar that didn't move
the air vibrated with the transformations spreading through his huge clan
and i who live on ellis island could hear him singing in italian

the great italian melodies seem to go on forever to a last note the most sweet
they arch over an entire sea of separation between grandmother and grandchild
i listen to some of them as if i were in the cradle of a woman i never knew

she cast her spells through daughters and daughters sons and sons and sons
and they call out p'o mare napule quant'armunia saglie cielo e 'ncielo sentono

26.11–26.12

26.12

the island turns as the rushing estuary tide arrives at its high still flood
its point that plowed the current will soon leave a wake of tiny whirlpools
for an hour the fullness seems to grow so that you think it will burst the banks

along the river buildings radiate light brightening the sky
over the spilling tides the fish rich air pours onto the streets
you can see directly into people's hearts

nothing seems to have any weight when forces stand at equilibrium
now you hear the man who sharpens knives ringing his bell in the street
the old bread delivery truck groans after the milk truck and the vegetable wagon

the tongs look like french curves holding the great smoking block of ice
the glass window hearse carries a casket worked all over gold italian filigree
in the casket we place his cards his rubber ball his copy of plato's dialogues

the horse draws away from the church and the cortège stops before the house
under the cemetery gate all pause before we enter the kingdom of clay

ellis island

27. i was haunted by memories in a language i didn't know

27.1

the first wet sand uncovers shells of the angry dead
horseshoe crabs leave spikes and helmets as their traces on the plate of earth
the cemetery rocked wildly on either side of the carriage as we climbed the hill

i could hear a thousand people crying as if all of them were in my mouth
their shrieking fell out of my ears and lay beating on the quilted cushions
their large melodies hung from my hair howling and cursing with grief

a woman sat next to me and calmly tore her shirt straight down the middle
then she held her hands up to the sky and began a fierce wailing and vibrating
soon she was stamping her feet against the carriage floor

outside on the grass grandchildren walk silently in the brilliant sunlight
no one hears the woman beat her head against the coffin
when she faints i go to catch her falling but of course she is not there

i walk holding onto things hiding rage in a pretense of age
if the young people knew what you were thinking they might never sleep again

27.1–27.2

27.2

i am the woman who never came to america
going down from here my children disappeared into the blue air
she walks around the outside the house for years trying to get in

one day she finds a crack in the wall and after that the family recovers
for this we have prepared an offering to thank saint anthony and la madonna
some nights i sit at the table beating a tambourine for hours

her children when they were dancing used to think of how she danced
they would pray forgiveness for having left her
on their knees they followed the procession licking the dust where people walked

at weddings into the small hours they waltzed their melancholy waltzes
eventually everything returns as grass and roses
she mothers all who mother even in the shadowy doorways of death

some recite the rosaries and others braid the thick hair of all that happens
one morning they look up and there she stands smiling at them

27.3

everywhere i looked i had built a heap of possible power
all my weapons systems made great impressions though most were incomplete
red clouds swirl descending into the valley as cowboys choke to death

an unshaven angry universe stretches and catches its breath
other ways to keep things orderly include polite requests
you often will also accept that another person does not do what you wanted

feeling and choosing can melt many solid obstacles into disappearance and dust
just think about how to love yourself valuing your powers as they deserve
touch the people you love and keep choosing the work you love

keep doing the work you love and caress the people you love
then you can bid goodbye to the sinking destroyers and blasted triremes
not that they have no charms but you need the room to get around inside the house

a rising and defeated expectation sings well but can make for depressing company
but if you do that to yourself that's what you get so focus choose succeed

27.3–27.4

27.4

i had been wondering how to touch and choose
and the answer came first feel the beating of your own heart
then your heart can choose

your heart desires poem country woman children
make music in the streets but focus on your heart
you must love yourself and approve yourself and enjoy your own life

out of this kindness flows kindness to others which we call the holy ghost
the father in you loves the son in you producing love for others
in water up to my ankles i watch little fiddler crabs carrying their huge claws

in you father and son joke with one another as they hunt together
each one has his own wigwam but naturally they do cooperate
as you treat yourself with great value you help him to admire his own value

most crab weaponry disappears into the water and feeds other living creatures
sometimes you find old ones pressed in clay that has turned to stone

27.5

the great south bay warms up early in the season because of how shallow it is
long island sound needs deep summer to reach its brief season of welcome
lake ronkonkoma warms the center of the island like a cup reflecting the sky

these dreaming waters once established much of my connection with the planet
i was always needing more because however much loving i got it left me dry
my therapist has compiled the usual short list of reasons

pine needles are my sort of conversation
they stroke each other on the slightest excuse of disturbance and so stay happy
morning noon and night the weather is always changing on long island

breezes from the deepest south in the ocean bring aristocratic bird geniuses
black feathered parrots hide when winds blowing sleet bear down from canada
summer bakes long island like a loaf of bread then electrocutes it like oklahoma

when i was a crab i would sun myself in wet rootlands under high spiky grasses
in those days i found the strength that carries you beyond loneliness

27.5–27.6

27.6

i remember victorian milanesi in frock coats at the opera who smelled like cats
perfume waved a larger fan at fashion then than now
true i have only inferred this memory from my grandfather's taste in crowds

certain ladies would roll nude in powder to protect their clothing from sweat
ecco ridente in cielo they would hum as the morning sun came in at the window
my grandfather with the face of a wooden indian listened to tosca on the radio

monsignor follows bishop into high lacquered carriage waiting where torches blaze
not every spasm nonetheless seems equally to matter
great beauty avec great athlete dancing under chandelier they call the painting

a fall from grace he cried with his cigar between two fingers a fall from grace
a next career may begin even with a tiny rise in fortune
howsoever gradual any changes in altitude will effect changes in daily living

a few of us ascend the opera humble among richer patrons but still rising
some strangers these days make italian bread that surprises us as not bad at all

27.7

things pass through people all day long invisible as radio programs
just today after breakfast i heard you transmitting speeches of fdr
your face forms a mask perfectly well known to aristotle as painful anger

i had just been reading the book about roman drama and i recognize that grimace
in the book it reminded me of my grandmother but on you it looks like the book
so who are you when all these different programs pass through you continually

wanting to answer this question need not imply even knowing what it means
who are you could be the title of a song about sadness
the real you may however not require questions but reveal bits of self in deeds

i watch messages rattling up the road of your eyes like trailer trucks
diesel fumes go with these messages the way a hamburger goes with a coke
i sit on the porch over the highway waiting for the message i will go along with

after supper i sit on a rock over the beach and watch the sun go down
the gnats at twilight drive you crazy but this is where the boats come in

27.7–27.8

27.8

every time i even turn my head towards my father i suffer
the fact is i do always not wish him well
the fact is i punish myself for not wishing him well

it seems he pays me no attention except to belittle me
afterwards i walk around feeling wounded but unable to say how deeply
is it rejected affection or a frustrated need for support that does this to me

perhaps some other force like sheer malevolence supplies him stratagems
can you imagine that he worries so much for himself he has no time for you
when you remember that then you give him presents as if you were paying tax

don't worry about the feeling but just keep yourself covered at all times
o you cry woe is me but you no longer need to play in the olympics
your medals although modest have the glint of genuine precious metal

beyond that just remember that it can hurt too when you give yourself support
your fear reflects anger so find ways to soothe anger and you will fear less

ellis island

27.9

the quiet when you wake up at three in the morning has the sound of beyond time
but when you put your head out the window you find things humming
another crew takes over in the summer dark

in the still air you smell long island jungle summer
here in brooklyn trees creepers grass great bushes mingle on the ocean hush
the seas here unload a heavy damp air that the gulfstream drags from the equator

now i have begun to understand that i have done well to write poetry
it has brought some comfort to some people and has eased their hearts sometimes
a sarcasm cam make for a healing poem

you never know what's going to help
it can hurt to be good to people who do not seem to appreciate it
so we begin to learn to try to show generosity even to those we fear

it's all in the sounds you almost hear
it's all in the lawn when it sleeps

27.10

whenever i work the market i come home thinking what did i do wrong
even when i did something right this happens
and though i thought i had seen through jealousy there it comes

i find fear where there ought to be gentle affection
is it safe to talk yet i asked him
then he said here why don't you write an unreadable book about it again

this puppet father hovers over every move i make mocking and belittling
i have placed this character in the bureau drawer where i keep old puppets
this morning i take out the new one that strokes my hair and says you will prevail

your stubbornness clears away confusion in moments like these
distinguish between the steel device and the actual beating heart
you have begun to row your own boat along the banks of the wide river

when you go into market you meet spirits and puppets by thousands
in the morning open the doors of your mind so they can escape

27.11

answer them when they call and then try to pay your bills
if you find that it is all too much you have probably been doing too much
poet novelist professor director executive officer president chair are your titles

each title requires maintenance like those houses in the country you don't have
father son brother husband cousin nephew neighbor also require maintenance
last night bill tonelli wrote in my copy of his book king of the viscusi nation

so there in private i have had this coronation by the king of the tonelli nation
he has a face that reminds me of napoleon or my mother or my father's mother
can i manage being king on top of all this other stuff

that is what i have been aiming at all along making my own world
now you have achieved it says the mother puppet and so now change your profile
in short you can approve yourself as what you really want to do

other things you can subordinate and delegate according to your need
as you read the bills think if you have been rewarding yourself kindly

27.11–27.12

27.12

you forgot italian and married someone other than an italian
but then you were ready to reach for the word italian
you went to rome like someone visiting the set of tosca

many people carry italian like an empty set marked nostalgia
inside it they put whatever they remember or think someone else remembered
i was haunted by memories in a language i didn't know

so my plan meant discovering yesterday as tomorrow
it was impossible but i drew satisfaction from even tiny acquisitions
i liked best the language then the gardens and then the processions

most others had given it up but i thought it is a place like anyplace else
you can go there and eat the food that made your grandparents
getting further than that required a science of inventing tomorrow

some doctors cure disease but others invent more ample forms of wellness
if you blow your trumpet into the empty air an entire opera rises up around you

28. streams flow backwards towards you out of the future from objects of your generosity

28.1

spend on those you see around you
don't wait to find out who they are
no need to monogram the luggage

spend on creatures that appear to live inside you
you may only feel them as a pulse
still try to answer

when these creatures suggest desires we supply them if we can
we cannot give more richly than we have received
nor can we receive further without giving

when we receive a pleasure we give thanks for it first and even beforehand
for what we are about to receive we thank thee we say lifting a fork
and afterwards o yes and my o my and thank you jesus

some ground may be nothing but stones
keep moving till you find a place to lie down

28.1–28.2

28.2

we have no need to remember measurements and titles
things come to you because you swim with them in life
when plato and aristotle speak of memory they speak of a restless worm

the next thing you knew we had all of us remembered a subterranean queen
and when the populous womb wishes us oblivion we shall forget
even magnetic memories live out of her magnet which we mistake for time

all writing imitates the secret folds of her body
every act of love passses in and out of her intricate palace tunnel network
invisible animals continually create all even memory

sancta maria ora pro nobis nunc et in hora mortis nostrae
for we know the animalculus so loved the world he gave it his own twin
the traffic between them sustains all life cresting the past rising into the future

the touch of the drum and the touch of the finger indicate reproduction
memory vibrates wet with new lives

28.3

at a certain point you catch on to what you might have been doing wrong
first had come the realization that you even might be doing something wrong
certain persons howl like bulls as you did

they stood up at the dinner table and began to shout tenor with soprano
they sang long slow melodies beginning one dawn lasting till the following dawn
certain people never seemed to speak except through bodies resonant as churches

their mothers had been praying and singing all morning and cooking all day
at belltower tempo they passed through all the dining halls from youth to age
their softest conversations shrieked head tones and chest tones

i could never stay with them
everything they did had so much heavy beauty in it that it weighed me down
i preferred bare diet conscious therapist voices with no production values

one morning my voice suddenly cracked and shattered into a thousand pieces
afterwards i did less screaming and more laughing

28.3–28.4

28.4

a large relationship between different kinds of songs characterizes an opera
any opera implies the whole set of human possibilities some closer than others
in tosca mario cavaradossi sings of desire and death

svanì per sempre sogno mio d'amore l'ora è fuggita e muoio disperato
e muoio disperato e non ho amato mai tanto la vita
the third act rests upon an e that is the lowest sounding bell of saint peter's

puccini here rejected a hymn to life and art illica or giacosa had written
composer and writers would settle arguments in giulio ricordi's publishing office
hollywood later as milano had done constructed music dramas using teams of pros

some things only a working group can decide or find the will or power to launch
in the year nineteen ought five one million italians climbed into forever ships
i used to hear them humming the tunes from madama butterfly while they worked

distorted screams and weeping have an honorable place in our history of language
we try to find the principle that helps them produce results we can love

ellis island

28.5

they understood benito mussolini as a baritone in an opera about rome
he made peace with the pope and signed a pact with the diavolo tedesco
in the salons long necked women tried to look like art nouveau tiger lilies

when i was three mussolini's ghost slipped out of italy on a broken down mule
into the garden he rode whistling the march from aida under the pumpkin vines
the old men buried his shattered statues because he had tried to revive rome

state zitt' e mangiar became the only italian our grandmothers would sing
mussolini appears on the balcony gesticulating but you can't hear him
for a long time everyone will look in one direction and then they turn

now no more can they imagine things they used to see every day when they woke up
mussolini falls out of the clouds among bombs that make night whiter than noon
napoleon has actually won at marengo but papal police sing a te deum by mistake

we hear tosca murder baron scarpia in a black mass on saturday radio
bells ringing from all seven hills italy washes up on the shore unrecognizable

28.5-28.6

28.6

every wall in rome exists somewhere else in the form of a drawing
laws changing across centuries govern window sizes and thickness of walls
half rome devotes its working hours to regulating the other half

in the tower of interpretations you receive definitive rulings at ground level
higher up in some rooms you find guides who may or may not admit you to archives
bishops patrol parapet balconies looking for signs to guide interpretation

at the summit the high priest dictates letters and thinks about his vacation
napoleon forced the pope out of rome in the name of la république
make peace with everybody they preach but hide the silver under the cellar floor

grand opera mostly records papal preoccupations since the barberini invented it
eternal and universal mother and head of all churches stands on the lateran hill
from san giovanni the papal seat looks out at the statue of saint francis

little brown bronze pauper preacher pleads at the pope from among the sparrows
everywhere you go in rome you encounter the night sweats of guilty apostles

28.7

looking to find my way back to italy i heard priests speaking in latin
this would bring me back to an italy older than popes i soon decided
an altar boy then studied with jesuits to become a scholar and return to rome

every morning i wept over another generation of dead in the deep world cemetery
priests in crisp linen go up and down among sanctuaries they have long maintained
they planted their altars on top of roman altars they had ruined in rages of revenge

my own apostolic nightmares leapt out of a box i had carried since childhood
inside the jack was carrying a hammer but i kept shutting it tight back down
and i kept looking for the rome that preceded the arrival of these fathers

popes had ravaged the forum leaving the archaeologists nothing but chicken bones
a bronze lava spirals up and down at the corners of saint peter's high altar
barberini melted pantheon porch metal of all gods to make his god this canopy

then i found hadrian's island constructed in a fake lake laid inside a library
this sacred pool has outlived christian furies to touch your gaze as it did his

28.7–28.8

28.8

i have started an imaginary painting one hundred meters square
divide each twenty five hundred square meter quadrant into four squares
each quadrant twenty five meters squared will add up to six two five in a square

passing through the sixteen panels of this huge representation proceeds history
her each new change of clothes fills another square with distinct divinities
an audience of one million sitting in a valley gazes up at the backlit panorama

they occupy this brilliant painting or does this brilliant painting occupy them
in the great hall at ellis island police lay out each million in layers under oil
sixteen million persons looking at this painting make one full level

i can't count how may levels there are but the number runs to awkward infinities
my painting then acquires the texture of sand in summer solstice afternoon heat
a solid continental chaos of ancient watercourses here melts embracing the globe

we came from inside the earth and first lived in volcano lips six miles down
we brought an ancient light with us as we strove towards the solar world out here

ellis island

28.9

small smooth stones make fine proverbs
skim them across nonexistent lakes where memories sink to the bottom
patience patience say to yourself i am coming to bring you help

meanwhile you stagger under the weight of what is that thick wet canvas
things you never wanted to do became things you never forgot to do
things you always wanted to do became things you never would do

on this table i place my passports diplomas fellowships degrees distinctions
reaching in i draw out a long manycolored silk scarf my poet's license
i slip away into the dark of production to help another poem come into existence

they call it inventing the universe but finding a stone or polishing one will do
then i return to the clearing where the gypsies are building a fort out of mud
where have you been they grumble but i try not to argue with them

every poem has a chance to arrange the irritants so that they leave you alone
here you say handing yourself one try this and see what happens

28.9–28.10

28.10

the most important thing to remember is that most people are drunk all the time
very few need illicit intoxicants because legal ones do the job
coffee and cigarettes stupefy though nothing stupefies like commuting to work

by the time you listen to car or train hum for an hour you enter a glass trance
some run riptides of self abuse across their own naked skins to fall down stoned
but whatever they do be sure they wake back up before you take advice from them

drunken opinions often make perfect sense but rarely suit the situation
sober listeners can sit still an hour or two before they say a word
psychodiscipline requires that they learn to sit calmly like hills or lakes

the tense stillness of the lake frames each flown leaf as a completed design
some poems do their best work listening to other poems
i find my own anxieties in the voices of others

the dog barks out of my childhood
the window frames a world i see and only i

28.11

one half truth says talent will let you do almost whatever you please
the other half points out the one thing excluded is the one you actually want
wanting it excludes it unless you can believe in your own wanting as productive

at first i did not see my gift expressing its power as desire
now i have new habits and let desire drive the poem between markers i set out
great desire pours pearly brilliance into the darkness making mind's first light

rough seas call for perseverance true but above all they require art
skies of art fill with light that rises through granite mountains at your touch
if the world is your prism then you have learned how you come from the sun

you practice art when you sit to your desk and your instruments
the memorandum has a touch of poetry because poems act to require acts of memory
we give shape to relationships with acts of memory bringing forth more poems

one can write poems for every projection from garden to kitchen to study to tower
we create selves for daily use but also to frame or demonstrate the lines of time

28.11–28.12

28.12

now you sit down to plan your move using colored pencils to articulate streams
streams flow backwards to you out of the future from objects of your generosity
they send back all you give them plus miracles born of your mutual commitment

these miracles you tend and love because as children do they have absolute rights
some commitments in life must last as long as their childhood and upbringing
other commitments last as long as the relationship between those who made it

in my prayers i ask the lord to show me the way when i can't see it
one step at a time good enough for me cardinal newman wrote in lead kindly light
try not to anticipate problems or magnify difficulties

changes of course often more apparent than real vary the journey to the goal
blue heavens that the butterfly sees present their own webs of illusion
the lord speaks to me one way and another showing me the beauty of his creation

philosophers say the lord is not one but is the process of becoming one
that is what we have philosophers for to remind us how our words slip away

29. with the wind in our sails we set out for the island in the pond ten feet away

29.1

who knows the meaning of things the philosopher shouted into the audience
i am conducting an epic conversation or classical education
i aim now to find those who desire exactly that conversation

in many humanities institutes have i conversed with philosophers
i am usually more lost than anyone in the epic quest for understanding
when i was young i learned to feign humility dialectically but now i feel it

my travels have seen me fall against walls demons and obstacles of all kinds
in the fear of the lord begins wisdom according to ancient hebrew sages
as we sink into wisdom the fear grows more familiar a habit in fact

i trip on a boa constrictor and skip away
this is how we like to begin the conversation in my institute
conversation divides our time with contemplation and composition

what ignorance i used to imitate now i recognize as mine
in our trade professing ignorance keeps us limber

29.1–29.2

29.2

everyone you look at has a plan an opinion and a time to leave
nothing lasts very long in anything like the same condition
most change comes in subtle increments till one day you need a new battery

you threaten yourself with every piece of bad news people repeat
but return to steering the boat and dancing in place
you don't know what's coming but the techniques you have learned will help you

guiding you your subtle passion planted deeper than the pyramids orients you
take your stand on the rostrum and raise your hands in welcome to your audience
assure them that you and they have something important in common

then state your position clearly with due emphasis but without undue emphasis
choose an intensity only after reflecting upon your actual urgency
when you aim at contemplation for example most dramatic inflection becomes comic

strength of assertion comes from meaning what you say when you state your theme
sometimes you can then sit right down though other times you need to talk an hour

29.3

in the magic kingdom they crown a mouse who appoints a duck as premier
rabbit or swan may acquire dignities at the rank of philosophical consuls here
humans become vegetarians in deference to animals who ascend thrones of thought

we see the empire transfigured entire in each single body enjoying the world
reading our body messages we begin walking through a gallery counting mistakes
ah well we remind ourselves mistakes are part of how we get where we are going

when we try this path every wall we knock down leads to a higher wall
one day we say to ourselves it looks like this path is made of only walls
the seaweed islands look good but will not hold you up if you jump into them

under the rolling hills other faces of the world roll otherwise
heroes who feel purposes and walk through time exerting them explain little
we begin to hang on for dear life and no longer remember our facsimile pride

we fix our minds on holding hands
thus when the earth flexes we flex with it

29.3–29.4

29.4

thirty seven of the seventy days have gone by and the plan has often changed
you said i am inside my skin already and prefer to wear it wherever i go
at this moment the body of your current life fell around you like a heavy cloak

can it be that you will spend the rest of your years fighting with yourself
do you even know what you are fighting about anymore
imagined dyings twitter and buzz and they throb you all day long

platoons carry axes and pommels up your arms and then expeditions dig your chest
i thought all right i will go but i will take the entire establishment along
i once failed at that so i hope i am smarter now because i used to be stronger

that is to protect myself from weakness i will assume a greater burden i said
then i thought no the only answer is love but it flickers like a weak candle
still i keep lighting the flame every day for the ritual period to signify love

in the end you hear the same advice for the first time fresh and new every time
calm down and work while waiting for dinner

29.5

we were removing selves like layers of masks and layers of coats
then layers of shirts imperceptibly gave way to layers of strategic postures
after i took off all my clothes with susan on the mountain i nearly died of fear

we made love among trees on the sunlit steep smelling of grass hot under the sun
it was the week before woodstock which i got sick right after though i didn't go
that mass public transgression enlarged my guilt for the earlier private act

the next day a mysterious infection commenced in me that no doctor could cure
eventually a urologist tamed it and only five years later it seemed wholly gone
it left a weakness for pain near my kidneys that occasionally would flare up

a few years ago i started taking off all the clothes i wore inside my body
one day i peeled off the bruised rubber suit i had worn as victim of sexual zeus
now i unchain this christopher columbus double crucifix breaking my shoulders

the deadweight guilt hurts in my arms and across the neck and even in my fingers
someone come and soothe my shoulders i sing

29.5-29.6

29.6

columbus finishes his famous inspirational speech called profits from tragedy
attendants rush out from the wings as the orchestra raises its amorous nocturne
they unbuckle his huge helmet and carry it out on a velvet cushion

columbus sweats rivers and can hardly be heard asking them to free his hands
oiling ten heavy berubied knucklers off his thick fingers gives him joy of motion
patiently they unlace the platinum and red gold elbow sleeves that kept him still

worked into his gold breastplate they see the brilliant sacred imperial diagram
his heavy stressful curving bellowed backplate displays islands against sunset
removing these from columbus they place them as if pots for palms in the lobby

they set thighplates shinguards ankle mantles on thresholds as if for scrapers
now they lift away from his shoulders sheet after sheet of chainmail
but what is that mass of jade you balance on your naked head they ask him

he is supposed to say christ and then put back all his armor for the next trip
instead of answering he walks away and the jade falls into the sand and disappears

29.7

look says columbus we no longer kill each other over whose idea of god is right
along route nine little shops sell glass cobwebs as images of eternal light
in our motel pilgrimage we try another pattern every night

say god and the very word causes my mind to twist suddenly taking a new shape
along the island shores we see people chained to icons in bizarre configurations
our boat which looks like a city street continues sliding past all this history

some people do not like me but still i manage to enjoy my day walking around
if i had the trick of pleasing and of accepting people as they are it would help
while our island rubs along other islands we can cross into patches of sprouts

i was lying on the ground trying to remember times i used to be happy among beans
shall i sneak back to take some bits of armor to mount on my walls and shelves
wait a minute they ask me where are you going now please tell us

the fact is i am at sea on the ocean of transformation and don't know where i am
as in an opera house i move one part of the platform to another making up reality

29.7–29.8

29.8

who is your god then and what journey are you making
it is the feeling of my mother's skin and the sweetness of the air she breathed
into a universe of abased desire i fell when she abandoned me to my father

he treated me like an enemy threatening to chop my hands off
when i complained to her she called him a monster and then sent me back to him
i never acknowledged my desire but played it like a broken piano

i constructed a wall of stone empires and mafia histories against him
records briefs and methodologies i sang wearing my scholar troubador lawyer cloak
it has placketed navy buttons and brass lion frogs on the collar holding a chain

but of course no one sustains you in battle like the lord of hosts
i marched to the table every night pompous as the pope and draped in rosaries
touch me they said and your hands will fall limp and your head turn to soup

in my poetry soccer game i am near the third of four fifteen year periods
my journey follows constantine's god as if he could give me this victory

ellis island

29.9

so to the question who is your god i answer god defends me against my father
god takes the place of someone whose shadow shapes even what i can see of god
out the patriarchy door i see daisies grow between cracks in flying buttresses

sometimes i venture into the fields even now even if gimpy twisted and shuddering
oh yes they said now it is time to remove your saint christopher medal
the entire delicate operation you will be awake but remember nothing afterwards

you see this sacred device first hung on your neck in childhood has since spread
a silver film finer than on a photographer's plate covers your entire body
it enables you to carry lightning four ways like the powerful axes of a crucifix

rivers of feeling ran through saint francis roaring like torrents in a canyon
saint anthony made a circuit giving comfort to the child which returns stronger
in the fields the beauties have another geometry all center and all periphery

after we finish the intervention your skin grows more comfortable and intelligent
we reconstitute the saint christopher medals as pills which we still sell cheap

29.9–29.10

29.10

in tutto che fai in all that you do dovunque ci vai wherever you go
blu come stai how you are blue sarà tutto che sai will be all that you know
woven word work windows wash water between two worlds while you wait

fenestre d'intrecci di verbolavoro lavano dell'acqua tra due mondi mentre aspetti
cracking one sort of granite against another we reconfigure concrete
spaccando d'una specie di granito contro l'altra riconfiguriamo il concreto

concreto in un altro uso della nozione indicherà una cosa solida o compatta
concrete in another use of the notion will indicate something solid or compact
and all such substances we know how to reduce to sand

e tutto ciò sappiamo ridurre in sabbia
dove mi trovo laddove mi diverto sto proseguendo dal mar al deserto
wherever i am i enjoy myself there carrying on from la mer au désert

concrete the idea makes the hardest way il concreto l'idea fa la strada più dura
ora faremo una pasta più sicura now shall we make a surer clay

29.11

stonco ccà i am here la luna nova ncopp' a lu mare the new moon over the sea
how beautiful is first love only comm'è bella lu prim'ammore sulamente
uocchie affatate enchanted eyes are shining so' lucente

nu pianefforte sona a piano plays nnanze 'a feneste aperta before an open window
i had been reading neapolitan poetry all afternoon occasionally picking up a word
at this moment from out of my innermost being came an entire self cast in gold

it was one of those baby boy god angel urinating fountain spouts of forever
wait a minute i said is this thing real gold or just composite
could it be plastic rock lookalike with old fashioned anodized balloonery skin

whatever it was we lost it when we cut the anchor rope which we had to do
with the wind in our sails we set out for the island in the pond ten feet away
i was small enough i could have drowned next to that paperweight divinity caesar

but when we reached the sharp bladed shore of the rocky island the god returned
i am neither metal nor imagination he said uocchie affatate i am the life in you

29.11–29.12

29.12

ebony balusters crown one hundred rough pink granite steps rising to an arch
below in the gardens the orchestra rustles out a long stiff rossini crescendo
bayonets fixed carabinieri chase my grandfather down the stairs dodging the draft

libera animas omnium fidelium defunctorum de poenis inferni et de profundo lacu
from hell's pains and deep lake free the souls of all who have died in the faith
libera eas de ore leonis from the lion's mouth free them to escape across the sea

e ce ne costa lacreme st'america this america costs us tears a nuie napuletane
to us nabuletans how it is bitter this bread comme é amaro 'stu ppane
ne absorbeat eas tartarus nor let tartarus swallow them ne cadant in obscurum

nor fall to dark sed signifer sanctus michael repraesentat eas in lucem sanctam
but let the standard bearer michael bring them to the holy light
contre nous de la tyrannie against us tyranny's bloody étendard has been raised

he called it tyranny but was always ashamed he had not stayed to fight for italy
at night he would pray mars red god of war to forgive him this crime

30. liberty changes you as rain soaks you just doing what it does

30.1

liberté liberté chérie combats avec tes défenseurs
liberty dear liberty fight with your defenders and what does with mean exactly
a new nation wearing its first red bandana goes settling ancient debts insanely

i had the choice of justifying italy's ways to my grandfather or else his to her
policeboats circle manhattan but can't find him among so many similar immigrants
at the italian consulate soirée everyone who stands up claims to speak for italy

marchons marchons qu'un sang impure abreuve nos sillons
let us march march till foreign blood feeds our fields
gestures of exclusion stand on whatever they keep out

you can't justify italy's ways because there is no single italy with ways
one morning i slip into the archivio di stato and stamp his file forgotten
in her dialectic torch liberty has consumed him and reissued him

that goddess makes more children among the immigrants than she can count
if they go back their divine motherhood nimbus eyes startle and offend italians

30.1–30.2

30.2

questi tipi non se ne andarono come schiavi didn't these guys leave as slaves
liberty in italian means a style of architecture or else a pricey english silk
liberty vuol dire uno stile dell'architettura ovvero una seta costosa inglese

we have a story about how little birds storming out of trees do their politics
three daughters scrub the bronze duke green but swallows stain him white anyhow
this parable means many italians secretly do worship liberty as well as la patria

as you go on you meet a million piecework italies each with ways you cannot learn
i have come to this hell for my grandfather you say please where have you put him
ahimé che sfortuna è bruciato l'archivio dice il sindaco ma ecco la tavola calda

alas bad luck the archive has burnt down the mayor says but here is steam table
if you find him here you can take him away se lo trova qua può portarlo via
the mayor doesn't mean your grandfather is food but he thinks only of business

ancient nobles raised liberty a goddess with pieces of burning sun in her hands
all their children married shopkeepers in the middle ages so no nobles remain

30.3

à la fête pour quatorze juillet chez giulio ricordi we sang alla napoletana
quanno fa notte o' sole se ne scenne when night comes the sun goes down
are you seriously telling me your mother is a goddess asks la contessa contralto

before i reply la commessa the clerk calls the beauty to a white telephone inside
waiting i finger monteverdi verdi puccini heavy paper edition opera scores
i imagine her phonecall no bullshit italian american can be rich the way we are

though he has plenty of spending money tonight she says and hangs up
some italians believe they invented money and use it as skillfully as knives
for example rich italians patronized painters who showed rich italians as gods

gods go through the world rich in compassion that transforms the humblest objects
deucalion and pyrrha on parnassus after the flood had nothing and no one
buddha advised cast your mother's bones behind you but they refused to break tabu

now the goddess compassion told them mother earth gives us her bones for stones
every stone they threw became another living creature with the eyes of a goddess

30.3–30.4

30.4

rome was born anew the day they carried quintilian across the tiber
so immigrants became children of the goddess when they passed though ellis island
loooking at her all day and all night they suffered a passion for possession

one day usually sufficed though some people stayed weeks and months
some never knew what hit them till they saw how their children grew up
others felt it rise up through them like the flowering of a volcano

it changed anyone and anything to cross the ocean and join a new religion
the usamerican religion jefferson designed was more tolerant than ancient rome's
you are a full member whatever you believe if you declare independence

you declare independence being born into it or pledging allegiance to the flag
then you can go to any church but liberty is your goddess
in the liberty religion you are free not to believe in liberty ideal or divinity

as you approach the statue its vast hot humidity dissolves and resolves you
liberty changes you as rain soaks you just doing what it does

ellis island

30.5

all right hell has receded to the proportions of pebbles on the path
instead what you see is that getting what you want entails paying a price
paying though sometimes it causes anxiety really means exercising your power

your power may have limits smaller than your fantasy but it still does work
you remember the violence of your grandfather's imagination breaking people
they killed and killed and killed and killed and killed and killed and killed

a lifetime of such days filled the stairwells with rifle butts and bayonets
but you have learned less perpendicular forms of persuasion merging in rome
circles entering circles spool out into the mutable current

thus our people survives centuries despite fools and misfortunes
as one enters a circle he walks alongside the others and one leaves sometimes
many prizes fall into your hands as you walk this march because they have matured

watch as the river changes and never returns to its former condition
when you find the right current you go surprising distances with surprising ease

30.5–30.6

30.6

giving up too soon as other cynicisms do implies hopelessness
nothing good happens to me anytime anyhow anyway but don't expect me to like it
saying words like those he sticks up a finger and goes

let yourself enjoy any good that comes to you before you think to put it aside
thick summer air pours honey over you standing bare covered with sweat
splash airconditioning onto your wet head like a cloud of icy leaves

every person tastes of spices if you open your nostrils
every imaginary italy tumbles out balls of marco polo spun into exquisite yarn
it slides through you like naturally smooth fingers angel lovers have

out of an iced coffee a movie star fills the screen as a silhouette in feminique
then a woman with the soul of an eagle appears on horseback behind the titles
a man basks in her pride walking down the street next to her astonishing glory

a string of pansies dressed as roses climbs down a ninety foot monkey bar trellis
bang bang they have nailed it together splash splash they have painted it red

30.7

desire his diadem he drove his mule up the narrow path cut into the mountain
those who keep these trails open return to town once each summer for a week
winters they restore equipment but during either july or august they will feast

when they take the saint out of the dark sanctuary all colors deepen
with evening the saint's golden veils glimmer against the pulsating sky
we hold our torches before us going down to follow love into the caverns of night

the sound of an oar stroking gently into water causes a fine long echo here
we make love in a boat growing rigid with our pleasure rocking it
in the morning children hang flowers on garden gates

at the cemetery we change water and flowers burn incense and light new candles
we teach the children stories of the long time ago yesterdays never to return
where am i going he cries suddenly awake and the mule keeps walking the cut path

you have the energy mr prestigiacomo's last words to me i carried at his funeral
caming home i bowed in gratitude placing the phrase at the center of the table

30.7–30.8

30.8

three times forever i looked without finding you
forever times who knows how many will i seek for you again without finding you
you are the meaning of life

on a certain morning i placed my freedom upon your head like a sunbeam
ma n'atu sole cchiù bello ohiné o' sole mio sta 'nfronte 'a te
there is a more beautiful sun than the sun o my sun rests upon your brow

where you walk i have been sweeping the pavement
where you lie i have covered the bed with roses she replies
in modo francese io te vurria vasà i would like to give you a french kiss

long hours i sit still on the mountain afraid you have left me forever
after he died she followed him up the mountain never finding him
one day as the sun rose upon the horizon she found his face in the face of god

some lives the two of them meet as women and other lives as hummingbirds
mother and daughter father and son king and queen any two children may hold hands

30.9

things remained bearable because my ambition promised something wonderful
i thought ordinary human happiness less rare or important than fame
ambition does not come from outside but inhabits the ordinary golden circle

my mother taught me to respect thieves because everyone has a right to happiness
anyway people thought my ambition laughable if they heard of it at all
arrogant little bastard they would laugh no one knows what he's talking about

so some people think it is stupid i thought it will be interesting to others
i had looked among the papers of the immigrants to find out what it felt like
emanuel carnevali knew himself another broken deck chair

carnevali like all sons of liberty also thought himself the one and only god
how could they possibly assess the magnitude of what was happening to them
they came carrying political philosophers shaped like cheap binoculars

they tried to explain everything but much of it only now is coming into view
i am trying to explain what this seems like now as it is happening before my eyes

30.10

finding a person not good for you makes the person not evil just not for you
it means you may declare your independence which can happen very early in life
you send a postcard of congratulations now and then but have set off on your own

at the first turn of the hill the chorus of italians cried lie down and shut up
after that came tremendous pain in my shoulders as if i had been carrying a cross
operating on me as it had operated through me my great italian fear descended

i call it my italian disease but others call it inherited defeat
such defeat produces chronic great promises followed by failures to deliver
failures cause great panic because in this disease they always mean catastrophe

other people fail without pain because they do not inherit this trait
think of a cross between a sliding pond and a performance of aida with elephants
italian defeat slides from trumpet parade down to slow death in a tomb

if you decide to leave the fastest way out of here is the swings
i chose the safest way from shower to towel to train to poetry ocean liner epic

30.11

my father hated the idea of poetry wanting me to do something totally awesome
study physics or mathematics or electronics he said that's where the future is
but i could not explain to him who had been seven years old in 1914

in those days boys expected to conquer the world as gladiators
his mother and father lived in high adultery like antony and cleopatra on a barge
but when i was a boy they hunted down and shot my grandpa's mussolini god like a dog

my god became christ of the bleeding sorrows with seven swords through him
all the gladiators sono stati sdraiati were laid out in the foro romano imperiale
they had swords sticking up through their backs in the baths of caracalla

forty years later i still found betrayal there in every shadow of every arcata
after the war my grandparents lived buried in the cellar like aida and rhadames
they had a little factory there and never came out of it for long

all the stories of defeat which i took in how would i ever live with them
i chose jesus as a boy poetry when i became a man because only magic would do

30.11–30.12

30.12

the poet makes new frames for moving through the music of tempest symphonies
my father could still enjoy strauss waltzes without a sense of bitter irony
boyhood in the imperial sunset made his soul perennial bronze

for grandpa who felt the defeat and for me who inherited it only toscanini spoke
toscanini rewrote bruckner's and mahler's beethoven as vivaldi becoming rossini
this large panic architecture became for me the history of music

every movement has passages underground with priests tiptoeing through them
they hold their skirts up from the puddles
men march down the domes of churches wearing adhesive boots and shooting everyone

the poet takes all these historical dreams and pulps them into a salami stuffing
he calls upon the goddess justice whom we revere and her sister wisdom
he calls upon the goddess memory to tell him the story

in the story we who were wounded are healed in mountaintop victory festivals
on every snowy alp gods and goddesses continue peering out of inaccessible caves

ellis island

31. they say you are changing you should feel better about it but the basics remain

31.1

in the dead of summer i lay asleep counting turns of the bicycle pedals
up hunterspoint ave from thirty ninth street to forty eighth we used to climb
then we turned and cruised down in the wind's embrace towards the church steeple

my right leg grew weak the bicycle went sideways and i was afraid to keep going
coming back down the hill i remembered my mother has been dead ten years
the high steeple splendidly black against the purple sky i woke up crying

anything will do to change the subject false pains books movies
i don't want to leave and i don't want to stay
they say there is no quick fix but is there even a slow fix

they say you are changing you should feel better about it but the basics remain
changing does not mean changing the subject but accepting the subject as it is
calm and centered you need fewer defense machines and are freer to think

the entire dream dramatic skyline mother bike suddenly turns into water and falls
our rivers of collapsed illusions continue to move relentlessly towards the sea

31.1–31.2

31.2

i had written by now an encyclopedia of collapses because that's all i saw
to me the nineteen eighties were a period of unremitting sadness
it pursued me everywhere i went like a bad smell i was giving off

all my stratagems for winning back my mother had failed leaving me destitute
i should never have wanted such a thing anyway i kept telling myself
meanwhile my wife and children kept looking to me for sunshine

i could give it to them but then i would fail again because sadness drowned me
i kept saying well you are not perfect and that turns the switch to off
but it was the sadness that wells up in me twice a day like tides

my mother and i spoke english together though our dialect is a sort of neapolitan
abruzzese they call it and they call my father's nabuletan
but now at last i learn napolitano sideways having first acquired italian

i have always known this language i realize but never could use it
this knowledge useless like a bag of wet rocks clung to me and made me sad

31.3

we spoke to each other in that house in the american we made up
it differed from the american of the americans but i still can't tell you how
we made the sentences rounder and stronger than the americans made them

my mother's sentences came across the room like invisible comets fire and ice
my father's sentences settled into places like a large hairy beast
to look at them she was a tempestuous beauty and he was a logical scientist

in conversation she was mercury and a greek fury spun into a single dervish
he was a boy perpetually coming home from school with a long story about himself
he had opinions about you and she had opinions about everyone else

as for me i kept coming home with stories no one seemed to hear
everyone seemed to resent me and i didn't know why
for a nickname they called me professor meaning for christ's sake shut up

when i became a professor in a college the old meaning of the word hung over me
speak to your childhood in its own language and you can start making distinctions

31.3–31.4

31.4

money was only the beginning of the difference between then and now
if i went to italy now i went as one who had made a contribution however small
in the old days people could say he'll never amount to anything but not now

i led a modest charge in the italian american revolution
we began in a wastepaper basket and after years of struggle occupied a small desk
it doesn't amount to much but i could point to it as something i'd actually done

professor means you believe something well enough they license you to teach it
instead of believe we used to say know as in knowing something very well
but now we say believing very well meaning to know intimately with great passion

to know intimately with great passion between a man and a woman begins a child
following that child through forests and mountains means believing very well
professing means espousing an explanation or a story or even a question

i profess questions doubts confusions reversals sarcasms and twisted stories
the hero comes around the corner and meets himself fleeing from where he is going

31.5

i will tell you the blue jade mountain palace of ten thousand balconies story
the queen of heaven emerges from death as a beetle to explore the jewel universe
breathing out emerald and ruby dust she climbs and descends its transparent walls

all the billions of rooms have numbers but all these numbers have been challenged
you thought we would have a perfect accurate map of everything to guide you with
we maintain roman bath scrap paper archives forever but can't find much in them

sometimes with luck the number seems clearly to answer some set of directions
fortunately the number affects nothing anyway so many choices may turn out well
you stretch your arms parallel to the horizon and turn in a thousand circles

with each turn you breathe air which is a large jewel we inhabit express and are
the air having its own memory tells its own blue jade mountain palace history
we infiltrate water's thick hide which as we do uses air but does so differently

great water plumes as well remember rise in your every mysterious breath of life
if you never leave your room you breathe out of and into the entire world

31.5–31.6

31.6

some people study literary history better to understand books they read
others study that they too may write literary history
anthologists cut literary history into bits and rearrange these in new patterns

i study to learn how to make literary history
the process includes writing but it also includes acting upon the public stage
some people write literary history in order to teach other people

some people teach by writing literary history or they teach how to write it
i teach by forming a group and then making literary history together
the process has four separate stages

first to join the group sound an ancient word in a language sacred to the group
second form a circle of communication sharing together
third learn to live with differing and taking opposing positions

fourth produce comedies that summarize and give back the variety of communication
comedy civilizes teaching us to imagine our actual diversity of desire and deed

31.7

we read dante alighieri because he teaches the complexity of comedy
comedy puts us into how many different kinds of people there are
then do we feel all over the body how to occupy another position

san francesco d'assisi taught us how all god's children belong to one another
who slipped us out of oblivion us also has made sun us moon stars rivers siblings
we recognize our common destinies no matter how differently we take form and body

sun fog log bug dog and moon love you as sisters and brothers
you step onto the platform of existence one universal sibling more
it turns out you are not so large as you have taught yourself to imagine

ministering spirits everywhere hover in the eaves like bunches of violets
the absolute number of souls continually increases
many of these love and will help you at all hours but you must ask first

iago the professing mind of soldier otello believes in a cruel god
but even when you do stupid things saint anthony knows millions who will help you

31.7-31.8

31.8

every time i get angry i can hurt someone so what can i do with this anger
conditions of the dumpster offend my sense of dignity but better if you shut up
i am lying in a garbage can of history

italy joined forces with germany and many italian jews died
my cousin's father died defending jewish italians and what about him
please do not put me in the garbage can of crimes i never committed

italian immigrants joined forces to control the waterfront and the numbers
my grandma said italians starved us and americans blamed us for the inquisition
i am not responsible for crimes other people commit against the likes of me

listen i am only a guy who at age three opened his eyes in the statue of liberty
from my father's shoulders through windows in her crown i looked out for freedom
the big green statue from the inside is the body of a large puppet including us

national italian guilt ties us with strings that make us jumpy
in italian american freedom school we first study untying of knots

ellis island

31.9

these knots all sit in a museum awaiting resolution
the knot of medieval authority forever paralyzing italians all over again
nowadays they sit in their cars and think at last we are getting rid of thieves

political squads climb walls into gardens and cars explode on highways
the main thing is do not believe too much in democratic method they say
the trouble with you americans is you have too much liberty

i heard all this when i was small and now i hear it again
i use freedom as a reply even though it requires more skill in use than i possess
adepts learn to employ freedom as an ingredient as a condition as a boundary

so when someone freely says a yes how we miss mussolini we freely answer
what do you miss using the police to beat people up for bad opinions
he sent people around the world to silence his opponents

any country may have leaders like this like knots in its memory
after they die they grow stronger unless you take them apart piece by piece

31.10

second knot is when people start feeling the desire for freedom they grow anxious
someone has taught them that freedom will spill them off the edge of the world
many of the immigrants thought exactly this had happened to them

l'america 'mpazzita america the crazed managgia l'america damn america they said
the american possibilities were so great these italians huddled together in hives
they kept busy with a million rules so as not to know what was going on outside

inside italian america they built a golden temple to their kitchen garden brides
american freedom still tumbles down niagaras of apprehension
drugs abortions guns block out pleasure reason and civility so you can't see them

but if we study how americans built freedom we see it does not mean wild abandon
it means many legal guarantees and options that limit the power of the state
the statue will remain immobile if immigrants slip away into the green continent

instead if we make mistakes we invoke the old rules sit still shut up do nothing
misery so distracts us that we overlook our freedom chances and stay in the hive

31.11

the third knot is inherited humiliation from the thousand year empire
italians ruled the world a long time but afterwards they became a subject people
the french and the arabs and the spanish and the germans have dominated them

the english and the americans have violated italian sanctuaries and persons
part of what italians feel comes from centuries of rape pillage and subordination
that smiling servant may love you but be also covering up resentment even inside

against sorry failures rise shadow caesars riding chariot shadows of scorn
we were such as you can never dream of being again they sneer
can you capture them and put them in a movie

as it is these torturers have the free reign of back alleys around your mind
every empire rises and falls according to laws which we can scarcely imagine
therefore consider wisdom more precious than any pain it has cost your acquiring

empires compared with wisdom shrink to ashy powder blown by random gusts of wind
ruined acqueducts stand in the empty fields

31.11–31.12

31.12

the fourth knot is ignorance
italians in america found their own past so painful they forgot almost all of it
they put the italian language in the ground with the immigrants' children

after that they spoke slept inside a slippery american groove fifty feet deep
the walls of the groove ripple causing the phonograph to emit crooning voices
italian americans rest in layers impacted like clay in geological core samples

if you ask them about italy they think you mean soccer wine or shoes or travel
instead we are calling now out of the dark freedom we have attempted
we call out italia memoria tristezza della gloria italy memory sadness of glory

italy before you raise yourself from the dead again think of other italies
are you doomed to revive regimes of murderers inquisitors and dictators
wisdom asks you to consider the materials for thought the word italy invokes

early romans invented a partnership of classes in the public interest res publica
that was before conquering the world when they still had minds open to good sense

32. our own freedom includes our freedom from someone else's idea of italy

32.1

the whole trouble with you came over your body in waves
it seemed the usual panic with its usual marks of being worse than any before it
so how would you ever know the rehearsal from the actual show

it was not to depend upon your efforts alone howsoever dedicated or effective
instead a certain voice would rise from the crowd and say yes thank you
from that moment forward your poem would become a sort of public property

they would sing it in the audience and give you back solidarity
you would perform it for them aiming at ever greater clarity and delight
together you would achieve the self control that makes for dependable works of art

it might not be easy but might need a hundred telephone calls every week or more
passion in principle principal goal different samenesses sing from your soul
you would coin a new slogan every hour for a year as a way of emptying your mind

giving yourself to others need not mean death only but can mean life as well
that river continually washes whatever falls into it

32.1–32.2

32.2

these dances come and go and we often stay home to sing together
you don't need infinite mountains of money but you do need one another
the snow falls and the herbivores hide near roots in the cellar under the kitchen

care for what you may some day need and offer your sufferings up to god
he meant for you to have better sex than you have had lately
anyway growing up sometimes includes substantial detours

odysseus took twenty years ten to go to war and ten more to get back
a long trip for a bottle of milk penelope said on the way into the bedroom
homer says she refused every goodlooking man in ancient greece all those years

là làlala là dòn't you belìeve it là làlala là whò can conceìve it
là làlala là check is in the mail ship is in the water and time has come to sail
she tied him to the bed and tickled him for hours

she flayed him ripe and red and rubbed him right with flowers
old people say it is evenings of this caliber will keep a man happy at home

32.3

our own freedom includes our freedom from someone else's idea of italy
some take the liberty to say italy means the mature study of life
many other people's italies may dance and parade too but we only ask them this

we ask them come into the open sometimes to enunciate clearly your idea of italy
if any people want to explain their own italies then the rest of us will listen
now we will sing and then discuss the words of fratelli d'italia

fratelli d'italia l'italia s'è desta brothers of italy italy has awakened
dell'elmo di scipio s'è cinta la testa with scipio's helmet her head is girt
dov'è la vittoria le porga la chioma where is victory to her let her bow the mane

ché schiava di roma l'iddio la creò because as slave of rome god her created
the syntax of the poem leaves one question hard to resolve who is the slave
is it victory that is rome's slave or is it italy

victory the goddess once was slave of rome but my idea of italy is a wild woman
italy is a wild man as well and both equally have glorious manes to show

32.3–32.4

32.4

to tell the truth my idea of italy has a bone to pick with scipio's helmet anyhow
fascists loved saying scipio was called africanus after defeating the africans
still hannibal and his africans had fought first up and down italia sixteen years

when they finished they had endowed all modern italians with african ancestors
the line schiava di roma l'iddio la creò does it mean god created rome a slave
its own slave we could say because the syntax does not limit slavery to victory

when we sing the song we just remember things connected to all these words
believe me many italians remember plenty of slavery alongside rome and victory
a latin slogan expressed this resentment roma amor rome capital of backwards love

anna magnani when they called her roma madre said io sono una vecchia puttana
calling rome an old whore enslaved to backwards love is a roman habit
new romes abound blood red as blossoms on vines when you really learn a language

you unfold the ivory paper and write using words from other people
very ancient words change color on the page like drying blood

32.5

my father believed in school and my mother believed in my father
but she remembered teachers had humiliated her because she only spoke italian
her mamma said whata you want all strangers are devils all teachers are strangers

as president of the pta my mother played anita garibaldi against the teachers
bitch snobs with their teapots she said what do they know about being a woman
women work like mamma roma in the whorehouse cleaning washing keeping a man happy

teachers were class criminals who wanted her to clean their houses for them
my father went around a mad professor which she complained about but admired
out of this i decided to be a mad professor poet brazilian guerilla anita myself

teachers adored my mad professor but then i would spit my amazon anita at them
a teacher had us scribble blindfolded to music then find pictures in the scribble
i found a large parrot i colored brilliant as any brazil toucan orinoco snake

jungle tongue my mother said go sing your thunder in the alley
to get into my fort on the school fire escape you have to say a word in italian

32.5-32.6

32.6

my father laid out and installed four banks of twenty five knitting machines each
with fiberglas thread they knitted sleeves to protect electrical connectors
in radios airplanes bombs suflex sleeves in coded colors guided wire installation

he took his three year old son to visit this coordinated mechanical force
any time i close my eyes i still hear the sleeve room fighter plane roaring on
the first years of my life our rivers flowed thick with destroyers

we were fighting for the king of england according to vera lynn on the radio
my mother's name was vera and so i took up anglophilia as an infant
even my italian patriot grandfather loved the well madeness of english clothing

we used blackout shades in case the germans managed to fly across the atlantic
in that crazy war another couple of years would have meant the end of us all
since then everywhere in the world human beings have not stopped quaking

in the universities we are constantly generating wars of signification
these can replace at least large scale economic terrorism we always hope

32.7

i wrote my doctoral dissertation in english on the tory anarchist max beerbohm
it gave me great solace in college to discover this writer as incoherent as i
how can you be both english and italian i asked

max wrote a comic epic using dante and homer to tell an english story
so i studied all these incoherences in order to learn about my own
every clue helps but you have to live to be old to get it all straight

well i am writing this ellis island epic in honor of divided loyalties
one part of me is the wings of a b fifty two and another monte cassino
i hate mussolini's whole horror show but i still feel the pain of seeing him dead

at the age of four you don't really understand politics or good and evil
but you cannot help understanding evisceration when you see it in life magazine
when your name viscusi looks like italian evisceration you can't help flinching

they tear us in pieces every night when we lie down to fry on the stove
we are dion and frankie who become kings of american rock'n'roll in the fifties

32.7–32.8

32.8

italian stands divided by contrary desire from american in one of us
american wants italian family good food deep connection with the past
italian wants american car house fame money boat frequent flier gold card

conflicting persons talk out of both sides of my mouth every night at supper
in sleep we flock back and forth between italian chicken coop and american barn
thunder rips the sky raining down on houses smelly wet cardboard cumulus clouds

after hiroshima the sky grew deadly to many people who turned colors and died
before that the night had always opened at day's end its great camellia
may the moon drop away the lace of skeletons shadowing her light

we lie together in the grass imagining mountains covered with white flowers
we produce new thought recognizing how division is internal and war is useless
now on hot days we already sometimes smell the air perspire coming back to life

in a torn heart an italian shoots at an american from behind a crack in the wall
american bombs shake the sleeping house though i awaken to the sound of crickets

32.9

my grandparents called it the other side as if everyone had died when they left
the newsreels showed italy as an underworld where these dead were still suffering
they used to sleep in stone houses with goats and donkeys to keep them warm

the germans mowed a family of thirteen people down to silence
american artillery made houses collapse in dust puffs as if nothing had happened
when the germans suspected treachery men hid in wells to avoid getting shot

from deep caves little children heard airplanes rise whining over the black trees
every friday my father tied a huge box tight and drove it to the post office
princess aida was a slave in egypt when pharoah made war on her father's kingdom

when our relatives came on ocean liners in 1949 we could not look them in the eye
but as they danced tangos in cafés they began to forget their humiliation
we meanwhile became a force of nature mutiplying by means of wedding tarantellas

italy returned to life now oddly stylish exactly where she used to be poorest
we too rose from our guilt as tommygun gods in movieland

32.9–32.10

32.10

some liners lie rusting at anchor and others do cruises painted white
the transatlantic jet invented a new planet of privilege
people with passes moved freely between what used to be worlds separated by death

when my grandmother crossed the ocean she vomited every day and prayed to die
the flat hot steel sky outside gave no escape from the stinking prison inside
she told us going back meant sinking into that airless box

when you fly in a jet the death is painless as if it had never happened
and what they take out of you is minimal on any given passage between worlds
take recovery time before crossing again and it is as if nothing had happened

we always run the risk of mystification when we speak of changing classes
but class progress remains a favorite italian american song in my family
we used live with donkeys and now we live with dogs

my cousin in the mountains owns twenty million logs
i had a pass for the airplane and when i came back i could speak tuscan

32.11

when you change countries you change classes
even if wordshapes remain firm the things they mean can differ wildly
truthtelling becomes unimaginable when you no longer know what words are saying

countryclass truth remains possible under certain strict conditions
you give up every hope of telling other people what to do
instead you concentrate upon asking yourself what is your class story anyway

we climbed out of a cave in italy and into a cubicle in the cargo hold
leaving the ellis island sorting bin we graduated to airy rooms in north queens
large college classrooms opened out onto palladian balconies in the veneto

from a long terrace in rome i could see tivoli where my grandmother was born
ottobre romano eighty kilometers away gleamed la maiella where my mother was born
we climbed out of dark animal enclosures into high capitoline brilliance in rome

we made all these places american simply through our circulation there
in america we began to put out gleaming italian tables under sidewalk umbrellas

32.11–32.12

32.12

our story is we wanted a better life and for our children
we have enacted parades of triumph up and down the avenues of rome and new york
class struggle occurs not only then but every time a waiter hands you a menu

you eventually get used to it provided you first admit to yourself what it is
afterwards you start to play the twelve tone piano in two then three voices
everything has its music including the sweetness of ordinary pleasure

counterpoint includes long silences distributing themselves throughout the choir
each voice listens and each voice can hear itself in an answering voice
when the fourth voice enters and the fugue doubles the mutuality electrifies

i have been hearing you in myself and hearing myself in you
you cannot call this love but you certainly can call it friendship
the woman moves to an island and the man learns the art of sailing

now we stand in a museum examining mounds of blossoms shaped as parts of us
look you say i see your finger ah yes i reply what is that perfume

33. the main thing we refused to doubt we were italians

33.1

when i hear the word unconscious i think of the sound of a trumpet in the night
the word trumpet brings to mind richard wagner's overture to rienzi
cola di rienzo revived the glory of rome in the 1340s but died humiliated

my unconscious has used a large variety of humiliation tactics to keep me down
in the 1940s my grandfather taught me the glory of rome before mussolini's fate
in my museum of struggle i man the ramparts of rome from my high terrace

down that scorched valley the temple of fortuna primigenia sits above ancient palestrina
nationu cratia reads the archaic latin meaning for offspring
i have made this primitive story the opera of transatlantic infancy

grandpa says here carry our family gods into the next century
grandson walks around london paris new york and rome with gods under his coat
one day he lifts up the god columbus and the people cry gangster fascist murderer

listen he sings you must be kidding and please remember all the other guilty parties too
rienzi was wagner's pun on rossini who invented figaro the modern italian

33.1-33.2

33.2

lorenzo da ponte mounted the first new york city italian opera in 1833
largo al factotum della città make way for the city's biggest operator
this barber figaro can and usually will arrange a thousand important affairs

tito gobbi sang barbiere before anything else on my graduation stereo in 1962
the new largeness of orchestra blew into my room astonishing my mother's mother
when i played don giovanni she claimed là ci darem was an abruzzese folksong

in 1969 my father's father who had taught me rossini now refused to recognize me
long hair and beard hung on my head like vineleaves that spoke the word disorder to him
i had begun performing an art of epic opera rag which should have made him happy

having started doing this at three years old not knowing what it was
in 44 when grandpa taught me the past i decided to make it a future
in 71 so he would bless me before dying i had the barber trim my hair and beard

il barbiere cuts a hair la bandiera waves the air la preghiera means the prayer
il mestiere means the art incominciare means to start il barbiere heals the heart

33.3

we never can tell how many people we are going to take with us when we die
some people die alone but other people guide smoky ocean liners onto the icebergs
the ancient judges have written huge tomes on the moral questions involved

thus sang don basilio the inhibitory music master every time you dropped a note
but figaro leaps over these little barriers because he is making money
money makes his mind pour forth volcanoes of inspiration

he needs all he can get because the forces of inhibition drive everyone crazy
figaro uses his mastery of mystery to circumvent obstacles and to free desire
the mystery consists mostly of saying what's this in my eye

nothing the matter with me he sings i am a good looking italian american educator
bartolo the old tutor joins in i am a good looking italian american educator too
and basilio the singing master i too am a good looking italian american educator

all the italians coming down off the steam liners sing in chorus we did not die
we are here we did not die we took a chance we did not die and here we are

33.3–33.4

33.4

what goodlooking italian american poet have the years crowned with a circle
oily locks pour from his head down his neck and beard foams out on either side
people can grow extensive as trees when they pass the age of fifty

in their faces you find a dark gaze that has seen faces you will never see
their many youths climb around them like vines decorating some mossy fountain
at a certain moment you see such a person as a public institution

you remember your grandmother over coffee passing judgment like queen margherita
chistellà the woman down the block sbaglia tutto has it all wrong
no marriage no wayward child no malingering spouse escaped this court

the women came in twos and threes until the room was full
tony picked up squeezebox and we all began to sing together even out on the porch
the men strolled up and down in long ellipses with their hands behind their backs

the ancient passeggiata closes the day passing between the sun and moon and stars
galaxies away all human generations seem to be flourishing in the same instant

33.5

yes they said we had no idea you felt so bad about it
i looked at them are you crazy or do you not remember faces of those long dead
the sharp smell of sudden cold air descended on a certain summer picnic morning

all these worlds have existed at the same instant as the present moment
you only know one direction through the worlds which effect we call real time
if it were actually real like a river or a dog we wouldn't need to insist on it

as the person grows older more cloudy worlds cluster under the gesturing hands
waves of the rocking tides ride up and down the flat boulder as if it were lava
a boulder's shoulders speak of languid pleasure rushing through there for aeons

as youth dances into fulfillment wildlife gnaws at the milky roots
on the hills the gold of a thousand harvests varies the moist green of the lawns
in moments of idleness the spirits invent subtle variations in the order of banquets

such ingenious beauty surrounds you that you recognize artifice has many levels
trail your hand back along time till you find where they put pleasure mountain

33.5–33.6

33.6

from one side of the house stretches out the ocean from the other the great park
in the distant north you find williamsburg but to the west rises the great bridge
this house has been situated symmetrically within the four walls of brooklyn

i write facing the ocean to the south with the continent off to my right
on my left long island and at my back the high cliffs of new york city
on a certain morning long ago i decided this would be the house he had lived in

i mean the poet was deciding in whose service i had enlisted myself as a child
active voices seek young persons of talent and dedication and speak through them
thus ended the opening discourse of the grammarian

later i gave up all this playacting and said all right i am a poet
they have delivered six velvet horses to my door every morning from then on
not all have wings because even a poet must spend a lot of time on the ground

every horse works four hours and then returns to the stables of memory
we fly the entire planetary system as turning years bring different parts close

33.7

assembling a public and assembling a poet you meet reservoirs of pleasure
in the uplands poets rest among pindaric lakes making love
at every gate out of the city you meet huge steel towers crawling with police

they call these towers suspension bridges because they hang people up
trying to live as a poet you condemned yourself every day to more hangups
at night you sat in your room reading about writers in paris reciting odes

some thick rivets have rusted away allowing large pieces to fall off your sides
you have a large pod fabricated of steel plates and high impact plastic sheets
for you the great bridge opens onto a prison larger than all prairies

whenever you step into another room new steel bars shoot out in all directions
one day you stroll down your mind to the inhibition office where the fat cop sits
he eats jelly donuts alone behind a desk because everyone else is retired or dead

take early pension you say shaking his hand then showing him out of the building
now you hear the cobbled aqueduct water rushing under every streetcorner

33.7–33.8

33.8

we envied fifties italians their knitted socks and command of roman slang
now we said we are going to start being italians too though differently
in secret we began to cultivate a rhetoric or operatic poetry

parte di rettorica part of rhetoric according to desanctis era la declamazione
declamation that is to say he said a solemn and harmonious manner of reciting
cioè a dire disse il de sanctis un modo di recitare solenne ed armonioso

he said the opera began when hearts grew empty so the words had nothing to mean
per difetto di sangue e di calore interno literature dies of inanition
muore la letteratura d'inanizione for lack of blood and of internal warmth

maybe this was true in 1600 but for us opera meant the undefeated voice of action
thus we survived the humiliation of living in a country that had bombed italy
much in us died of sorrow and shame but our voices stayed alive like shellfish

when we sing you can hear what it felt like to live underwater for fifty years
now that we leave our shells on the beach you can hear us loud and clear

ellis island

33.9

put italian things together out of envy hate and spite
put italian things together symptomatically contrite
put italian things together and don't worry if you're wrong

put italian things together and you'll feel completely strong
if you do what i say and you say what i do then i'll leave the apartment key
and i'll show you the gardener's corpse and the pardon and how to be gone and free

put your hand on your pocket and kick it and rock it and turn as you bend away
get the world in your feet as you stand and repeat what i'm whispering you to say
stavo in montagna oilé stavo in campagna oilé

stavo in italia oilé starò ancora in italia oilé
starò in montagna oilé starò in campagna oilé
starò in italia oilé come stavo in italia oilé

put italian things together whether me or whether you
put italian things together and that's all you have to do

33.10

first thing after a revolution you move people around
some of them go into the army some go on rafts to other countries
governments often improve things dramatically by taking things away from people

aha i turned watching that car shoot into the distance
i had just seen how my own government responds when i make a dramatic improvement
small shiny black sixties jags with four men in them carry off possibilities

in this forties british paranoid future version bureaucratic paranoia means god
next to this what the italians did in 1880 looks like pastoral poetry
they made a poor country rich by sending half its poor people to work abroad

outmigration raised real wages in italy while sharply increasing foreign exchange
no economist could resist net gains of such diluvial proportions
of course we were left to sort out the theological issues for ourselves

we sent money to the goddess italy who existed though we could not approach her
unshakeable faith in the enlightenment goddess italy gave us astonishing force

33.11

the main thing we refused to doubt we were italians
let them shit on us we said if that is the price of calling our children italian
when you step out the door with a vowel on the end of your name you go naked

if freud asks where are you going and it is to italy in german you say gen italia
we italians strut in cities of the new world as a race of purple bulls
we like to talk about our primitive force as if we could love the earth directly

on streetcorners we would brag my grandma can strangle chickens with one hand
joey's uncle slammed two men with a cement hoe and put them in the back yard
we still pour orange soda on the concrete where joey said his uncle put them

if strangers come down our block we sit like lizards looking them over
we always answer when they ask questions but most of them never come back
local fauna have tactical advantage plus you go gen italia when you come to us

we remind you of velvet collars leather vests satin sheets smooth skin
we know you but we still know too the things that do not talk in words

33.11–33.12

33.12

as soon as i think i did something right my father starts telling me my mistakes
he builds up to a raging coda and then i run to find my mother to console me
we repeat this drama many times a week even many a day for most of my boyhood

by age nine i have a fractal loop in my glands
it shapes things like a long blind spasm
by the hour the afternoon the day the week

know your hooks and learn to pass them by
first you see a mere unmatched seam in the air before you
perfect your serve if you can and get them off balance

but when you fall into a volley play it long and rhythmic and wait for an opening
you do even better after you get to where you can just rule them out of court
progress once in a while makes a great discovery when it blinks around a corner

but the phantom tribe of self distraction has lives at many levels
give yourself a little time to carry the news through all the passages and rooms

34. i wanted the old italians never to die because they knew the dignity of love

34.1

you now no longer need to consider heroic measures to prove your worth
while you have known this for some time the news has not penetrated the interior
approaching the inner reaches of your self you come upon a cement stoop

there are steep sharp edged steps and a stone cornice all around the brick house
you knock weakly on the wrought aluminum storm door outside the iron hinged oak
a small black lady peeks out from behind the horse and carriage filigree

is bobby home you ask but then you see him around the side of the house
he leads you into the basement past the pile where his grandpa shovels coal
touch the old man with your newspaper and he disappears into a clean gas furnace

upstairs his grandma's bedroom has a statue of san rocco pierced with arrows
as you whisper the news to the statue a bottle of iced champagne takes its place
a crew follows you around throwing all the tobacco stinking drapes into a bag

in his parents' bedroom you open a window for the smell of hot bodies to escape
after all this you are tired but you have certainly made a great start

34.1-34.2

34.2

toy shops mean most to people who know how to sit still and watch once in a while
men pour into piazza venezia from via dei fori imperiali and from via del corso
now pinocchio picks up his newspaper and strolls under the porch of the pantheon

great efforts rise and strain and push and fall and these stones still stand here
i am watching the whole puppet show of operatic history on the radio
the strings pause high in the air and then down comes the thundering lone ranger

our roman past twirls before the historian's eyes a large swiss repeater machine
wait till i tell you all the things you must put in this boat before you bury it
every slab of salmon becomes a marble lozenge bearing inscriptions about my life

the color resembles raw veal as does the effect of translucency
i will sit to wait for the tide to turn at some point when it is safe to slip out
think things out plainly and then fill in the details checking them twice

having placed the cemeteries in order the general took ship for the isles of joy
he expresses pleasure seeing red luck ribbons everywhere in great silk flowers

34.3

a certain failing repeats itself or do we have an instruction to this effect
the instruction runs do not do this worthy thing so we will know you what you are
regard inclinations not to do this thing as injunctions to punish yourself

or okay i will not do this thing you say and will cover my head with brown stain
feel the juice run down over your head and smell its bitter acid solvent
some of the primitive italian wildmen have been having at you from above

they shoot flaming arrows and they catapult stones the size of houses down at you
under their battlements men sweep and carry every morning before dawn for hours
macs had an instruction hide balloons click it and the balloons went away

horses run headlong and champions in gilt steel drive lances at one another
ah yes you say over your coffee we went to the festa last night
one man the harder he drove the hammer the less of a result he would get

these various plots will amuse you if you watch from a slight distance
behind a curtained arch they can less restrain your advancing towards your goal

34.3–34.4

34.4

moving your life forward leads to twenty call them interactions with people today
each contact booms and leaves a loud long echo you scarcely hear running around
but after you turn off the power machines the silent room roars at you for hours

to this fellow you showed your vanity and he will tell that as a story o no
can call him tomorrow and make fun of your vanity if you want
you surprised someone with a sarcastic remark but you can say something nice okay

a literary market activist expressed interest in your work so watch out
voices spring up everywhere like help balloons on a macintosh screen saying wrong
the mac has an instruction hide balloons you can click and the balloons go away

someone tried to paralyze you with guilt but it backfired because you refused
but treat people kindly and the same comes back to you
as for voices the air grows stiff with all the conversations in transmission

a great deal of life consists of tuning in a program that makes for happiness
then you don't need to filter out most noises because they don't really interfere

34.5

of course the program of happiness where can you find it
you need not know names and addresses for all the great questions and answers
as the day goes on the alps melt bald so you turn from sun to earth

we wished to propitiate all gods so we accepted the universal billpayer
we placed the image of this person on all manner of things we traded for credit
our religion had its power but like all mass movements it had its limits too

we preserved aristocracy as a corrective to the excesses of christian communism
according to this roman compromise some come to chapel and some to chalet
in the mountains we recognize the divinity because of its imposing shape

on an island the whole world counts as water because of its endless otherness
when i go broken with self interrupting guilt through my pleasures i end sadly
i am installing a program to take this guilt as it occurs and recode it as static

enter into a conversation with local gods who live in people you understand
this can make a much greater difference than you ever imagined

34.5–34.6

34.6

my mother's dissatisfaction with my father taught me to act differently from him
if he loved money i hated money and if he hated the city i loved the city
when i began to love money and hate the city i fell into crisis

i made steady progress but when my mother died i felt guilty for resenting her
she used me to console herself for disappointments and thus kept me tied down
i tried to transform everything into what she would like but rarely succeeded

i specialized in the dark of the poor and the shortcomings of their educations
so my schooling was a rope thick lace doily starched into a hundred foot pyramid
but now she had seen how money works better and began treating me as an ornament

i resisted being an ornament and began a real family real career real house
every inch of the way i met opposition from this sense that i cannot touch money
her guilt became my guilt when she would hit me repeatedly shrieking

did galley slaves in chains consummate by biting and hitting one another
did an abusive grownup ever impose a huge pile of shit on a child

34.7

look here is the story kid you need me even though i'm never around
no one can ever love you the way i love you though i don't love you
you are not allowed to touch money because you are above all that

your father will kill you if you do though he will make fun of you if you don't
these may not be perfect double binds but they came close enough
i could not keep from running back to her though there was nothing there

i sort of caught onto it while she was alive but once she died it seemed normal
but running to nothing can only mean you fill the space up with what is available
so I constructed a marital dance i have never been able to deconstruct

the idea was put a good face on things and everything will work out
while you are waiting however the bus arrives and she gets on and goes away
my new idea such as it is amounts to getting on a bus now and then too myself

you now can see my mother and her story on screen and video everywhere
i have sold the rights and used the money to start a business

34.7–34.8

34.8

philosophy of course awaits you every time you start asking questions
soon enough you descend into the fable of the signified seeking its signifier
you the signified don't know what to call yourself so you try everything you can

philosopher poet literary scholar gentleman revolutionary italian you say aloha
excellent fit the salesman says each time adjusting the shoulders
one day you say i am from brooklyn and the next day you say from ithaca

approaching certain places your signified body interior jumps out to look around
these places have signifier resonance that firmly plates a well shined signified
your suit of armor causes others to single you out with a hundred names

when many people call you names signifier resonance has grown intense
42nd and fifth called your mother's grandfather names so he went back to italy
when you tried to teach at the graduate center same address they called you names

the signifier is the abject desire of your mother object of your abject desire
wearing this armor you try to make yourself as desirable to her as she is to you

ellis island

34.9

on the last boat out of long island i saw you going away to connecticut
night fell and sand blew in my face off the cliffs from the beach
i was humming round round round round i get around as if i were rolling

i still sat still listening to fast music on the radio after the light changed
people will think you are boasting when you are just trying to approach them
you can feel very lonely despite everything you have in life

but if i get up and reassume speed things usually go well
you can look forward to goodness you will recognize but in forms always new
when i listen to figaro i think i can hear my grandparents talking

they would console me when my mother slipped away to have a little fun
come see the peppers my grandfather would say to me when i was crying
i would watch my grandmother making her constitutional ravioli

in such moments we taste a gentleness that heals many wounds
i keep trying to offer gentleness to others

34.10

i wanted the old italians never to die because they knew the dignity of love
e tu m'amavi per le mie sventure ed io t'amavo per la tua pietà they sang
and you loved me for my misfortunes and i loved you for your compassion

they gave each other kisses the way they fed birds
compassion fills the dawn with pink and orange surprises
the earth flowers continually because life has feelings

you can give yourself this compassion which will find its applications
you will feel it towards all other creatures
san francesco points out that the sun and comets are creatures as we are

if you say we are flung into existence this includes beings of other sorts
learned philosophers sent out rockets to see if there was life on other planets
life is other planets

even yourself discover spinning another ellipsoid under your feet some mornings
grab onto the emptiness handles and spin with it

34.11

i have been waiting for the clouds to lift but they have not
anything you want to see or say here let us not decide against it
other planets continue turning however so you need not panic

this crystalline weather bodes well for bookbinders
perhaps magnetic field disturbances that render computers useless will now begin
people try to make you feel like dirt if you best them at something

victors dress as mars so that others suppose them invulnerable
we always hope for that effect and many victories can in fact do you good
plumes of black ostrich follow your hands your shoulders your lifting head

the christian draping himself in guilt and sadness marches to a dirge
but his progress moves no less surely than the transit of mars
he desires he forces he travels forward

guilt the mountain slows you down but eventually you move into the clear
the river has a brilliance it takes directly out of the night sky and redefines

34.11–34.12

34.12

as distinguished guests trail down the lawn the madrigal group opens up
fà lala lala là fà lala lala là fà lalà la là
do you not know how mushrooms grow how salmon how geese

will you not stay don't go away we're not police
after the ball we'll meet in the hall like breezes on hills
after the storm we'll get very warm and swallow some pills

i published four volumes mezza voce he said without encountering much trouble
the one time i tried to whisper they announced it from skyscraper radio towers
well surely you love it here with your swimming pool the interviewer points out

thank you of course i am grateful for everything unworthy as i am
i didn't mean it that way the interviewer says and the poet smiles back
who ever thought they would be making a movie about my life little me

and though he has many things he always wanted he still wants others
you can get a new episode at your supermarket every monday

35. by habit i encouraged people to think of me as simply out of touch with reality

35.1

rossini master of simple repetition perfected the national emotional opera
madness fury and nationalisms interested artists after the revolution ended
like them i grew up thinking constantly now i will begin a great sweep of glory

when i stepped out the door i hoisted my sails like a five masted schooner
i could hear trumpets announcing here comes the italian american poet viscusi
but i so designed my life so that no one else heard these trumpets

by habit i encouraged people to think of me as simply out of touch with reality
now you know and i know since that time i have filled these words with sorrow
if it keeps leaching out into the surrounding parched gardens i pour more

it is only something to do like carrying water or sweeping the stairs
they gave me this job before i was three and i have been doing it ever since
i played the professor who speaks poetry and hopes someday to be a gentleman

do not be fooled by this act
all my forefathers descended from gentlemen even the slaves

35.1–35.2

35.2

i felt guilty because my mother sexualized me and i feel guilty for saying so
she used me as consolation but did not think very much about my point of view
when she would call me goodlooking i would defend myself by saying she was lying

the settled result was that any woman who liked my looks became my mother
and was lying and was using me for her own ends and my father would punish me
same went for women who lusted after power money fame or glory they saw in me

the only exception i made was for those who admired me for some moral standing
if they were right i was successfully punishing myself and needn't fear retribution
it all confused me for decades as a secure discomfort or comfortable insecurity

then one day i said this is killing me do i have any way out of this
for years i had been planning to emerge again as a poet
on my first go round in the sixties the anxiety flattened me cold

i battled success and defeated it in those days but now it has returned
this time i decided to accept friendship and return it as a gift to others

35.3

in friendship we seek immortality
seeking immortality we find the one true basis of friendship
you love me and i love you produces exchange and exchange produces increase

increase means our lives go on beyond our knowledge
it means we pass through the large web of time weaving and unweaving
what we give becomes the measure of what we receive

frequent trips to the universal waterfall amount to involuntary generosity often
which make believe yesterdays or tomorrows are you drinking tonight sally
in other words when people you know die parts of you die

you have finished one set of agenda and now you have taken up another
from this day forward you will be healthy intelligent and clear
passion bears compassion and compassion touches everything

shedding unnecessary skins caress the branch along which you slide into april
curl with the intricate progress of seasons

35.3–35.4

35.4

twice in the old days some italians invented world domination
after the roman empire fell the italian mercantile empire arose on its ashes
both times the ruling classes grew rich while disinheriting most other italians

ancient rome granted citizenship everywhere but still kept italy full of slaves
the medieval italian trade empire belonged to a network of big banking tribes
they got rich doing business with popes kings of spain france england portugal

some italians got rich discovering america working with these big time partners
other italians got tomatoes tobacco and coffee but no america
four hundred years later rich italians began exporting slave replacement italians

italian rich tell their children watch prices for differential fissures
buy cheap here what you sell there dear sell dear here what you buy cheap there
the rich earned bounties from railroad builders for slave replacement italians

the rich had bred them for durability thousands of years ago and now had too many
strong poor with short legs big shoulders hard skin fetched good prices abroad

ellis island

35.5

the concept of the naked italian grows from the italian wearing clothes
in america as vespucci pointed out everyone quickly grows brown and naked
when rich italians come here they spend all their time putting clothes back on

but bodies resist clothes in america
everything the italians apply dries hardens cracks and flakes away overnight
poor italians become naked too in america but they accept their naked bodies

as gods and goddesses they grew out of the earth in italy like stones
they left the mountains in many places empty of gods you now only find in america
caves vergil visited trembling with awe now shudder with loud dry echoes

how did naked italians in america open the fiery gates of underworld kingdoms
ignazio silone says that cafoni what we call poor italians exist everywhere
slaves and choctaw midwife chieftain horsetraders recognized cafoni as brothers

in italy and in colorado and in rio de la plata cafoni light night fires
they touch bodies under lakes of moon

35.5–35.6

35.6

i have been horny so long i think it is the normal state he said
well why don't you do something about it they asked him
as soon as he started trying he began to grow short of breath

his eyes hurt his back his liver his lungs his shoulders his arms
black shadow faces came to him as to so many others in the mirror
in other words you are carrying the leaden cloak of someone else's story

now you unfasten the clasps that hold the cloak in place
now your heart beats like a deer at the gate leading to the forest
you plan how to get through the emotional bad weather patient and warmly dressed

at every turn twenty tar stained sailors stick their heads out of the portholes
not that they sing in chorus not there not here they cry not you not her
sometimes you just sit still behind the rain spattered panes of the glass porch

in the distance the whistle echoes between the eastern mountains
suddenly you are on your way to the underworld station

35.7

we all thought in terms of old fashioned warfare with our shoulders together
kipling mussolini roosevelt churchill stalin hitler we shouted in unison
at this writing i am putting pencil to pad here in cement hell

thirteen days without sleep i am here interviewing ghosts from the 1914 war
yes i lived from 1987 through 92 as a scarsdale lawyer one of them told me
they come back to earth whenever they want he said but it doesn't help

we are looking for what we died for but you can't even imagine what it was
we can't imagine what you are looking for either so i don't want to be unfair
i have written down many hours of these guiltridden ghost epistemologies

indirectly i suggest to them that what we are looking for we know as one another
one person steps out of the black rivers of nonexistence to recognize another
these recognitions pass through participants like lightning bolts

all reveals itself in an instant of mutual recognition after twenty years
changes occur before you see what they supersede recede

35.7–35.8

35.8

every time i get off the train in hell i find myself preaching to the inhabitants
you can make all of this better i say if only you just let me shut up and go away
after i perform my oration a complete stranger kisses my hand

you can make all of this better i say if you just think of it differently
accept that italian american now has recognized standing in the perfume market
essence manufacturers have designed five thousand italian coffee flavors

let us call my act the ambulatory or strolling italian
imagine a doric colonnade where the ancient philosophers argued all day
the strolling italian has a perspective of streets and arcades behind him

all of all of all of this he sings just make it better with a kiss
tambourines rise slapping on the air behind him as he plays
each time he performs he includes songs of the strolling italian

we are piecing ourselves together he sings using spears of bitter weather
this crafty use of contrasting textures makes for a remarkably refreshing salad

ellis island

35.9

how dare you write about anything important
who do you think you are with your messy room
the only thing is i can't seem to work except in a stable

a skinny old man came to me in a dream wearing a plaid bathrobe
who are you and what do you want of me again
i am the ghost he said of your great great grandson

have you come to ask me about my poems i said after all these centuries
i have come to tell you he said we think you did a decent job
what's it like down out across there in the distant italian american future

he sat down at my godfather's table where i do all my work
you have sacrificed upon this altar for years he asked why
we are seeking the terms of a decent settlement in america i replied

to which he i'm come to tell you you achieved it
and reader i believed it

35.10

i was working on a global understanding with an angry writer but it has faltered
she doesn't seem to understand that i have feelings too
her sense of grievance and her consequent resentment sometimes overwhelm her

she sends me money to handle for her but i don't want to do it
i have written her a poem of congratulation upon your new book
but do not give me your money affairs to manage as i have enough work with my own

she was engaged in an act of trust but i in an act of prudence
too many novels by anthony trollope have made me careful of other people's money
people feel i have earned their trust even though i do suffer for it

the global understanding must include this aspect
either accept trust or do not accept it but get it all clear
anyway i continue to love your poems my dear

you think straight about things you think about
seeing how things are you put it so bluntly you sometimes knock us over

35.11

one year i spent entirely seeking a white antelope in a footnote
and i never found it and gradually began to think myself foolish and drift away
when the white antelope cry would go up i would raise my fist but then drop back

i resisted the temptation to write a book about people who seek white antelopes
it would have been easy to satirize their flaws because i had all of them
other times of course i compiled encyclopedias about my former enthusiasms

regrets i've had a few the poet anka writes but then again too few to mention
i study to imitate as form if not as sincere feeling this modesty
i would love to be proud but i do wonder if i am coherent enough even for modesty

that poet would say give it up bob you are as coherent as a bank statement
yes i reply but bank statement coherence always self contradicts
bank statements are narratives of flow and of subtended undertow

another year i spent making love like a lion in the forest
that was a good year but not modest in any known sense of the word

35.11–35.12

35.12

silence speaks sermons only silence can understand and only when itself silent
as you count exhaling each parcel of air grows large and substantial
you leave stony rivers behind you down valleys with faint lights in the distance

trains rumble through tunnels on their way to find things or to leave them behind
horses in hundreds step across the face of history lying there on the sidewalk
the boat sinking could not find the bottom which is twice carpeted with wrecks

down here on the seafloor you will find not peace but the houses of defeat
every creature trails gauze in the heavy current tugging at death
from the sanatorium balcony you see pearly air shrouding green mountains

we rest sometimes five years the inmates say and sometimes much longer
under porta santa barbara the stranger stops and begins preaching the gospel
soon statues are seen moving at night and strange cries emerge from cemeteries

once you break the silence it is like rising out of the stickiness viscusi
you begin to deploy the name instead of offering yourself upon its altar

36. the statue cries at night

36.1

the statue cries at night
did you call the lawyer
is that cash in the bank

has joey come home she wants to know
did marie's boyfriend make bail
is that priest sniffing around my daughter

i think i am dying of fear
you you bastard
you were in my dream

my best friend is sleeping with her doctor
his wife is fucking joey
my joey

we are going to need a thousand lawyers
and i can't sleep any more

36.1–36.2

36.2

she has a slot in the back of her neck
joey collects beercan deposits
they build a house of soda bottles

his wife stands in the kitchen spilling pennies
there is a hole in her hand
the floor is wet with pennies

joey's wife the statue of compound interest
has a slot in her foot
some years she sleeps only with women

the doctor's wife has left town more than once
joey is worn to a nub
sometimes he brings home paint cans

you can't sell them for anything
you can plant them with germaniums

36.3

her sister's getting married
she needs a dress
joey climbs roofs at night

steals the green copper flashing
gutters leaders pipes
he is fucking her sister

the statue never sits
she stands by the stove and fries
she stands by the sink and runs water

she reads books against the bedroom wall
the case of the slipcover stains
the harvard guide to the lower back

at the wedding she steps on his foot
good luck she says buona fortuna

36.3–36.4

36.4

grandma lived in an opera
i live with a canvas of astoria ferry
as if the future were called italy

at the temple of new ideas they display things italians supposedly invented
the temple is vecchia old inside with glass chandeliers and frescoed ceilings
we examine pistols telescopes catapults cement and the nicene creed

italians have made life easier for everyone men wearing boutonnières announce
where is the booth where they show you how to make a new life for yourself
palpate living matter to make life the pastrycook sculptor says

each work as it leaves your hands assumes the figure of a body part
olive oil garlic spaghetti greens compose a portrait on the round white plate
each form adds dignity to the conduct of affairs though alone it resolves little

we never return to certain places because they are gone when we get there
others and even some persons have staying power even if only in the mind

ellis island

36.5

in the country of italian perspective large houses stand next to small
the proscenium arch has a horn of plenty above happy and sad eyehole masks
a man blows in from another city to unload an unhappy wife

he helps others fall in love with her
magnanimously he allows her to go leaving house and children to him
feeling happy improves her disposition and she stops infuriating everyone

he acquires with money young sweet thing and poetry competition prize
the audience enjoys it because wife and husband both end happily
in the second play of the evening he tells her look this isn't working

the next thing you know the stage fills up with lawyers
he finishes alone wearing a rain barrel while she has house money and kids
both are miserable lonely broke angry resentful hopeless and feel doomed

in the third play of the evening husband and wife mud wrestle
every morning they go to work with little smiles on their faces

36.5–36.6

36.6

why do you call your perspective italian anymore
que pasa nueva york the dj shrieks at the mike
try something fresh

grandma abandoned her husband
grandpa left wives and children behind
and had to

wash their hands in american water the minute they landed
the slave worked behind the plate glass window at the whorehouse in italy
in america they didn't use plate glass and the slave opened his own whorehouse

my parents practically broke their necks and ours getting respectable
i don't know what it did for them but me it confused
they drew the line at church but us they sent

jesus had plenty to say about priests
none of it good

36.7

racket clatter in the closet means october when skeletons mate
in someone's pumpkin i recognized the adulterous smirk of a cerain uncle
when i danced on the rooftops with raccoons you saw my grandfather's red scarf

across calvary cemetery a lone towering cypress joins skyline and sky together
electrified cards of sky tumble by jabbering in ten thousand languages
you can't write it down but it all makes sense

when they say silence they mean a roar of pain so loud it colors the sky white
listen he hissed at me it's one thing to be pope and another to fuck soap
our new situation comedy he calls breaking your balls

did you see the hallowe'en episode where they finally get it on
he was calling her by his mother's name and she called him by her father's
and she was like i don't know if this is a good idea dear and he was like yes

later that evening he went looking for his grandmother now in her early twenties
he was like listen let's you and me try to rhyme again this time

36.7–36.8

36.8

what do we see when you go free said the cat to the rat as he spat spat spat
cat come catch my act real soon tango palace august moon
i love you and you love pat i am thin but you are fat

that tablespoon of clotted prune explodes below a black typhoon
take off clothes and polish hose blossom rose until it flows
that gliding tune on the lagoon is cruising down the afternoon

you dip your toes in all the shows and still suppose that no one knows
cry out deny the sigh just lie just let that spy go fry and die
when royal crows decompose do not expose the naked nose

their fingers fly immensely high grinding acorns into pie
the company is how you chat he prints in red around his hat
what you imply you never fly but when you buy you do know why

at times the sky is black and flat but not that not but not not that
for every brat that hatched a bat she sat and wove a scratching mat

36.9

things i saw my father do made it clear what was the problem
so how would i do different
i can bring you food

not break you down like a log run
we can talk
you can drift like a breeze

could be the brilliant musk of sunset will tell you take a look
walk in my piney woods
where mosquitoes patrol the air by night

the walls are wet but we snuggle under the blue quilt
have no fear the harbor gate is open
we can sail all day

slowly at first gulls squalling ropes squealing through pulleys raise heavy sheets
these snap into large roundnesses and the prow dips as the ship strains forward

36.9–36.10

36.10

one advantage of the new condition is to have more freedom in museums
under sklyights stroll among sets of totems until we find one upside down
here we lie on the floor

champagne sipping sitting on bedrolls unpack knapsack pâté
our slogan is use what you like reproduce it or sanctify it or just let it rot
everyday reality depends upon the operation of blanket systems

the world is a jail where miracles occasionally disturb the puddles
constellations overlap across every sentence as in a cubist wall hanging
though you can never know all truth your ship keeps driving forward for years

out the window country after country passes you licking your chicken fingers
usually you can shape an hour at a time well enough though interruptions do occur
systems snap adjustments flattening tablecloth creases unseating the odd goblet

wrap yourself in webs and consider your satisfactory performances and rewards
a good night's sleep under an artful quilt can soften your wounded heart

36.11

now we have the ship in ellis island motion dipping plunging hawsers screaming
this is an allegory of a life that has begun to move forward towards a purpose
get up on the wall and paint your insides stretching scraping soaking steaming

do not forget that other you carry around in you will disapprove of every picture
they candied the corpse of louis napoleon crooning framing posing seeming
this is an allegory of what it means to model yourself after a consummate model

harpo harps the migrant song dancing leering pinching scheming
this is an allegory of how a bad attitude can turn a gondola into a slave ship
they come from lebanon and turkey talking frowning spitting beaming

when you fail try to remember that no one really gets it right all the time
it's raining people now in thousands frowning hoping shouting dreaming
this is an allegory of all the voices echoing down caverns into your poem

they're climbing out of subway tunnels counting checking timing teeming
the statue frees a bedroom thought rippling roiling rising gleaming

36.11–36.12

36.12

you don't need to be stupid in order to allow yourself pleasure
just shed whatever awkward clothes cause you stiff necks or make your arms ache
nor need you torture yourself in order to feel like a responsible parent

rather think out other people through your sense of whatever flair they have
every person who can sit or stand or walk erect takes pleasure in it
study to find your own flair through the sorts of thing you can do nourishing it

on the blues charts of life i found your old hit single called samson and delilah
later he wrote a hip hop universal house proverb anthology called frankie the rat
he had distinct insight into rhetoric human relations music art food common sense

i am a man who came back from the dead i am the foam on the water of time
i am the rope in the rigging of rhyme i am the dead who came out of the bed
here you rise up out of death into life she's singing melody you hit the chords

you do the king the sword and the wife while i do the fish and the ironing boards
tomorrow we'll choose up to see which of us plays chimpanzee and which unicycle

ellis island

37. by ellis island i mean existing simultaneously in two worlds at once

37.1

children want to feel someone understanding providing protecting them
you do best with house job money food affectionate attention
they recognize your recognition

attend to your own development as it can help others if you share it
at present I find myself in that arena where they award grudging recognition
in these conditions you can still find something satisfying to do

your next step slides you past another curtain in the waterfall of tomorrow
please do not fear the rattle of trains going by marking the passage of years
you hum through each minute with a billion bees and flies in a cloud

you may now stop punishing yourself for the deaths of others
for years i believed that my anger at my father had rebounded killing my godfather
only a child at play can afford these pompous imaginings

i used to relive my mother's death constantly to stave off other deaths
now i center on exercise modest food and a humbler mind

37.1-37.2

37.2

tricks i want to see i may yet not have enunciated straight in what i write
when they finished the irrigation system the desert turned a silvery green
fear can concentrate you but whipping yourself with fear can cause aching bones

every moment you have many choices so why pick this one
on exposed ground you turn to look for love but find only terror
love and fear while they get a lot of ink do not exhaust the list

you can turn to organizing your perpetual messes
then reflect on the meaning of a life given to poetry at night
if you write your poems by daylight you will do other things by night

again do not dig with the crocodile tooth of your misspent youth
consider everything from the position of your strong attachments
anything good is free to happen once you stop tugging at it

the flow of desire is the dark animal swarming bees make none of them can see
it wraps itself around roses while in the act of exchanging sweetness with them

37.3

to distinguish real badness from imagined firmly apply your title sticker
you have attained better than average position in life whether you deserve it or not
even modest heights provide strategic advantages you'd best deploy when needed

plot campaigns through the uppermost window of your mind to see things coming
let's not meet without first deciding the agenda you tell the local troublemakers
repeat the rhyme winter comes and winter goes wind the windman blues she blows

tactically watch weather phenomena wash away sand in watery waves
shift buoys leading your enemies down oblivion bay where old men bore them blind
a navigator who understands flow deftly positions one convoy to suggest sixty

even two or three small galleons spied unexpectedly around a cove can seem an armada
invasion theaters impose upon the people illusions of omnipresence omnipotence
markets cower at the shdow of the general officer who lays hands on random throats

when he begins believing his own illusions we impose rest and recreation
i pitch anchor in porpoise channel for a winter of weaving cattails into hats

37.3–37.4

37.4

crazy mary you better get up she answered back i am confused
crazy mary you better get up they're drinking wine out of your shoes
if you kiss a banana man he'll go and come come and go his fat banana in his hand

if you take off all your clothes he'll stroke the petals of your rose
o mammà pisce fritte baccalà ue cumpà fà lalàla lalà lalà
palm trees rustle in the steady roar of hoarse old airconditioner fans

the house specialty involves rum oranges cinnamon and your own brown skin
che dolcezza è questa you pant repeatedly as she shouts out a spiral of pleasure
her smile says she has not spent a night as good as what she expects from you

before you touch her you begin to feel already part of a larger together movement
desire drew you to earth on a slow river thick with weeds
her eyes speak and her hips speak and her laughter speaks

as you move towards her you feel your step plunging into the grass
broken swords and bucklers tumble down the steep magnetic cliffs

37.5

when you do good things rewards may or may not follow quickly
you had a year of appetite a year of driving rain a year of death
how many mornings of ice have glazed the twigs and branches in your yard

a reward arrives with its thin black velvet silk veil draping the lip of the cup
you may remove it or leave it there now as it suits your need
it slides soundless into your palm for you softly to pocket it

spy movies vary in rhythm but the plot remains grab your dragon by the tail
you turn his every thrust against him simply retaining your focus and balance
afterwards they announce one day that you have inherited a bronze symbol

it looks like a token for crossing the triborough bridge into the mass of land
mountains and oceans of arable symphonies play as you breakfast there
the storm king sits next to you at dinner and puts his arm around your shoulders

domine non sum dignus said the centurion ut intres sub tectum meum
lord i am not worthy dixit centurio that you should come in under my roof

37.5–37.6

37.6

when you do things people don't like they protest in different ways
some just go away while others fight you to the death
harsh treatment produces harsh treatment if not always in a flat mirror

you married an angel you thought but she turned out to be a too quiet woman
she made endless amounts of noise only because there were things she didn't say
so you remained confused about things because she was confused too

was she saying to you come stay with me all the time i want you
or was she saying get away closer because your heart is not pure enough for me
in short this angel had fallen and now had become for you a hint of hell

it became her habit to guess at sinful desires in you
she did this partly reassuring herself you would stay close
maybe someday she would stop feeling so angry and start just liking herself

if she felt her dignity straightforwardly she would express desire that way too
we make heaven and hell the way we invent parts for ourselves to play

37.7

of course the problem wasn't she wasn't speaking but was he wasn't listening
your heart had closed like an iron lid trapping you inside the narrator said
as you could not love even when you wanted the music got faster and more intense

people you loved could not hear you crying no matter how loud you sang
maybe christ could make it out but even to him you would almost never call
you thought yourself too disgusting for words down there in the stone bowl

you strangled your own desires suspecting filth horror and death everywhere
nightmare priests writhing in hopeless shame tumbled through your sleeping head
across the clean sheets you twitched moaning and whimpering every night

oh i did sometimes love it being you anyway with your nasty masterpieces
now i'm trying to get a fix on which pieces of bronze plate to use which to store
i tried wearing monster breast columbus but found it too big for daily use

instead i walk among falling leaves listening for my heart and for others' hearts
weeping sweeping sleeping echoing in every step i keep changing my mind

37.7–37.8

37.8

what you wanted out here you would have had trouble finding anywhere
you hampered yourself at every turn of the corner in those rotted conditions
but now you begin to acquire the silverback silence that flows from clear thought

you stand red as a flower under a lamp in a doorway
whenever you swim in a swamp of the past you scrub and rinse yourself afterwards
this tunes your capacity to recognize and respond to life's challenges

light on hair negotiates charmingly together with you completing circuits
paying attention you hear what the person looks for and then offer it as an aroma
it might distill a serious figment of sleep intensity desire

when you smile at someone reflect the full sunlight that falls on you
this reflection may return to you mingled with the other person's light
second sunlight infused with delight creates magnetisms between you

each can be as hard and soft and hurled rapidly forward as any eternal planet
i suspect your excellence when your hands express needs

ellis island

37.9

by ellis island i mean existing in two worlds at the same time
some pieces break off in one world and go on living there
other fragments move on to a next world and there flourish

on ellis island they have erected an altar to the goddess of separation
this goddess's daughter divorce raises her bronze sword over north america
slices of time lie together here while others go elsewhere to blossom

i mean a piece feels itself come apart from one place to flourish in a new place
on ellis island pain rises at times above insensibility's wall
whistles blow all night in your dreams of ships that leave on the morning tide

the water slides so gently by you might never understand its power to dissolve
it can carry arrange rearrange uncover recover sink and raise from the depths
oceans make us many people many places many nights and many days away

on the sky our fingers trace outlines that turn to wrought iron
no one wants to enter these confines of confusion more than once

37.9–37.10

37.10

do you mean to suggest that ellis island is the gateway of a huge madhouse
each person who enters the americas from abroad slave or free loses some mind
most sponsor tribes of further persons who lose more

o tempi antichi perduti when the wise perfected us ways to act
when we came through the ocean of which ellis island is an effect we lost memories
some the water took but we lost others when we tried to use them in a hostile place

gradually we descended to the level of machines good for work but not for action
though they declared us free again every year on july fourth we did not move
we had money and muscle enough but our undertstanding was sawdust in the breeze

we returned to ellis island seeking mind we think we might have had
we found broken beams of it that we employed to start sorting out our condition
we consult the ancient wise but we consult ourselves and one another more

we found enough of the wisdom there to guess at the scope of our loss
it became a place of fitting broken parts together

37.11

the mind lives through the body though it partakes of things outside the body
in ellis island insides often became outsides and rest upon the harbor now ghosts
shapes rising at water's edge attract and summarize spirit millions every morning

when you return here lost shapes for instants of time make themselves available
living and dead millions mark traces on old photographers' plates
if you want to see them take the velvet bag off the cage of your apprehension

if you elevate me to the rank of a god i will fail you every time
nonetheless i will try to arrange some small facilitations
i can only do that though it isn't much as the most of my mind is in shambles

sometimes i think the mind may have grown rich but lacks for body
thus do i exercise and sleep and wash and care for the pearly clawed animal i am
on gray mornings i ask you to thank me for your warm beds and dry ceilings

just now in the world a woman with teeth for fingernails tapped your shoulder
she says i will infuriate you so you won't be able to stop thinking of me

37.11–37.12

37.12

in this moment the single light begins to shine in a simple talk rhythm
the fact is you say to her i do not need you to survive
about the money be sure you get your fair share

remember you each will need enough to mount a new life and help it flourish
the fact is you say to the world i am ready to enjoy life more
enjoyment stimulates production so you can leave the moral worries out of it

if you gave a hundred for each of two hundred that would be twenty thousand
if you took a hundred for each of two hundred that would be twenty thousand
so take forty thousand and divide it in two

remember money buys pleasures satisfactions freedoms
once you have the money taking the freedom requires its own attention
when you are ready to do this you wake up one morning with an appetite to do it

your project of mutual commitment changes shape on ellis island
you have near ones but also now construct variable distance credit structures

38. second by ellis island i mean states of persons changing shape or mode of being

38.1

after they hear a poem some people say wow
this means they think it sounds powerful but do not understand a word of it
jesus if you know what you're talking about you are either crazy or a genius

or are you just full of shit like nero writing epics
of course there is always the chance a nero might have written well
he seems to have had excellent taste in architects which is a promising sign

but when people say wow it means they would love to undertstand but do not
it occurs to me to include instructions to make that part easier
first of all every single line aims to be an entire freestanding unit

i wrote this poem in a period of wild interruptions so its parts had to be short
proverbs and quotations dictionaries held a powerful fascination for me in youth
second by ellis island i mean states of persons changing shape or mode of being

third a person tries to make sense of the world even as it too is changing
the plot of this poem can be summarized in the question what next

38.1–38.2

38.2

when they speak of the starship enterprise they mean a floating island
you develop a set of collective sensors which your enemies call an empire
each one of these creatures has its own adaptive strategies

we meet with our friends and write their names on the carte du jour
today's orders indicate four of you must sing at noon two at three pm
seven of us will be observed walking past the restaurant window at dinnertime

and of course we prescribe ourselves similar lists of regulated moves to make
rules of engagement guide our every meeting against the black sky of history
as i shoot down the defile of planets i find the portal of the damned

i avoid it and do many sly maneuvers allowing you to pass into it unawares
charlemagne arranges his greatest warriors along the orbit you assume
he sees to it you find one another that his champions may thwart your progress

even the gate of hell has an assembly disassembly schedule
since we have erected it again we can also take it down

38.3

i was thinking of a tarantella composed of letters and books
you would send me a book i would read making notes in it and then sending it on
we could start with ten people each sending a book in a circular motion

along with each book goes a circular letter to which each reader adds something
at completion of circuit we deposit each book and letter in a central library
every so often we stop and exchange the same book twice between each two readers

when general circulation resumes these two sometimes go on to other joint acts
other times we reverse the order of circulation so that we see some books twice
when each reader has seen a book at least once it drops out of formal circulation

as years go by but one book at a time comes out but if we all read it we can talk
provided everyone met obligations the circles could grow larger than ten
another way would be to have everyone buy the same book every month

after a very little while a momentum would begin to grow
you see soon a great narrative paisley spermatomorph on the face of the silk tie

38.3–38.4

38.4

we speak of how a literary history takes shape as if it were a hatching leviathan
that is we laid our seed forms like shadows across brilliant egg forms years ago
the shell hardens and darkens eventually from brittle white to hard dark olive

one day a three armed crack like the symbol trinacria appears on the upper side
 the tips of these cracks connect through other cracks so jagged pieces fall off
we speak of the emerging creature as if it were a navigator with three lives

colombo the crusader plus vespucci the banker make verrazzano the conquistador
christians use subject populations as collateral for letters of credit
our literary history begins with the totem of a galleon in piazza della navicella

prehistoric sailors with impermeable horny skin dance along our sunrise lines
many bankers lie upon jasper bas reliefs and bronze intaglio in our temples
against their empires of terraced vineyards do we measure our achievements

they have mastered the past with money which is labor time and we must do less
like them we harvest the future in advance in order to rent our ancient fields

ellis island

38.5

there is such a thing as class oppression and what does it look like
i love lucy grunting under the marlboro man
class kibbitzing our parents like a laugh track

in renaissance comedy marriage each person deceives a deceiver
they wiggled down the sweaty chute to a wet coal gas cellar of hopeless wedlock
but some others undaunted still try to construct marriages based upon mutuality

they don't exactly believe equality exists but find the idea useful as a gauge
balancing numbers of childrearing cooking cleaning hours starts us toward parity
then some marriage contractors take conscious private affirmative action as well

everything begins with position since how people feel shapes how they think
what you are looking for predetermines your result the way prayers find answers
you only get the sense of getting what you want if you know what it is

some intentions have escape clauses carrying you confused to their own back doors
turn knob walk through hall open front door look down steps and think it all over

38.5-38.6

38.6

now that you have a position please close your eyes
do a breathing mantra four times
open your eyes

in this house you have been living and shouting fifteen years minus one in rome
you have not yet integrated your operatic voice with your spoken voice
we will never hear gianlorenzo bernini singing but your voices have a chance

you won a doctorate or license for professorship the day after buying the house
artium baccalaureatus cost four fordham years cornell master of arts only one
philosophiae doctor at new york university exacted sixteen more yes sixteen

coursework and comprehensives took three years taming my prose style another nine
then i wrote four years while teaching marrying traveling fathering housebuying
my thesis studied an english writer in italy who died saying grazie per tutto

closing the masterslave transaction and reversing positions i have danced along
the trick is to keep changing places according to the needs of the job at hand

38.7

do you mean to say yes to shouting and singing
i affirm it good to interweave them with whispers and calm voices
laughter does well as an uncoupling device when you need to shift tones

emanations occur intended or not requiring that you begin examining them
stop arguing with devils and simply tell your story
their wrongness can keep you from confronting your own vulnerability

in my new opera i play the ellis rôle of leopard poet
i decide which baritone commodity to model as i work to support my family
professor critic novelist administrator composer performer poet help one another

it is vital to sort message elements into distinct kinds and groups
in reassembly you can then use just the stuff you need and leave the rest aside
purple red and crimson do not always work together as necessary companions

one gold piece one gold piece one gold piece one red one red i use in an eyebrow
i make a cloak out of orange pieces using green and brown for depth shadows

38.7–38.8

38.8

some people are always afraid to die while others bull right through to the end
people who die sometimes take life out of entire worlds they have inhabited
many white nations have gone into the further beyond already

as for me i picked up my centurion's breastplate and raised it on his behalf
though i can do many things i do them only in his service so he will not die
if i enter the next century may i do so giving continued life to my captain

my godfather uncle mike taught me how a man orders coffee and gives joy to others
his sicilian eyes still hold a stone world in florid balance long after his death
his gaze produces green parrots tall palms latinizing my any possible america

planets follow paths that reflect their respective weights
when you think of motion think of how it gives the earth its steady ocean glaze
think of an image that unlocks the door of your body

your body can come out of its prison when you use it sensibly
as it works it grows more beautiful and or its clothes make more sense

38.9

although there are a billion rooms there is only one room
but this one room no matter how many repetitions it has is unlike all the others
its unlikeness to others is its one universal feature wherever it recurs

mrs viscusi has placed a thanksgiving turkey in the refrigerator to cook tomorrow
each of these things we do has its own trajectory and its own valence
others do the same thing at the same time each in a way entirely unique

what history does that action have is a question with many answers looking alike
each like answer however as the person gives it takes its place in a story
dividing money has a clean method but dividing stories usually makes a mess

a learned folklorist may disaggregate a story into a million pieces
holy cow the folklorist aims to eat all stories but they devour him instead
stories march onto the horizon and carve out possibilities of change

in our case it is a question of deciding on being in a slave ship or not
if you decide to stay it is because the deal really appeals to you a lot

38.9–38.10

38.10

you moved to wherever it was and made a lot of money in real estate
at this moment i have been enjoying how you ran away from me
it opened the way to a new sort of middle age

though i spent a great deal of time complaining about you i did not mean it
actually i thought you had done well to avoid a quarter century of hypocrisy
now i need to buy a car but have not decided which best suits me

she plans to paint house and i to buy children computers
we stay together day by day always on the edge of separating
we continually have made choices to avoid feeling like prisoners of one another

in one way we have been together but in many others we have been each of us alone
how can we go on being together that way but not being alone the rest of the time
we can be together the rest of the time with each other or with others

in this way we might construct a mountain of eternal marriages of brief duration
we trace each as it forms forever in the crystal undergrowth of human consequence

38.11

i wanted to call our team eldorado jaguars in every sport where we competed
like petey's red studebaker stevey's fat black buick had cracked leather seats
barry bought a big wide nash and i used a staid ford my father passed me down

with vinny joey and joey i planned a singing group with buddy and andrew a band
instead we produced one accountant three policeman two professors
our parents said just take the trolley every day to where they give out the money

it was too soon for a group but now this name on the shelf suddenly comes alive
i hope eldorado means when you turn fifty because you acquire a golden light
indians call the fierce black spotted yellow forest cat great dangerous yaguara

the american leopard body three to four feet long ranges from texas to patagonia
unnoticed gold yaguara slips a soft paw onto the glass table among your drinks
hermanos i have entered the large green coolness with the king of playing cards

in the clearing beyond the trees barefoot drummers have been drumming for days
after the king says you have the energy you dance a week on the flat ground

38.11–38.12

38.12

don't forget everything i taught you on the trip last summer
when you dance the masterslave reciprocation work and pleasure change places
each house has an altar a rooftree a pediment prow and a porch with columns

one in the porch greet strangers where two the pediment protects the interactors
the rooftree three tells the stranger you have raised angle to the height of your intention
at the altar four all bow and pour sacrifices to the family dragon

before you make an expedition ask your shadows four to bless your enterprise
three make sure the managers of the estate have all they need to manage well
two consult the acroterion cresting the pediment to orient your journey plans

one on either side of the porch columns stand for armies that march with you
you are each of your armies and survive despite even sometimes tiresome setbacks
when you pitch camp you perform orientations protections meetings and sacrifices

one two three two four three four one two one three four four three one two
take your time and your gods will lead you to know and understand all you need

39. my conflicting feelings move me back and forth between by now familiar locations

39.1

my first large italian american pow wow was at the washington hilton in may 1979
in the district of columbia the national italian american foundation convened
hundreds paid a fee to discuss a national italian american agenda for the 1980s

that spring i had been teaching the italian american novel at brooklyn college
pietro di donato in march had spoken with my students about christ in concrete
he had shown them his vision of a cruel america resembling don corleone's

nietzsche he had taught said most men live in herds as most italian americans do
but he asserted that the old immigrant paisani had been not herd animals but gods
di donato gave us an agenda for 1980s and for centuries leading into the mist

from this day forward he had said when you go as an italian american go as a god
di donato of the sandpaper bricklayer hands touched you
he said we peed on our hands to heal the cracking after a day of work

your streetsweeper grandfather was osiris looking for his lost broken pieces
one piece fell so far into the murk of time that only as you has it reappeared

39.1–39.2

39.2

funerals carried so much freight because sorrow needed more outlets than it had
today with all these large icons gone to storage in jersey we use blank stages
we have spent fifteen years wishing we knew what we were doing in making a family

being a god belongs to making a family because you have a god's responsibility
you might need help of a different kind than you have had as even gods need help
would someone mother your children energetically for you when you were not there

we begin from the different rules people bring to interactions
these may seem systematic but people also make them up or get them in dreams
for this reason you study desire as a rule making device for interpreting rules

his fear of dinosaurs did not stop him from writing large books about them
this weekend we have been slapping up huge sets for an outdoor family spectacle
after every war the winners tell the losers it was wrong to fight back

while all this noise was going on i noticed someone had left the door unlocked
i wanted to leave but all of a sudden my hands got cold buzzes so i felt frozen

39.3

a god is one in whom forces of destiny operate clearly
thus all women and all men may be gods but we cannot perceive this in all cases
on the other hand we are supplicants so you wonder which hand is working at any given time

one god will often supplicate another in the manner of bureaucrats
so you think can your brokenness complete itself gloriously next to her brokenness
no message completion lasts long though you make thousands of them all day

my conflicting feelings move me back and forth between by now familiar locations
how can you write about forces of destiny that you never name
you need to say this sense of destiny comes from my own sense of myself

make new small choices and they soon enough present you with new large choices
you may play a god in moments of self definition but recompose as a breeze later
not every commission you receive requires your acceptance so do not feel obliged

i have been sitting back to contemplate all the incompletions on the horizon
conversation can be interesting even if you don't get much done

39.3–39.4

39.4

the best thing you can do at times like this is sit still and calm down
my greatest problem is that when i think i can start something i think it's over
no i say it's too late no you're sick no you're dying no don't bother to try

yes i get going anyway but some things i don't try after all this discouragement
when the great paranoia descends even that is now only a way of staying alive
if you think about it you will find it easier to abandon your diseases

instead you begin tuning your piano body mind your strumento italiano
listen for the answers that simply came out too fast too strong too loud
your mind is equipped with swinging doors you may now unfasten

oil the silver hinges lovingly for when these doors swing free you can find calm
ordinarily they form part of the eggshell membrane of life your brain configures
but when there is a disturbance they move ever so slightly to adjust the pressure

thus you maintain an equilibrium meaning remember what your project explains
it knows most of what you need to know and is happy to discuss changes of plan

39.5

when you concentrate on the stone in the path you help all that flows around you
you begin to see people work together effectively
then when you are listening to another person listen for the harmonies

some of what they say will go well with some of what you say
you will also differ but do not use that alone as it works like bonding cement
enough difference should feel as comfortable as clothes should feel

harmony when you experience it may seem so strange you are not sure what to do
stay calm and enjoy it remaining alert of course but focus on the pavement
people who say they are looking for the meaning of life often only need new shoes

in designing a park give space for others as well as you to walk there
the most successful designs have many people moving them along in different ways
at this point i really have to spend a couple of days on end of month chores

doing these things gives me a nice steady feeling about my work
every moon you live is another paradise of feelings

39.5–39.6

39.6

the voices move in many directions like great tribes of fish in the gulf stream
some come from the south of your mind near the warm ocean birth source
other times you hear the echo of catastrophes some years into the future

occasionally a voice comes to you recirculating something you said an hour back
as you learn to tune your reception more finely the instruments grow distinct
when you listen crudely it all sounds like one voice in the loud eternal present

as you shift your angle of perception the signals begin to reveal individualities
in the end all writing is one but along the way you learn its manyness
at my present tilt i have been watching a lot of messages circling around me here

this poem resembles a huge vat of chocolate with a large paddle turning it
the circular drive paddle runs across almost the entire diameter of the vat
it moves the chocolate and the chocolate swirls behind the paddle's leading edge

no one can fully understand the dynamics of this mathematical exuberance
but if you tune yourself to its harmonies you may hear something you need to know

39.7

a charade comes to a close when all the actors dance in a circle
processions disestablish former realities in the process of establishing new ones
even your terrors are traditional realities established walking

processions include weddings and funerals and marching to class or the lunchroom
in college we do scurry processions between classes formal ones at year's ends
moving house is a processional activity in which everyone can have a role

assigning processional roles in a divorce can save everyone a lot of trouble
each person acquires newly crafted title to days places functions and inwardness
carrying things back and forth the procession helps each person self reconfigure

exchanging pieces of responsibilities gives each a dignity of self composition
like a college a divorce includes many scurry processions and a few formal ones
in scurry processions we exchange sound bites figure bites and we touch hands

formal procession plans consider each person's function in relation to the goal
each person raises a hood or moves a tassel from one side to the other

39.7–39.8

39.8

sometimes they take the dead king out and use his body to pass miracles
certain nights in this climate you can't be sure which of the four seasons it is
this is the way the world ends announces the saint raising his arms

ubicunque fuerit corpus wherever the body will have been
illic congregabuntur et aquilae there will eagles gather mittet angelos suos cum tuba
he will send out messengers with trumpets and thus you know it is at your gates

we were always afraid of the end of the world which we heard of in italian latin
when you see all these things then all the tribes of earth will wail
tum plangent omnes tribus terrae but who are the tribes of the earth

as everyone knows priests were oppressive though some of them treated us well
always watch what the priest wants and stay out of his way when it's not good
justus ut palma florebit some others shoot right up around you like palm trees

keep your instrument tempered and it can predict weather better than a television
preparing for winter you can't help crying no matter what tribe you belong to

ellis island

39.9

when my uncle mike died the whole world collapsed into the grave after him
i stood there beating the fender of somebody's station wagon with my hand
i see him at christmas dinner lift a bottle of champagne singing libiamo

one nervous rapid waltz after another moves the pizzicato forward in this film
his father and mother had skin like marble statues
his three beautiful sisters eleonora elvira and gilda sang just by looking at you

everything he said was brilliant come un'angelo like an angel i saw him
like the archangel michael he stood on the horizon of time with his great wings
after the first act we drank cinzano in the lobby watching for diors and whitneys

look said vito i see belphagor the greek orthodox bishop of bangor miane in mufti
a fat man wearing a long beard and a paisley cummerbund waddled into sherry's
often la traviata seemed longer than the ring except when they sang parigi o cara

you are in every statue garden of the known universe
o good and faithful servant serve bone fidelis

39.10

they disappeared with the float in the flat wet manhattan cement as it hardened
pumping itself into the sky the chrysler building sucked them out of their bodies
men ran and hid on porous long island sand banks where the tide rose around them

in the dark westchester hills long white flints lie at angles where they fell
all the italians died expecting the next sound would come from the orchestra pit
delle belle turbando al riposo great beauties disturbing their rest they shivered

many folded themselves into the red california hills as the plow turned the earth
aching battalions lay flat along the dry colorado so trains could run across them
in panama some had arrived already boxed and layered like anchovy fillets in oil

vanderbilt orsini opened a sack of paesani and poured them into the portland mix
sometimes i play opera music for them the way you leave cocoa for santa claus
along the east river they threw italians into the water weighted with rocks

waterfalls of iron horse sewing machines howled and roared down rows of women
the phonograph needle hiss calls out from fifty years ago as if they were in hell

39.11

now damp december wails in a minor key and all our new dead wander the world
lachrymosa dies illa qua resurget ex favilla judicandus homo reus
one tearful day the guilty human who is to be judged shall rise from the ashes

spare this human huic ergo parce deus pie iesu domine dona eis requiem amen amen
loving jesus give them rest amen amen amen amen i now live where they sing hebrew
i am humming mmmm aut patriam aut mmmm parentes amen alios sanguine coniunctos

amen homeland amen family amen others joined in blood cicero advises us to bless
performing the rituals correctly will cleanse and free the sky of drained spirits
when high walls open on jewelled heaven lost souls burn as light back to the sun

jewish chinese italian doctors wrote all these stories down when writing came in
aztec maya inca astrologers could read the family dramas of gods among the stars
ibo bantu tagàlog secrets explain burial of the dead as how we construct time

i have myself served mass under a pastor who learned to do it in the 19th century
before dawn he strikes the new fire echoing the huge creation about to begin

39.11–39.12

39.12

do you mean the age of arithmetic is over said the children from under the desks
the siren had sounded and we returned to grazing on latin verbs and maps of snow
no one even bothered to boycott handel's oratorio on the death of hitler any more

later on they sat us down and whispered no one can tell if it will ever end
all night long people whose imaginations remained alive cried in their rooms
lord save my mother father sister brother wife husband daughter son that day

libera me domine de morte eterna in die illa free me lord from eternal death
we read books about how eternal death would look feel smell sound and taste
so we filled the black distances of spent light with family radio comic operas

in certain periods severe rules apply allowing only comedian and laugh track
giving the audience lines to say makes the drama ever so much more interesting
nowadays heroes emerge from the crowd and challenge champions in loud sneers

these diversions may serve us with parables of the broken family
the family itself serves us as a warning against eternal life

40. we no longer deal with indecision but we deal with starting slowly

40.1

certain ideas flower without much effort from who thinks them
others proliferate with no help at all
you go looking for a blossom that includes every single aspect you had in mind

once you find it you may as well cook it for supper as keep it some other way
spend love freely hanging onto what you need but not every damn thing
guilt seeming to defend love instead builds fear with narcissist horror masks

if you know how to say things that occur to you then freely do so
most of us most of the time find ourselves hard put to get any of them into words
so we inadvertently skip it slipping forward to the next thing we know how to say

generally that moves us but not necessarily where we wanted to go
words work as keel and sail and rudder on the steep seas of life
they negotiate our aim on the disappearing dark mountains below

we brace our arms to the wheel as the ship tilts drastically forward into a swell
weeping men strain the mainsail steady rising on the storm as if they were birds

40.1–40.2

40.2

new orleans united states music has latin chords african rhythms and arab tunes
slave shouts shout shòut shout shòut shout shòut shout shòut shout shòut shòut
african circles do latin symmetries coming down broken arab staircase melodies

swaying in the net from the boom over the hold the white statues of italy descend
under the mercury lamps the marmo di brecciano has the color of snow on a grave
a tall man raises one hand high pointing up and spreads his wide marble wings

start with a statue of some pontifex maximus caius as the messenger god mercurius
large added angel wings recall merchandise from at least as far east as persia
romans wore loose fitting clothing as did carthaginians across in north africa

rome occupied a position along a world configured around an elliptical sea
rival carthage from its twin position looked east to egypt as did rome to greece
at the western end the pillars of hercules opened on outer space

the greeks and egyptians in their turn look back into their mountain pasts
from kilimanjaro they drifted east as later from tibet towards tierra del fuego

40.3

general hamilcar first saw rome from carthage hidden behind islands and capes
afterwards his son reconfigured it as it would look from an elephant on the alps
hamilcar had already circled the ellipse along the coast all the way to spain

now his son hannibal's elephants crossed southern france to die in the snow
for him they worked as parachutes bringing him and his gear most of the way there
in italy he laid down catastrophes against rome from etruria to apulia

this immortal general pitched camp in the luxurious city of capua on the volturno
rome never defeated him but after all those years he left italy without reaching rome
in the volturno lowlands mosquitoes only spare those with an african blood trait

hannibal planted an african homeland in greek campania making neapolitans
when southern italians speak you hear great greece and when they sing great africa
garibaldi stopped his army at that same volturno and gave over to the northerners

my family has lived many centuries along the volturno like water buffalo
we share a blood trait and a black persistence that scares some people

40.3–40.4

40.4

when you run out of space maneuver advance attack fall back leaving traps behind
if you don't know what to do next sometimes you sleep days weeks months years
after engagements win or lose you want to readjust attitude and material support

each musician specializes in a given instrument in an army
even general officers focus on certain sets of operations or higher up sets of sets
the waters pound against the same cliffs and then against the same other cliffs

the most general general pays the greatest attention to smallest signs detectable
they first detect large changes among tiny objects almost beneath notice
if clay slightly shifts some bricks come loose and some buildings come down

don't be afraid of tomorrow when the evergreen forest runs down your block
yesterdays of every creature have occurred on the same spot again tomorrow
we cannot explain how these things happen but they happen anyway

most of the time a decent amount of attention suffices
reward all your officers after every engagement and probe them after campaigns

ellis island

40.5

now we are beginning to organize things in a large room by room way
if she flags i turn the hollow flaking map sphere on its rusty axis anyway
sometimes i hang a chain onto an equator hook then fasten it to a jeep and pull

once you overcome an obstacle the river runs along quite freely even to the sea
monkeys race up and down the steamer ladders smelling of soup and gasoline
bàng bang bàng bang bàng bàng bàng albino baboon punches wheelhouse roof

now use finesse as you turn prevailing conditions to your benefit
but wait do you really want to do this it's not too late to turn around
when you come to the back of your own infantry you find it still marching away

these big decisions grow best out of small decisions you make in reorganizing
one day you suddenly know exactly what to do because you see it in front of you
such recognition scenes have an absolute quality like stones in a riverbed

only afterwards does it even occur to you what you have already joined up with
yet in the moment you saw it you at last came to a decision

40.5–40.6

40.6

my hesitations seem to have to do with the fear of hell
if you leave your wife you will pay a terrible price
you will grow sick and suffer and die all alone

you will die and go to hell where you will suffer bodily pain forever
so is it really so bad to stay where you are
you will not be alone even though you may be lonely together

you may end in hell anyway but not for leaving your wife
in the next world you will be rewarded for all this suffering and pain
this reckless talk sounds like a football rally so try something more calibrated

if you and your wife do not love each other well you do better to part amicably
your children suffer either way and you will have to deal with that guilt
at least hear and share their feelings so that you do not add insult to injury

as for your own sin though it is real it will not be mortal if you choose to live
the sunshine continues to come down from the left right through the branches

40.7

tuning an engine an orchestra or a human body one studies proportions
harmonious figures produce deep mirror resonances the ear can see lined up
any tuned instrument hums its sharp focus over the waves or up the hill

a chaos of drums keeps breaking out of the garage in the middle of the night
you don't have a garage any more they keep telling and he weeps don't i know it
any act of tuning begins by noticing the discords then noting their distribution

each string snapping into its role increases the sound of the army when it calls
now they are coming on horses row after row in an astonishing unison of hoofs
some women weep behind beds and washstands and cowsheds but others paint their nails

brave deeds often fall into the category of sins but they also sometimes win wars
if you want to commit a sin consider whether you are not in fact leading an army
long ago you fell out of the category incubator and began your singular wandering

already you belong to the four winds and the seven seas and the twelve months
a radio rich sky around you fills with stars every time you sit still to breathe

40.7–40.8

40.8

when you return to the feeling of not being able to do things remember this
superego ego and id are not necessarily father son and holy ghost
in fact father son and holy ghost are all complex ideas and not clearly related

i was always one of those italians who puts you down before you open your mouth
when people responded in kind i either didn't like it or fell in love with it
in the first case i felt passions of hypocrisy in the second i acted the slave

my opening gesture had the sort of nervous content of a dog's barking
someone is at the perimeter it announces but it often provokes bad feelings
nowadays i speak more softly not to be someone else but to fulfill my own desire

i compose myself to hear people gently allowing them to reveal themselves
glass circle on my coffee table reflects a great lake of light
superego ego and id are mapping devices like mountain sand and sea

along the aisles of department stores they hang the fathers on christmas trees
gothic arches throw shadows across the path of the manfully striding away fellow

40.9

once you recognize that everything you do has this assembled quality you relax
you can begin to recognize that not everything you put in a museum belongs there
you don't need to throw things away but you can assign them relative importance

some things you used to worship may now gather dust or serve as bootscrapers
others get left behind if you forget them as you learn to make new values
you can mold them like cookies or gelatin gods of quivering receptivity

ah italy you say when they hand you the dish full of dust clotted marble grapes
on the second day of christmas my true love gave to me two dead rattlesnakes
the first is for the roman empire and the second for the roman church she said

students of mary baker eddy made her monument a plotted grid of towering pines
it signified how thought lounges along interspiritual axes
i have been ordering bits of my life every day now as if writing a menu

each part of the day has the shape of a poem including a question and a reply
even hopelessly wrong answers use music as a healing oil all over you

40.9–40.10

40.10

suddenly i stopped writing this poem for many months
i was finishing one book and publishing another
i was unable to stop returning to the well for more infinity

when you live inside a long poem it changes everything around you
but if the poem is about changing everything around you everything stands still
so i had to stop writing so that things could begin the actual process of change

a roaring harmonious chorus pours out of the many colored globe
it swings spinning down the elliptical channels of the void as you watch
no one can hear it but the movement of change is perpetual

the one thing i am afraid of now is my own habit of self obstruction
the way this works is it makes me do what i want and then ruin it
as your finger lands on the wrong note slide it across to the right one

for the listener this creates an effect we call appoggiatura
in retrospect the rightness of the resolution was supporting the melody all along

40.11

we no longer deal with indecision but we deal with starting slowly
now i am learning to do a small thing for myself without stopping
later i will try something larger using the principle of appoggiatura

appoggiatura allows for the standard variances
always rest the foot on a good support before beginning
we search for footings continually as we walk

we learn uncertainties of sand and of mist when they lightly film the pavement
in those passages we walk with greater care
in the clear dry sunshine we stretch our muscles and move boldly forward

every march includes dancing as music sounds everywhere
the good walker hears it with every muscle
every walking part answers the hearing parts and so intensifies the messages

keep going and you will find the going world go with you
first steps can give pause but after movement answers movement you'll be swinging

40.11–40.12

40.12

parrots have colonized brooklyn college and the tree lined side streets
they have the green a leaf has as a shaft of light shifts between two shadows
turning the corner i heard a raucous dispute emerging from a lofty maple thicket

slowly i approached the sound and stood looking up at the cloud of squawking
green confused abundant early summer did not want to reveal them to me
but eventually i saw five or six hover conversing under and over a single branch

they live on the tops of mercury lamp stanchions alpine over the playing fields
each nest holds many of these tropical birds who control the flowering campus
cherry lilac magnolia elm and chestnut walnut weeping pine and bitter apple

they investigate the flowering cabbages in december and they never go away
what were they saying among the maples where avenue i meets ocean avenue
one of them was telling the others about life in the swamps of south carolina

the young who have not seen alligators or tree frogs believe nothing he says
they believe god made brooklyn college and made them with it

41. choosing to stay means leaving but choosing to leave means to stay

41.1

apart we remember how we were separated throughout those years together
you would say to me the real world doesn't go that way and i would say too bad
the real world opened out in front of me as so many palaces on the water

you could hear feet scraping along the pavement of large squares in venice
i made a plan after i heard someone typing over a deserted garden in giudecca
why do you write in this difficult way they said to me

i did not mean to write difficult work but when i came up against the page i did
i wish i had a simple definition of what it means to see around corners in dreams
writing gives you the habit of seeing tablecloths and sneakers in six dimensions

after height and depth and width came number four the snakeskin of elapsed time
everything has a fifth dimension showing who put it together with what labor
and sixth belongs to the masters kings and gods in a row envisioning objects

fine you say to me you have proved that you are ready to write an epic
now tell me why you chose ellis island

41.1–41.2

41.2

the first thing to remember about an epic is why people read epics
you want to know how the world came to be the way it was when you were born
this poem explains that

in the old days before the revolution the rich were rich and the rest were not
some people began to get so rich the old rich resisted so they made a revolution
they cut off the head of the king and after that the new rich had no more problem

when you would get rich they would let you be rich just like the old rich
the revolution also did something for the poor although it did not make them rich
of course some of them got rich anyway but the revolution might not have been why

what the revolution did for the poor was to put them in crates and send them away
they had a chance to root in new soil and see what happened
a lot of the experiments failed and the people died

the many successes in physical recombination made new noses houses highways foods
one kind of skin attracts another kind of eyes

41.3

stone hip bones clog the path between you and getting what you want
you need to say no to others and to do so gently
recognize in them centers of accumulation even as the rain washes over them

the rain did not come from you but from the past or from the sky or from strangers
if you stop rubbing your hands on the barnacles your scrape marks will go away
sit quietly and think about the whole business of statues

statues think of themselves and they don't want to hear about you
and when they do think of you they do so according to the gospel of marble blocks
limestone reasonings land on your spirit crushing it in the name of lymph nodes

each creature has its enormous presence carved out of living kidneys and balls
you too have expressed the bladder of urine that has set you in play
an old lady prayed for you before birth to to gleam with her jaundiced wisdom

when you step before crowds they see her yellow in the whites of your eyese
oh she says never let them forget that they too have been slaves for an eternity

41.3–41.4

41.4

before rome every village had its king who won slaves in battle
each tribe raided the neighboring tribe and whom they caught they enslaved
if they caught a rich person then rich relatives would buy that person's freedom

people without rich relatives had to stay alert or they would end in bondage
then under the caesars slavery needed to become a large scale social organization
after the romans had conquered egypt they began to compete with the pharoahs

augustus marked his victory with obelisks and altars to himself as an erect penis
the old rome of wood and brick now disappeared under a famous tide of marble and bronze
slave teams cut mountains to measure and animal teams dragged immobilities miles

slaves living on hannibal's old campsites hammered swords for slave gladiators
later italians belonged to later italians down the saracen and spanish centuries
in short and to begin with we italians carry marks showing an aeon of subjection

we came to america to acquire mastery and dignity
it turned out to be possible for some not for all

41.5

down at the language laboratory i said teach me to write like shakespeare
okay they said into the contraption so in i went and when i came out there i was
it took about twenty five years start to finish and i learned a lot along the way

from shakespeare i went on to max beerbohm henry james gertrude stein
john ashbery kenneth koch and frank o'hara were stations out in the burbs
i also spent summers at camp stendhal camp manzoni camp dickens

this year i have been hiking across the canadian swamps with margaret mitchell
the whole idea of the civil war in canada has been marching in my mind
more important i am thinking about how to give my literary name some neon

astoria came out in stores two months ago and i am launching it every month
in may we did cafes and in june bookstores and in july a professional group
it has a publication date on august fifteenth birthday of augustus and napoleon

priests call it the feast of the assumption of the virgin's body into heaven
and now it is the birthday of astoria and a million alley cats

41.5–41.6

41.6

i sang the triple empire of napoleon augustus and the street
then it was time to launch this sucker as if it were orlando furioso
we had a pageant and a puppet show

should there be a movie or would you prefer a play
the most important part would then be the dialogue
in gone with the wind scarlett is torn between the old south and the new

she never stops desiring ashley the old south but chooses rhett instead
through her we watch the new unfold and the old unravel both self consciously
in astoria the dialogue is between italy and america

always desiring italy the hero always chooses america
at the end when he thinks he has found italy he turns it into a theme park
in the beginning he finds paris and makes it part of astoria in new york city

he calls this doing of one thing while wanting of another by the name terror
once he finally arrives in ancient rome he makes it part of florida

41.7

in this poem the dialogue is between choosing to leave and choosing to stay
choosing to stay means leaving but choosing to leave means to stay
after a long trip ellis island is the place where the division at last occurs

some people return to start and lead a different life than they lived before
we have heard about the ones who went forward into the land of the iroquois
those who returned to oscan villages in the italian mountains went forward too

today and recently i have been saying yes i return to the family estate
i go back to the conditions of professor and father because how can i leave them
is it because i don't feel strong enough to cross the water or am i afraid

or is this is the turning point in a love story
something in him not his ego wants his family
the ego doesn't know where to sit

the crossing is terror when you are not prepared but otherwise usually goes well
you may cross frequently in a stateroom in a dining room in a lounge if you like

41.7–41.8

41.8

the next day he was at the bus station
listen he said to the lawyer i don't know how to live on nothing
listen the lawyer said it won't be nothing and you'll figure it out

there is a long list of instructions which if you follow it leads you home
home has a very different character than where you have been staying
you have been in exile for a decade a century a millennium an aeon

what you call your memory resembles a bedroom full of old postcards
your actual memory distributes itself equally throughout your body
do not try to remember things with your mind but let your mind review memory

your body advises your using not only memory but also desire
when you feel like running run and when like jumping jump
as the energy flows through it flushes out your so called basic problems

your new life comes through this pulsing river of energy
you find home as a dinosaur a crayfish ecstasy under the water filter of the sun

41.9

i want to write about how badly you treat me
whenever you do whatever you do you make everyone else pay
has someone been raising your rent again

why expect anything from someone who has always given so little
you go on for years suffering as if it were going to add up to something
and the you i am speaking to is not my father or my wife but my own bad habits

i used to go in for a lot of this screaming at myself though i do not know why
i was stopped at life's gateway age three not to come in except by remote control
then one day i turned around and found myself in my own body standing up

how did this happen you wonder and of course no one can say but i have a guess
i built this teddy monster parent with some strong features of my real parents
it sometimes looks like them but has more of a decomposing cubist edgy sharpness

one day i said jesus christ can't we replace this smell with something healthy
i put aside this first mask of things and let examination light blind me

41.9–41.10

41.10

when they come down to the wavelet waters in the morning you can smell petroleum
stoves lamps cars outboard motors whiten the lake with texas chemical perfumes
into the water imagination they plow noisily returning fishless

when she said that you were hungry how could you know which way to reply
all around the shore campfires dramatize issues of subordination within families
traffic jams fireworks scenes of transformation celebrate american summer

in italy we had burning rosemary infused fat of spitted suckling smoke to smell
now we winter with georgia cousins in panama city florida on a big cruiser
i was reading the paper when i heard the propeller groan on a big bloody fish

machine oil droplets intensify blue pacific haze san diego bay sunrise
i have a mind to do something about this foolishness
clean the air clean the air till it's healthy everywhere

we now are planning to issue a cd on that theme and with that title
the prize for this task should you choose to complete it is a house in the hills

41.11

allora they sing sei un mito perchè o yes you're the great pretender
in the final quarter hour of the millennium all revelations stop
a sharper silence falls around the himalayan lodge looking out at the stars

what is that sound i can't hear in the sky the children call out from the dark
the blade of the timekeeper whispering by the call of the dove to the ark
what is the message i feel on my hand the monk has a power of light

the mystery queen impassive and bland drinks deep of the water of night
an emptier emptiness opens inside while the blaze of confusion grows strong
nothing can climax or ever subside except as a war or a song

i let my potassium chloride crystals fall through my fingers into the acid
it can be better to open the windows at midnight if you are afraid
hire musicians to suffer for you whenever you possibly can i read

every day i had to put on my shiny yellow raincoat and ride up the escalator
we were preparing to sail over the barrier into the new millennium

41.11–41.12

41.12

this is the beginning of the story of the immortal gods my grandparents
out of the ocean they came wearing rags with saints in their pockets
when my grandfather opened his hand a bird flew out singing torna a surriento

when my grandmother opened her hand flour flew out snowing on the ravioli dough
they were the god mars and the goddess italia at the ends of their table speaking italian
the wind came through the windows thick with pollen in thick hot afternoon waves

the nightmare train whistle echoed on the polished granite faces of headstones
wet cemetery grass thirstily drank the howling midnight echoes as they fell
slimy puddle shaped creatures evaporated under intensifying reflected light

it was raining from the height of laurel hill and the rain came out of the trees
it was screaming from the slate steeple on thompson hill
the couch smelled of the dog's urine the baby's urine and of something else

the immortal gods turned in their sleep to the sounds of saxophone and trumpet
the baby trying to sleep lying on a wooden stool looked into the dog's big eyes

42. when italians approach an irish horizon in the mind they acquire new outline

42.1

making things terrible became a specialty of mine on saturday mornings
i would close myself off in the living dining room and listen to records
heights of fantasy included father crashing in shouting o my god

what are you doing in here draped in curtains he didn't call me a king or a chief
i was trying to unthink the whole world around me and replace it
my grandfather believed in italy and my father believed in america

their contest twisted me into contortions around my own core
every day i escaped to movieland on our big empty lots hill hollywood set
joey was cochise and i was geronimo and frankie was the blue cavalry captain

a big stone was for fires and another black glistening mica was the shiprock
standing on it we announced our discoveries as we sailed into tropical bays
in my japanese fighter i roared down the flat shiprock aircraft carrier strip

is there refuge anywhere in the world you asked
you threw a rock and hit cochise

41.2–42.2

42.2

i decided to rewrite the world from the native point of view when i was three
age two i had learned from my grandfather the dante ambition
invent a language for italians in america and write an epic in that language

the summer i was three we went to beach lake pennsylvania indian burial grounds
between the graves a spring made a little flow of water we knelt to drink
american soldiers had shot the lenni lenape as now they obliterated mussolini

my grandfather the wounded god staggered through the rooms holding his crotch
i was cochise on a horse picking its way up a hill with loose rocks rolling down
it wasn't americans who did it he said it was italians

in the lots the squaw tied the tent flap down so no one would come in on us
dark brown light fell on the silky pelts of her bed as she rose to caress me
i am dreaming of you whenever you are dreaming of me she said

through her long black braid i breathed her teaching in the deerskin teepee
maybe it isn't too late after all because i wanted to go on and not give up

42.3

an uncomfortable silence that landed on me refused to budge
what can ail thee knight at arms she hummed she hummed hummed she
she looked like a devil i saw in a cold sweat vomiting

her shadows flowered the corners and darkened my sense of the next morning
i was holding onto the walls as i worked my way out of the building
every sentence possibly connects billions of compromised networks

ever since our imaginary native wedding on the mountaintop i was suffering
would bigfoot want to see you shaking your ass under the bright mountaintop sky
i thought so but after i did it switches began whining down in my mind

what happened out there the cleanup crews shouted from deep in his intestines
now i was seeking my way down the second house stairs of the old law tenement
it's a good thing i have a car to get out of here with i said to myself

anything can happen i used to think so it may be that things will get worse
when i saw her the next day she was prettier than ever

42.3–42.4

42.4

the question is does my body still labor under a curse
it has passed through twenty six years now since that day on the mountaintop
conditions of blood and of urine come with diabetes to afflict me

diabetes a disease of sugar means you take more than your body can digest
your body craves sweetness because it yearns for love it does not let itself have
to have love means to give love and receive it freely

you laid down a bumpy road for love where broken sidewalk slabs jut up at bikes
now you want to learn you think but you are not sure about even that
you think of loving as a set of categories like encyclopedia articles

anything can help good loving even impolite words and sounds but it all depends
we differ with difference in time so the rule is speak to the present difference
even as it disappears it leaves a golden line aflame with satisfaction

we acquired a taste for these elegant fireworks at a theme park in florida
the fall of your enemies will cause rejoicing at your friends' campfire

ellis island

42.5

have i laid a curse upon my own body in the form of a stone heart
around the stone heart i put another stone heart so that i was buried in life
i believed the social system holds us firmly in place at any given point

entering the social system needs a stone heart i thought so i can stand it
however take the stone heart away and the system still holds you but differently
now you are one of the fish that swims among old stone hearts seeking other fish

water you do not exactly see holds you as you follow these centers of brilliance
afternoon among smoky sunlight reeds shows colors weaving one another
sometimes you connect but other times you eat tiny creatures that seek your mouth

i left a casket full of old money old jewelry old boots next to my stone heart
as i imagined it we would have a large ceremony of departure but then i forgot
a red and yellow gourami with a black stripe down her spine caught my attention

i know it's along here somewhere but the moss waves in rows so you can't tell
the next time we come down this way i definitely am going to find it

42.5–42.6

42.6

when you began to develop an intellectual style they gave you a command
you can know how to lead because you know where to go they said
treat your crew kindly and let them tell you their troubles

a leader who explores the riches of the human heart does not grasp at glory
glory comes to him and places a hand in the leader's hand and says take hold
well not exactly it's more that he dangles his hand till someone clasps it firmly

in his heart the leader shares his pain and his treasures with those of his heart
and sometimes another suit will be trumps either diamonds clubs or spades
to lead well with diamonds requires a mathematical head

who use clubs play a quick game and who spades a methodical
heart and diamond club and spade that's the way the world is made
spade and diamond club and heart every method plays its part

drive to dallas all alone talking on the telephone
bathing lead them from the tub heart and diamond spade and club

42.7

my italy belongs to the industrious family of paper italies
it has a capital in columbus for veneration a capital for poetry in new york
it has two money capitals palm springs and palm beach

these capitals also shadow other capitals in earth italy
some people call earth italy another paper italy like argentina or constantinople
but paper italy nonetheless includes earth italy

you say earth includes paper and the sources of paper
earth includes ideas and the fields where we form ideas and us that form them
paper italy meets and touches earth italy the same way we form earth into paper

paper italy's passion for recovered time can find satisfaction in earth italy
some people say you cannot recover time but you can
large stone abutments of time pierce the mouth of earth italy

tourists come home to paper italy leading time on strong ropes like elephants
it fills up with recovered time so in places you can't tell it from earth italy

42.7–42.8

42.8

in paper italy we do not expect anyone to know we are paper italians
how thin and brittle is paper people say as if to erase their love of smells
every book stirs nervous systems making electricity flow as desire and thought

paper means we made it from sweet smelling trunks we cut down still wet with life
we use it to make packages and to send things and to organize sending of messages
absorbent paper removes unwanted secretions leaving skin healthy clean and dry

our plans exist on paper and debating them on paper we resolve debates on paper
every morning we make a new paper italy putting coffee in the paper filter
thus we move ships from brazil to europe full of lumber and beans

other paper italies we make in the evening with oil we pour from a freighter
boot and shoe italies descend to our carpets from great steel cranes in bayonne
as long as some of the money ends in the hands of the priests we have no trouble

our paper pope appeals to the pale rider singing let my people live
he scares away plague giving very good value for what he costs in cash and grief

42.9

one paper italy i had a lot of trouble with because it kept coming back to life
in this paper italy they castrated benito mussolini and hung him upside down
next to him they hung his mistress clara petacci and violated her body as well

i saw these pictures in the american magazines at the barber shop
mussolini's mutilation still smells to me like vitalis hair oil
later on i grew morbidly reluctant to take haircuts

my fascist grandfather refused to recognize me with long hair however
i cut my hair the day before i saw him for the last time
he loved me when i was small and throughout my youth

he had not been able to love his own stepsons but treated them violently
they all stayed together on the principle that they preferred hell to the street
and they loved their mother despite the man that she made them put up with

because he loved me i suffered for his pain even hating what mussolini had done
finally knowing this for a paper italy too i folded it and put it away on a shelf

42.9–42.10

42.10

things people used to know they will need to learn again so keep this book
herein i have rwritten down old clues i have received
call me fortune cookie machine

moving into a large building visit all passages you can open as well as secret ones
in planning a marriage calculate the weight of the roof when it is heavy with snow
every twenty years reconsider all the laws and customs

i sat on the tombstones of calvary cemetery and the wind taught me old sayings
under factory windows i saw my classmate's father drunk at nine in the morning
women with husbands get fat or athletic but the others grow pale and thin

marie told roger's candy store counter coffee smokers tom gave her the black eye
we did not speak to colleen whose father had the bar next to nolan's funeral home
joanne's father belonged to the union so he let her go out with union italians

he didn't like it but the italians didn't like it either so they were even
these irish italian marriages have produced strange amazing new understandings

42.11

they run noisy machines all night in the italians factory
making italians requires bunting music paper brass spurs straw hats
moustache combs high wheeled lancia touring cars balconies spilling oleander

movie theaters collanders steaming pasta black shirts running with benito
a tribe of italians two hundred fifty six were stamping the tarantella together
làlalàla làlalà làlalàlalalalalalà lalalalàla lalalalàla lalala làlala làlala là

the irish argue a case strenuously as if they mean to end the question for good
in slushy march they march shilellaghs and bagpipes down millionaire fifth avenue
red faced they throw glass mugs at mirrors shards on the floor meaning good party

father devlin drinks his face redder than pentecost and keels over on the altar
irish politics is a cargo cult using bluster high horses and a british accent
thus do kennedys melt into gangster police lawford crashlanding attorney generals

europe rubs against africa bringing forth tarantella italy mountains in the sea
english north versus south struggles triangulate policeman ireland sailing west

42.11–42.12

42.12

firehouse irishmen cook ziti alla siciliana under the charm of male bonding
world elliptical shadows by michelangelo exaggerate parabolas across the piazza
charles prince of wales makes separate trips to each of italy's twenty regions

when the mothers speak irish the children recognize the memory of suffering
italians suffer musically ritually magically and hysterically the opera of life
irish fathers look for the uncluttered horizon and the hand of the black and tan

these are the queens and kings county irish italian comedy characters i know best
queens boulevard and kings highway root these boroughs to the british crown
irish types and italian types had long preexistences on the london stage

american newspapers remade us as vaudeville immigrant marx brother jester cities
then many old cultural translation formulae we acquired began to breed new ones
when italians approach an irish horizon in the mind they strike a new profile

irish in italian families find food rituals differently powerful from their own
political planets revolving proliferate before the american irish italian child

43. i wrote a story of a scholar poet who changed his life by writing a story

43.1

i was reading the map of possible consequences
in and out of my pocket it had grown creased at points illegible
most of the intersections that concerned me lay eradicated in those folds

what would it matter even if you could read them
a map is only how the thing looked when they took its picture
you change things by what you do and how you see

you think so anyway and that's only partly a delusion
events and consequences scrape at each other's heels
some of them have your name on the back but others are blank

age and weather and new people appear at the end of the walk
you designed the highway but they mixed the wrong amount of lime
under the warm relentless rain pieces broke off and slid down the embankment

in the archive old signatures disappeared after the river rose
in the ocean you cannot even find the river but you can look for me

43.1–43.2

43.2

i gave you a cup of coffee for a piccolo
the piccolo was good enough to buy a house
the house required work for which i gave some lessons

the work improved the house so much i sold it for a fleet of trucks
the trucks were in argentina so i did not need to smell them
instead i sold half the fleet for a café bar in the alps

while i was seeking a buyer the other half of the fleet disappeared
i filed a claim with the insurers in zurich
now my claim and my bar were in the same country

nonetheless everything else that mattered to me was in new york
the claim went at ten cents on the dollar and the bar at half the assessed value
all i could think about was whether to take the dog to the groomer

i gave the groomer one percent of the bar yielding eight per cent per annum
it's not a lot but it covers the hair and nails

43.3

i only wanted to say i loved him in spite of everything
and i wanted to tell carole this too
i wanted them all to know that they didn't need to be so angry at me

i don't know how that happened
i was too young when it started and by the time i figured it out i was grown up
and by that time i guess i was truly unbearable anyway

nothing special about that because a young man is supposed to be an outsider
on the streetcorners of long island city we stood in motorcycle jackets
we dressed our hair with liberal pomades of vaseline and girls kissed us

the very things that made my family simmer led me to victory in examination rooms
we filed our teeth and inserted diamonds in our nails for turning textbook pages
the bodies of slain competitors lay along the highways to ithaca and cambridge

pride is like a rock
easier to throw it than to catch

43.3–43.4

43.4

the day i was conceived they had a fight
i told myself that story many times
a thousand ways for every restless night

i said the rosary of family crimes
a bastard rockefeller came to stay
who coined us nickel steel and cardboard dimes

my grandpa filled the house the factory way
machines in cellar workers rent upstairs
their wives do not get rich on piecework pay

but save the bus and subway fares
we lived in lines by salary and size
in smaller bigger houses blocks and squares

my stories told of terrorists and spies
my sadness came from systematic lies

43.5

now i was going to have to learn patience and suffering
i took these things in as body attitude pain memory twitch boredom programs
waiting for buses in a bad mood gave me diabetes

my body scrunched together in a fist of terror when my mother lay wounded dying
resentments from others though mild enough rained as acid on my raw nerve endings
since that time i have been seeking to cure my soul of its hungry sadness

now i have gone back to reconstruct my mother's protection
when i lost her in fact my body tried to change its form
this internalized passion of terror became a hysterical solidification

my body turned to steel leather marble granite porphyry even lapiz lazuli as I slept
living in rome i occasionally felt the intense heat crumble me into heaps of moss
such moments gave some relief but now i have simply abandoned the shell

pains light up the map of the paris subway in strings along lines of force
events occur frequently in a capital and yet the city rests serene

43.5–43.6

43.6

in the kingdom of kindness they love scholar poets
i came here with a palm and a plumed hat seeking a place
after many trials the masters allowed me to share at their table

things change when you find that you no longer have enough money to live one way
make a new plan that will increase income and reduce expense as well
begin by lying on the floor to feel the current flow

and afterwards allow the flow to charge your body warm and red in every cell
i wrote a story of a scholar poet who changed his life by writing a story
at certain writing moments i feel the earth evolving

we used to say the earth didn't know what it was doing and neither did we
now human smells baste our apprehensions in beer
i was so afraid of the earth it almost killed me a thousand times

i have written a poem to the ocean my mother from an island my father
now i open the gates so that the sunlight plays along my walls

43.7

don't worry if people love you in one million different ways
flowers and butterflies speak variously of how the earth generates life
every day of your last moments will teach you another volume of these scriptures

and in these aeons you will discover the immense softness of time
human memory settles luxuriously into time as a cat silkily into a cushion
time expands subsides elides replies to pressure as it licks the pussy's tail

the morning i met the gods of time we were sitting on a terrace in oxfordshire
we smelled willow stroking ducal warm gentle trout abundant lake waters
once you enter this famous english sleepiness no amount of coffee can awaken you

a certain part of me slipped away into eighteenth century pastoral paintings
i understood what it means to sit at home and write poetry to the tree
another part of me actually lives on a rocketship to mars that left in 1976

each epic destiny has its place on one of the hundred sixty eight hour schedules
this television show fills every hour all year so you can always relax with it

43.7–43.8

43.8

now began the giving ceremonies organized on the other side of the ocean
i remembered my combination and once i had the locker open it was all still there
wonderful counselor the mighty god the everlasting father the prince of peace

yes i said these names we call any man who attends to the work of his family
each person is a monarch so it makes sense to say christ died for each alone
you may fail to understand this unless you think about how god means anything

god means as what is greater than all of us in each of us means
the whole of it all as it speaks to us all as we in fact hear things each alone
christ died for your sins because they are the only sins in the world

your sins remember means not only the sins you commit but those you inherit too
so all sins in the world are yours one way or other once you are born into it
we call what helps us christ or mary king or queen of heaven to suggest its power

whatever we do we say aloud earth sky and water have authorized us to do
all with one meet speak come to terms in the ceremonial touching of living

ellis island

43.9

when first i saw the whole of life at once
o wow i thought there must be some mistake
my brother said remember you're a dunce

below the waterfowl the limpid lake
gives hints of where the sweeter fishes swim
he said watch out don't waste another break

i waited for the detailed sky to dim
instead discovered there my constant guide
my cherubim my thrones my seraphim

my brother could not see what would not hide
a faint ellipse surrounded all i saw
a resonance of light from deep inside

they call this light the day they call it awe
they call it text and principle of law

43.10

at this point he first goes to california
dark blue light rolls in as sea clouds the cliffs welcome
the wet air of san francisco brings you microorganisms of asia and the dark ocean

reddish hair ice plants stubble breasts and thighs along high hill country roads
flying across the usa he sees only snow until he descends the sierra nevada
he lands on the rim of a warm pacific where humans learn arts of calm

hot philippine trenches continue to generate fish with lights in their mouths
california desert mountain valley shores belonged to another country not long ago
thanks to napoleon the united states purchased the entire center of the continent

after that it became difficult for mexico because spain no longer helped
the anglo jacksons were pretty soon marching in and taking over spreading west
meanwhile lost sailors light fires from chile to alaska

on the western hemisphere landmass edge he sees eastern world light flicker
his mother dying in new york he sees italy come to life in the berkeley hills

43.11

l'italia senza l'anima said toscanini over san francisco italy without the soul
did he mean without the pope or without certain hopes dreams and ancient feelings
whatever he meant perhaps he had not yet visited the mission at carmel

god's garden said father junipero serra naming his independence from the presidio
the protestant civilization of the californias has not kept this indedpendence
while the spanish perfected agriculture the anglos studied war

along the california coast deep silos maintain crackling armageddon syrup rockets
highways belong to aerodrome police in blimps controlling all traffic
ships of every kind stand armed and patrol the huge empty ocean like a schoolyard

among sea lions barking over rock real estate electronic messages scratch the air
domination is a word that means satellites organize domes of dissemination
usa destruction dominators still haven't understood fray serra's point

meanwhile the gardens continue to grow in watsonville and castroville
domes use money to buy places in the sun but the sun may have other plans

43.11–43.12

43.12

a dome gives the figure of a greedy hand
developers are part but the story is bigger
under the dome of sun water breeds mammalia

as a stone dome ages the scholars soften it
strolling in porticoes they teach the young
scholars sing meditation music under a dome

vines will climb in air weaving igloo domes
great shadow patterns will move streetplans
then will we harvest an excellent coherence

our words will pass through transformations
our transformations will pass through words
every lake will design itself a dome in air

thus will the ocean burn as a lens
and the planet grow us its glass extravagance

44. i have been trying to remember which is my desire and which someone else's

44.1

the victory appears before us in the smile of a buddhist italian blues pope
this person ordains women priests and anoints some bishops and cardinals
as pope he says i live on a plan slightly differing from any you have yet seen

i have chosen to marry he announces and would do it again
the collective of bishops and cardinals meets frequently in his rome
he has invented twelve new arrangements for these meetings

in one they use the large open space in san paolo fuori le mura for a banquet
afterwards they listen to tarantellas in the courtyard
then comes the day long seminar on tarantellas at castelgandolfo

in another version bishops appear in tv panel discussions twentyfour hours a day
people submit questions to the pope and he chooses some for bishops to debate
in his favorite version the pope lives in capri reading books

every day he answers some telephone calls has some meetings writes some letters
in the evenings and mornings his blues and his ragas resound in the courtyard

44.1–44.2

44.2

o the sun is rising behind wherever it is setting now he sings
and behind the place the sun is rising sets the sun
nine other arrangments for governing the church the pope will unfold

first allows him to maintain the papal newspaper on the universal kiosk
in the second he makes it impossible to know anything of the papacy forever
afterwards comes the third when they refabricate the papacy from memory

fourth the pope discovers a book written earlier contradicting the new version
fifth opposing armies kill one another for the pope's blessing
sixth the pope devises a new peace that consists of everyone's changing places

seventh one of the three billion peasants in the world conceals the pope
eighth the pope leads an army into toronto
ninth a band of four musicians includes the pope but never says so

gradually the papacy acquires the status of a fractal glint in every adult person
buddhist blues italians become desired breeding partners throughout the planet

44.3

buddhist blues italians win great wars through perseverance
their music gives them strength other armies only find in sleep
they sit along the vibrating rim of time emitting clouds in lavender strands

their path is to become for an aeon the middle path and for another the kingdom
only prayer allows for the emptiness of things to perform its perfections
it centers us and we swim down the vortex of time in its rush towards tomorrow

these are the ontological institutions who invented our sexual organs from within
no one knows all of their names but the hindu theologians have made a good start
anthropology belongs to confucius as christianity inherits jewish contract law

blues italians use buddhism to show how italian the blues are
italians are half a blue people and half a yellow people
blue people come from the yellow nile yellow people from the blue yalu

italians the green people tumble down half pale yellow half blue brown
oil of olives smoothes the skin draws it out and slips it in

44.3–44.4

44.4

i have been trying to remember which is my desire and which someone else's
teachers taught me put your desire at the service of others
this approach did not produce happiness though it often would ease the cramps

now i wonder which is the snow and which is the slippery marble
i have been the citizen of a well instituted confusion in my head
you don't want this it says but if you leave it you will die

you want that other it admits but if you have it you will die
not only have i believed this in my life but i have acted to make it true
whenever i stepped out of my yoke of self denial i risked destruction

a large force organizes itself in me at such moments you may call the stupid guy
the stupid guy whines moans argues and in general makes me look like a stupid guy
or else the stupid guy decides to get sick and stay home from life

anyway the secret of doing well is to do the thing you want to do
you can settle logistical and social questions better when you have a little satisfaction

ellis island

44.5

i thought that by now i would have this part clear
the water opened up before us as our little boat turned the hill crazy cape
out there lay infinite possibilites but would they do you harm

it turned out that despite appearances clarity had not yet pierced the wide air
although the atmosphere was without fog it contrived to show me nothing at first
a fisherman vibrates waiting as i did except that i was not fishing

no you need a purpose if you go to master indifferent universal walls
purpose cuts a path through the blinding transparent freedom of the flat ocean
for the poet the poem constructs a site of possibilities

when you read a poem you put your own purpose in place of the poem as a purpose
this does not teach you anything about either the poem or your purpose
but it distracts your attention and the poem enters so the purpose grows stronger

the poem and the purpose are two words for the same thing whatever you call it
it knows where to swim when expressing its nature

44.5–44.6

44.6

i have been exploring the ocean floor in my mind
people think that with all this water everything must be totally clean
it certainly helps that most fish have no fingers let alone opposable thumbs

all oceans mental or not are socially constructed of course but at a distance
the pacific and atlantic and indian and arctic and antarctic have social shapes
you may wonder what social forms shape any given bottomscape

consult a panoptic map of the ocean floor with pictures of what lives where
you will find such maps in good textbooks and they will help you think about it
once you learn to recognize localities you will travel more comfortably

the ocean floor of your mind also has places streets hills bridges tunnels
you ride through them on your bicycle at top speed dreaming of girls to marry
judy claire marie and joyce what an excellence of choice

when the lobster returns to the lobster rock he finds lobsters there to love
some returns are really worth the trouble if only to refresh the sense of purpose

44.7

on a cold morning i said now i have flattened myself financially
now i have flattened myself politically and bureaucratically
i have made difficult what was easier

no daily place seems easy to me any more neither the office nor home
this is a theological event for it is a matter of desire
i do not want to do the things i am doing not in the office not at home

the time has come to dispute every decision that takes you the wrong way
does this mean i will spend the best part of my life arguing
does this mean i will not spend the best part of my life bored and angry

punishing myself for my desires i force myself to take more of what i don't want
if i succeed in doing so i will be rewarded with yet more of the same
the time has come to take more of what i do want and less of what i do not

to satisfy desire cleans you out and burns away pains and harms
why am i barking orders at myself

44.7–44.8

44.8

here is something
he kept standing up
the snow was falling and he was standing up

he was standing there watching a car drive away
it was not out of the driveway yet
now it reached the stone pillars and turned

no one ever heard of him
it seemed perfectly sensible to live quietly after a thing like that anyway
disguised as a nobody he became centered in a somebody on whom the world hung

ta ta ta very slowly he said and sang to the grandson in the kitchen
the sun wrote pictures of his mother and father on the shiny linoleum floor
no he would say while he was eating with his head down no no no

after lunch he got up and walked around the kitchen to the window
it was snowing on the river too and he began to cry

44.9

the movie of bad moments threw me into a sort of panic
fear of death blew around my head as i would hear of people dying nearby
a little younger and a little older and yet i love what i do in other moments

i love to write texts perform them play music and publish all these things
dancing i love and making love with a beautiful woman
next thing on my agenda will be make toys and sell them

sell them as prototypes or in the form of a novel about toys
a toy may use defense or consolation as an added attraction
but a toy succeeds when it works as a tool to reconfigure the living space

a magic pad shows you living space differently and you reorganize it with cars
you change its features with video cameras or with feng shui
these things are not only toys but toys belong to the category of tools

when i write i use a toolkit
i am duplicating it and preparing copies for sale

44.9–44.10

44.10

people who might forgive you and people you might forgive are not the same people
i thought i had understood that but had not because things slipped away from me
it was necessary always to keep charging forward and i no longer knew how

i did not want to deal with yet another mountain of debt alone
then we learn it was no mountain it was a tin box full of secrets is all it was
we empty these out every time the box fills up

keep the paper moving means of course read the paper and understand it
you know how to do this well enough to hire attorneys with good prose styles
each such person should receive your calling card

in the course of ordinary conversation one inhabits many roles simultaneously
i am the infant king of pajamas happily arranging shadows on my bed
altar boy oedipus moves a vase on the table while family prince leans on desk

italian tribal chief on the professional road and humanist in at his desk in town
these performances play counterpoint in your conversational mind

44.11

when an actor masters a large repertory of parts each and all enrich one another
a touch of hamlet improves benedick as a touch of jane austen transforms faulkner
authors who died have returned as great performance anthologies

dickens haunts the anglo streets at christmas out emily dickinson's east dormer
popcorn masterpieces saturday at the bliss theater i learned many detective roles
as philip marlowe i later visited the vatican museum to study egyptian frescoes

the vatican frescoes were later in style than the ones on the walls at the bliss
on greenpoint avenue where george washington marched the bliss held head of hill
we entered that pharaonic lobby where now jehovah's witnesses enter

the watchtower society has kept some of these illustrations from the hebrew bible
as philip marlowe i learned that everything is connected to a lot of other things
you never get all of it straight i learned so it is important never to boast

as philip marlowe in the vatican i came to understand that a circus is a circus
but when you make it out of marble the expenditure strikes people dumb

44.11–44.12

44.12

so much dreaming and so much practicing at the screen of plans had i had
and withal too so much the sort of something we forget but then remember
i have spent a universe of traveling at this depth of life where you find me

here i have become like those small and large fish swimming the philippine trench
miles under the water miles under where sunlight stops the small feed the large
the small ones believe in light and the large ones have lights in their throats

in this the deepest part of the ocean we smell the basements of volcanoes
our myths teach that our lights come from the volcanoes that open up down here
we fly out of them as sparks from the intense light of the earth within

the brilliance within melts you back into the refraction of sunlight that you are
other stories say when you find the higher light you rise to it too
these narratives teach us how have died even those that live on hills

some tiny fish eat the luminescent moss that grows on a volcanic lip as it cools
we shine our lights brighter feeling these fish as they race down our throats

45. a man eventually begins to stagger wearing the spirit mask of an ambitious clan

45.1

italian america has fifteen bays corresponding to the mysteries of the rosary
five joyful mysteries annunciation america exists visitation so this is america
nativity our child was born in america circumcision i am an american

finding in the temple america is an italian invention
five sorrowful mysteries agony in the garden what shall i do in america
the scourging at the pillar i carried bricks to make america

the crowning with thorns i took on the guilt of the american empire
the carrying of the cross i began to read and write an american language
the crucifixion we died under an american stone

five glorious mysteries resurrection i became a new italian in america
ascension i became a new american in italia
descent of the holy ghost i learn the italian american language as i write it

assumption of the virgin into heaven italian transforms american
crowning of the virgin in heaven italian american transforms america

45.1–45.2

45.2

italian american language has many irish elements
many italians fell in love with irish in school and after school they married
many irish fell in love with italians who acquired much of the irish music

boston dublin brooklyn dodgers brogue belongs to italian american jimmy durante
another example is frank sinatra who speaks jersey city irish cop
irish american language has many african american elements

bing crosby sings saint louis blues african creole scat bop skiddoo hello ma baby
italian american language has african amercian louis prima strutters ball tongue
has irish american african american as in perry como's sicilianisms

i love to listen to dean martin and count the jewish comedians and irish nuns
he sees them in his voice and they hear him in their wedding dress photos
jesus himself speaks a kind of british african american irish italian american

you hardly ever see him except sideways and almost can't hear him speaking softly
he could be valentino

45.3

my friend anthony valerio has written a book about valentino
he explains how valentino captures the minds and bodies of italian americans
but jesus has also entered and behind him came the hypocrite

the italian american hypocrite praises generosity but does not practice it
hypocrisy results from a systematic dysfunction in makeup cleanser
christmas holidays require ritual masks we know but afterwards we wash them off

poor washing hardens skin if our excessive christmases allow mask residue buildup
pores wear stiff plates and the face changes into a firm fix that gradually sags
facial surgery often rejuvenates because it disturbs these systematic stiffnesses

the ancients say wash your body thoroughly and rub away clogged insincerity
other times the problem is some fixative attaching a mask to your body
social cementing arts evolve with humans so these compounds are tried and true

a man eventually begins to stagger wearing the spirit mask of an ambitious clan
new waters our symphonies say new waters new loves and the pleasures of new masks

45.3–45.4

45.4

you are the water and the saxophone i am the daughter and your mind
i am the uncle on the telephone i am the shadow going blind
the piano batters in the first class lounge on the cruise ship

she brings me a drink and i start to sing you don't know what it's like
after that we start writing each other letters to improve mutual understanding
on the telephone she sings you a song about starting to cry at a traffic light

every part of the winter we sit in our rooms dreaming of effective lies
now and then one of them functions and we slip away to the open city
once there we hover in doorways smoking illegal cigarettes

wet northeast wind reminds us that when we become masters we smoke in warm hogans
something always remains secret when we live together and make a home however
home howevers let us call them require expensive secrecy music

i am twilight in your bone i am finish i am die
now you face the world alone never wonder you are why

45.5

i am reborn for the first time an italian waking up every morning as a marchese
a grant to study robert browning in italy stumbled me into a bourgeois paradise
a noble family rented me a house frequented by browning henry james eleanora duse

counts duchesses princes queens pashas maharanis earls countesses ride the hills
dorsal cypress fins twist down the dolphin crests of deep baroque ravines
at the foot of a mountain the sculptor canova built himself a pantheon for a tomb

these are the pacified provinces where the very rich still have the whip hand
habsburg caution thoroughly soaks their sceptical curiosity about social progress
how very interesting you came from the working class in the united states

what let me in there was not the working class but a good american education
we continue exporting the american revolution to the europe we came from
scholar grandchildren of immigrants exhibit an expensively acquired curosity

grandchildren who remained behind have stayed in place and they envy our leisure
they use free time productively but we study talk write and read as nobles do

45.6

we lived at the corner of via roberto browning and via pietro bembo
browning invented the nineteenth century orientalist brown italian subaltern
bembo invented the sixteenth century high italian literary perfectionist

the house itself they call the villa la mura because it is part of the city wall
the medieval city wall is the figure for the systematics of italian literature
inside the wall la mura looked out on its hundreds of acres of meadow and garden

outside up the narrow hill street tourist workers labor up the hot sunday stroll
inside the italian language wall bembo discusses editions with lord david cecil
those who learn this language from early childhood possess the dialect of command

my serious beginnings in literary italian came to life in asolo
the dialect of command in american english gave me access to this embattled spot
i stood on the balcony in the piano nobile of palladio's villa barbaro at maser

in a meadow below a long haired girl ate an apple next to a long haired pony
ah said the soul of my grandfather gazing up at veronese's ceiling fresco

45.7

when a whale begins to fart the microenvironment registers the fact immediately
whales fart long chapters of the absolutely uncensored truth about something
it could be anything because these animals are extremely openminded

whales have no need for property and they travel the whole world thinking
their huge powerful brain bodies reflect the musculature of the ocean itself
as they go the whales think things through sometimes very difficult problems

they study music oratory and philosophy and some practice psychoanalysis
in whale the word for psychoanalysis and the word for farting are the same
to a whale the most important thing is to grow clear in feelings

great whales sing long sentimental epics concerning their affections and desires
some whales grow deeply interested in major currents as objects of meditation
these produce a hum that vibrates at very low frequency falling to the depths

down here i remember i heard a whale sing about the smell of a major exhalation
the earth lets out foul gases and whales explore the monumental seams they leave

45.7–45.8

45.8

in our third roman month we became irretrievably roman ourselves
ostia antica villa adriana via appia antica and the cellar of hadrian's tomb
i carried three year old victoria up the ninety five degree saint peter's dome

eight year old robert stood on the colosseum wall to pose for the camera
in santa maria maggiore he went to confession
we explored the countryside and the small cities of lazio

in great fireplace country restaurants they spitted goats and hogs
my inherited resentments afflicted many days as did the traffico romano
a boy and his father died in an accident on the festa dei morti 2 novembre

after that we bought a bmw because it was safer than their little fiat 500
a truck sliced their car in half on the way back from visiting grandparent graves
they had gone to rieti where the father was from and died on the via salaria

the boy was in my son's third grade class
i wonder how many men and boys have died along the via salaria

ellis island

45.9

a soul in torment approaches the altar of christmas cold romano
tall white marble walls cornice and acroterium shadow a flickering eternal flame
carries bags of figures from the stalls in on icy paving stones in piazza navona

all this seems so familiar to me he says but the whole country is behind glass
every forkful of fettucine wears quotations marks in his mouth
flies to new york returns five days later finds his daughter speaking italian

i still miss the point about priests are all of them queer is that it
and the italy we had imagined more resembled old new england than anything else
nobody ever sat back after a meal to make music except me the glee club baritone

i brought an electronic piano and sang protestant hymns in neapolitan salotti
delta blues sounded right on the meadows of limatola along the volturno
they play drums for volturnus the latin name for africus the sahara wind

hannibal stopped there and garibaldi so it is the african river of southern italy
we hunted fish fossils on a hilltop near there in the heat of new year's eve

45.10

i needed to free myself from chains of hatred
i hated my parents my sisters my wife and my children
friends and colleagues collaborators and competitors i hated too

i battled my hatred with a large edifice of generosity
many pennies i earned went for big family educations vacations shrinks
i made a career of promoting other people's work

nonetheless i had no generosity in my soul and i failed at this effort
i put others high on my list because i didn't want them there at all
but in my heart i knew you cannot give what you have not received

hatred does less harm they say than hypocrisy but i practiced hypocrisy too
max beerbohm's happy hypocrite changed himself by living up to a saint's mask
i did not wear a saint's mask but the mask of a husband and father and good guy

i lived this mask as an unfair chore all the time wishing myself elsewhere
ordinary responsibility left me naked to my own incompetence as i called it

45.11

in other words the pieces we are removing are only parts of masks
you have been competent enough to stay in business despite all this negativity
a healthy attitude ought to take you a lot farther a lot faster by now

when we begin to get rid of unwanted mental furniture our lives begin again
hatred sculptures weigh heavily upon the soft lawn and sink into tilt
clean out the yard and stop living like a hermit in the attic

suppose i like it here suppose it works for me
all right then stay there and enjoy it
other people become ordinary nuisances

why must you fear them so much you can't help hating them
i made a camp under one of the big mask fragments
but when people grew angry at me i didn't know what to do with it

i looked for reassurance from people who expected it from me
those i hoped would reassure me had not done so and now where would i find it

45.11–45.12

45.12

badly my clan judged my family my tribe judged my clan my nation judged my tribe
my sunnyside clan said my family did badly because i did badly at the head of it
my north queens tribe esteemed my clan but envied and minimized it badly

my italian american nation did not find my north queens tribe interesting
the world thought poorly yes badly of my italian american nation
i lived all these social judgments teeming with pain given and pain received

these and many other transacted judgments entered my every intimate task
the price of living inside a mask was to imagine the whole world enemy territory
removing the mask means removing resentments

to deal about important things you must admit your feelings
transforming your feelings means looking elsewhere
look at what you like and be glad you can see it

once you learn to replace them with gratitude even deeply toxic feelings blow off
the most splendid perfumes often have names that suggest illicit pleasures

46. the setting sun lights up our transatlantic clan spread out across a great log

46.1

writing immortalizes us because we see a person ten thousand years later reading
you communicate with that reader and with yet more distant readers by writing
i don't care whether they get it all wrong you say and i know how you feel

but i think if i can explain it to one of them maybe i can understand it myself
a tiny misspelling can perpetuate confusion for a million years
how can anyone dare to write at all under such circumstances

this is why we invented quotation marks and parentheses
these marks make it clear that we are simply drawing diagrams of echoes
the words we scratch on pages faintly suggest things we remember hearing

sometimes we said memorable things ourselves and sometimes other people said them
lawyers say it is very important to know who said it but we say who is who anyway
my first thing to say is i wish you and i had both been born better people

half the italians the oldest nation in europe went out into the world
they prepared the stage for the opera of the new millennium

46.1–46.2

46.2

when the nèw millennium arises and the old millennium goes down
you wànt the side that civilizes on the ruling side of town
so did the new italian americans sing in the election of the millennium

the directories of the millennium will fix for a long time the world's ruling class
families will use what they were at the millennium as an historical benchmark
how long will the memory matter you ask and of course that is another question

if there is an italian american party it campaigns on the civilization party platform
singing come to the restaurant learn to drink the right wine with the right dish
after dinner they will croon we invented the fork and the political scientists

vote the italian american party and bring style back to washington
no one can vogue the jefferson palladiums the way italians can
these american national opera houses come from the italian tourist board calendar

pompous washington porticoes on capitol hill are postcards of medieval rome
edgar allan poe stoned paints canal port new york as a dark colonial venice

46.3

italians always do well at the beginning of a world millennium
in periods of uncertainty the authority of style can seem self evident
for europeans italians mean the beginning while in the east we mean sunset

in both cases we are an extreme and people notice extremes
as a double extreme we can be unusually interesting
in italian expressive art east and west speak loudly towards one another

the messages mostly miss their targets and begin their long global peregrinations
some letters take centuries to arrive at their destinations
the intensity and ferocity of east west dialogics gives italian letters style

now as the millennium has begun to roll we think of horace and octavian
we remember ovid in dalmatia and tiberius amusing himself in capri
streets in rome are still known for armor they sent to jerusalem a thousand years later

those millennium crusades lasted centuries and entered a new chapter in 1492
the letters of columbus and vespucci are still continuing to arrive today

46.3–46.4

46.4

now we sink into the deep heat that baked our ancestors into forms
when i return from italy i understand i will eventually acquire a bronze profile
they will coin this journey because in it i coined a darkness of return

on the highlands surrounded by peaks at matese i saw herds of buffalo wandering
wandering carbonari a charcoal burning tribe had built shanties and mounds
fifty foot diameter fifteen foot high underbrush heap smoulders covered with sand

each mound burns a month so there are three one building one burning one unbuilding
plastic tablecloths covering plywood form the walls of the portable homes
the charcoal colors carbonari bodies black

nationalist revolutionaries called themselves carbonari and some wore blackface
my cousins spitted a goat and shared penne all'arrabbiata at the side of a stream
my daughter called out fratello mio for her brother to join the family photo

the setting sun lights up our transatlantic clan spread out across a great log
the carbonari have huge power cables running washing machines televisions pcs

46.5

the next thing was the women washing the clothes in the fountain as of old
plenty of people do not have much money but they need clean clothes anyway
the old social arrangements live even in how people lament their disappearance

architecture assures the continuous roman moulding of tribal populations
agglomerations large enough but not too large for glandular coagulation shout
the barrel vault returns their collective voice to them as the voice of god

thus the womb oven of holy mother sunday mass emits tribal loaves of people
italian homogeneity of style amounts to a collective masterpiece
from taormina to the gran ticino the leather sofa whispers to the glass table

in the alfa we inspect one another's clothes for heraldry of fashion
gucci pucci zegna armani as well as our formidably religious approach to food
this is a prison that keeps all of its locks oiled and all of their keys on file

for thousands of years in the face of brutal poverty italians celebrated christ
san francesco taught them to taste and know the sweetness in every breath of life

46.5–46.6

46.6

when i returned to the united states i had read goethe and knew i had changed
goethe in italy became monumental and i had at least assumed a firm outline
no longer would i wear the mask of the englishman in italy

now i would act the italian in the english speaking empire
from this time forward we spoke no longer of masquerade but of action
in italy i had sketched the history of a revolution that was yet to take place

the first step leaving italy i had now taken as my grandfather before me
i might have stayed but i chose instead to make america and make a revolution
the second step would be to choose italian makings for america

which italian things would america find useful in the coming days i asked myself
the third step would be to monumentalize or at least to commodify those things
this third step would include writing the poems i had been dreaming of

they would include first to discover how to publish astoria
this book gave a history in advance of the entire revolution i intended to make

46.7

i brought home la storia della letteratura italiana by alberto asor rosa
at the opening of every chapter he treats i gruppi intellettuali
intellectual groups make a literary history i thought and started looking for one

i found tom belmonte helen barolini fred gardaphé diana cavallo peter carravetta
carol bonomo paolo giordano gloria salerno anthony tamburri theresa aiello gerber
emelise aleandri joseph papaleo vinnie marie d'ambrosio tony mancini geri de luca

i take those names off one list from right after i came back
the clearest point was that we needed intellectuals who were funded as such
they needed to get professoriates and spend many years thinking things over

at this stage of the game we started coming together like tribal chieftains
we need to make a great nation we said to one another
fred anthony paolo published from the margin writings in italiana americana

in every group each has the responsibility to elaborate an individual figure
as a writer i began to construct a pulpit as if i were building a brick porch

46.7–46.8

46.8

all these people treated me with astonishing generosity when i spoke
i said italian american literature now possessed the required financial basis
now we had begun to conquer educational positions we could establish a literature

these american universities work very well if you are willing to give them time
they have machinery for the diffusion of literary work
i opened a seminar room in the italian american experience

it had been filled to the ceiling with volleyballs that rolled into the hall
all right i said let me try another room
it is eight years since that time and i have tried thousands of rooms

i teach the need for an italian resonance in the united states of america
not only the italian americans need it but all the americans
the italians are the actors for whom the stage set of america was designed

they best know and remember the processions and feasts that glorify a colonnade
playing east to the west and west to the east has put dialogue in their hearts

46.9

i started a band and called it christ and the crusdaders
but i was too busy perfectionating my italian and trying to refocus on new york
my public life brought me into the work of the italian colonizer community there

diplomats professors international engineer bankers hold conferences
what does the future hold for the river of shoes they ask
italy wants to know how high will the tide of wine rise in the next decade

at the long dinner tables heavy with linen the borghesi trade jobs for clients
they discuss children cousins children of cousins wives and in laws of friends
persons wearing expensive watches organize financial campaigns

now she says quickly in here close the door pull the zipper kiss me there
i was too young because my fantasy life continued to distract me during meetings
those who achieve a center of gravity in their lives should have public roles

frivolous people such as myself sit still as a penance for thinking bad thoughts
my new level of rsponsibility took me to a new line of infantile defenses

46.9–46.10

46.10

now we began the campaign of beginnings
i sketched a long row of roman arches along the lines of dominant perspective
here we will put the old and here the very young

this row of splendor pavilions will house many students of law
these vast quadrangles of terraced gables will shelter doctors who cure souls
welcome to lincoln center in the upper west side of manhattan

at fordham university my children studied science on saturday mornings
during the week they went to school in italian at bleecker and leroy streets
in carmine street i remember carrying my infant son to see lights at the feast

each morning i drop them off and have a cappuccino at rocco's before driving home
but why are you working for a nation that cannot express its gratitude to you
i think of this as time i am investing as one does to produce wine and olives

i industriously weave italian things into my life because they keep me strong
i am roaring down the river of shoes and the rapids of silk ties

46.11

never you mind i cried out as the plaza began to open up geometrically
octagon octagon we grew waxy with eight sided cells they screamed
don't forget me as you make the empire flourish boys and girls together

every letter that came in i can hardly remember anymore
i devoted many days to lying in a pit of ashes practicing for eternal damnation
these monkeys must sleep on wet grass every night or they will never mate he said

many squishing sounds come into play now but we don't know what we are afraid of
what used to be a high savannah has sunken under this winter's wild tides
dog dog the doctor's dick ding dong forget me quick

i worried about leaving big enough tips while my children saw me as a monster
should they have this or have that but they wanted more control
meanwhile i had power authority and rank and scarcely an idea of what it was for

i began making energetic mistakes that have produced some results even for me
at the same time the line of my major argument lay before me like a road

46.11–46.12

46.12

revise the entire plan and present it to the world
every time you do this someone else seems to swallow hard
you know that this may be an effect not only of youth but of thought as well

i do not want to march in an army but i do not choose to stay home
all right i say to tell the story means to live the story as well
i begin to try to change things and make history move differently

i join a group that plans to promote a phd in italian for the city university
they elect me leader and i start trying to lead
soon i am writing documents by the dozen and losing friends on a daily basis

the inertia i am trying to move gazes at me blandly
it wants to be loved but i don't know how to love it
indeed i am carrying a burden of hatred i have suffered

family hatred sinks its root into me like a wisdom tooth
every step forward the pain makes me cry out

47. when i began returning to my body i found its parts all still in working order

47.1

formerly magnificent banners now hang rotting off the ends of tree limbs
we know a lot about baroque disillusion architecture experiments
for centuries people have often built with broken pieces to get these effects

one thing that surprises us is how optimistic we are likely to get anyway
some enterprising party givers will always decorate ruins and have atmosphere
most people still prefer the proper sort of salon with fluted white pilasters

look she said i am totally at the end of my tether i don't care how you do it
just get it right for once she pleaded as the orchestra piped up a lively foxtrot
guests began arriving for the dance but many of them were weeping

a sad fog striated with expensive perfume drugs and incense filled the room
look i said nothing will ever come of it but let's give it a try
we need to be strong in order to go on but our strength does not come from us

strength flows through things easily when you respect their logic
your desire to write a universal history every minute is a plain symptom of anxiety

47.1–47.2

47.2

i have been remembering the great vomit of my youth
1969 we had come home to avenue a from the stones madison square garden concert
she had been nineteen jean seberg lookalike i said hello to on eighth street

i twenty eight and we had gone home to my big apartment in university heights
she had been around and once married by a navajo priest at a denver lovein
her father was a photographer of models while she lived with her baglady mother

she had made herself intensely desirable i thought hopelessly seeking father
we had made love one day wearing navajo beads on the top of a hill at a commune
afterwards i had gotten very sick and felt the gods of place had stabbed my body

did her navajo ceremony husband's god or some other husband's god stab me
i had just broken off a long guilt heavy affair with a married woman
guilt i could not face and so i wondered had i sent it ahead to meet me in the back

now it was november and i was throwing up empty in her tiny back building toilet
she was a drugged nineteen year old devil and i was in hell

47.3

the eternal punishment style of interior decoration includes a lot of shouting
ixion revolves on a fiery wheel because once he slept with the wife of zeus
sisyphus rolls a boulder up the hill and almost gets it there when down it rolls

large screen color television has made the maintenance of personal hells easier
the internet has lowered the cost of personalized operations and that pleases stockholders
national and international hell systems managers teleconference daily worldwide

every woman i loved would begin to broadcast similar hell management bulletins
at a certain point i lay down and accepted my card in the hell union
yes you will marry be a good citizen professor taxpayer father husband

eventually people will think of you as zeus flinger of fiery bolts
in fact you prometheus will suffer daily for the fire of your own desire
in another refinement of pain people will mistake you for your own worst enemy

all this started to change when i began studying the philosophy of set design
now i recognized that every angle of vision is a shrine to something

47.3–47.4

47.4

yes i know i am projecting it but how can i avoid that
the first thing to do is examine the holograms
catalogue the holy places you encounter going around your daily life

i live in a neighborhood that considers itself sacred to the messiah yet to come
at my college the library glass walls and tower declare the enlightenment
using spray snow on our stormdoor our son has written the words charles dickens

a house of writers dumas et fils viscusi and children is a shrine of writers
thousands of books my sister linda says there should be a velvet rope
avoiding malocchio i have constructed shrines of spiritual evacuation

i chose as my study a room with a closet that has a hinged window facing north
i open it north and blow spirits into the wind and so i stay healthy in hell
where do you go for a parole from a self imposed sentence

to accomplish this end find or build one of these chapels
human life plays best on an appropriate set

ellis island

47.5

i have decided to lay a perimeter of books around me twice
book book cozy nook file file half a mile
records music pictures cameras slides radios tapes stereos lamps cars

electric piano and screen printer computer wires all emerge from surge protectors
on this set i rehearse my usual public opera i call genius at work in monkey suit
on my wooden table i act the chancellor of my exchequer a royal function

real estate means the king's estate and all i have belongs to the king
i have yet to find out who the king is but i hold it all as his steward
they tell me that in my body a king has lived all these many years

i now turn myself over to dramatic kingship with every paying of bills
i was trained to treat the spending of money as a tragic penance
then come boxes of projects as large as liners freighters and ocean going tugs

my three room study floor resembles new york harbor in 1951 full of water traffic
they mean not really king so much as monarch or one ruler that fits the body

47.5–47.6

47.6

now we have begun to concentrate upon our purposes the doubts are loitering at the door
some are wearing purple sleeves and others orange lipstick
these phantasms just as quickly subside into the black bay of meditation

when i began returning to my body i found its parts all still in working order
some functioned at impaired degrees of sharpness but most were doing well enough
a marked quickness of movement may betray systematic impatience but no one minds

at this moment the child enters the man and the man receives the child
i will give my strength freely to what i do now because i have returned to myself
i feel on the inside of my body for wounds and for scars

some places reflect moments of pain and others have found clear pleasures
my youth has entered my own age returning as king to kingdom
the first thing i recovered of the old newness was the smell of the wash

many smells coming back follow shapes of actual body parts moving
flowers that bloom in the spring tralà he sang hiding under the couch cushions

47.7

now comes the other child singing the old song i am you and you are me
this time you can say no you are another child becoming a man but i am me
i have brought my child and man together in thought and they resonate

but how do you speak to that other child becoming a man when he has hurt you
you can hardly say much but simply let your feelings be known and move on
he may be so engrossed in his own sense of grievance that he sees nothing else

when the weather is lousy make sure your family has warm clothes and shelter
now that we see the ritual we can examine it as part of a stage set
the child says yes the computer you just bought me i left at the buddhist temple

i left all my books there without thinking oh well
the stage set is the kitchen where you are heating him a late supper eleven pm
was he really at the buddhist temple and will he ever see any of that stuff again

only tomorrow will tell but meanwhile what is the name of this opera
i am your torment i am your grief as long as you love me you'll have no relief

47.7–47.8

47.8

now i am ready for the total immersion course in the body
i take down the joy of sex planning to read it or at least study the pictures
everywhere i look people might scare me if i let them but i will not not again

in removing the armor i moved about half an inch forward in my body
it is as if i had held back from the surface and hadn't let sensations reach me
excess had terrified me and left me in fear of my life

i had tried to overcome my hesitations by making women my defenses
this is what i had learned to do as a boy but it didn't work so well for a man
i did not understand this however and blamed my problems on sex and the body

the body did not speak the way another person would have spoken
so i blamed my body for my problems with women which had to do with my parents
but in fact my body had served me beautifully and continued to do so

now i am curing my attitude and curing my body as well
it seems only reasonable to try to make up for years of bum raps

ellis island

47.9

sister stephanus used to beat the new public school transfer boys every morning
she called transfer girl virginia a slut for wearing a sleeveless blouse on a hot day
in the seventh grade everyone wants to look down an open armhole said sister

the principal sister justa came in and made virginia stand up and said look at the slut
there were fifty six seventh graders that hot september including six transfers
i had come from public school 80 while the other five had come from ps 76

all those sisters of saint joseph believed public school transfers must be inferior
josephite trained children behaved better they said and did better work
every ninety-nine or hundred i got on a test blasphemed against this boast

sister stephanus held my tie and slapped me till my cheeks were raw
virginia learned to cover her arms and i learned to retreat back behind my body
at lunchtime the lithuanian gang beat me up and pantsed me

so i helped big ray sanchez with homework in return for schoolyard protection
when i had to face the nuns my own body became big raymond and i hid behind it

47.10

the communists had put sharp things under father c's fingernails in lithuania
we saw him in life magazine testifying before the senate with a bag over his head
he was the moderator of the altar boys when i joined at age nine

he took us on a trip every year and at twelve i became master of the altar boys
a new irish priest came in and dethroned me for a tall irish basketball player
the priest drank and hit me with his walking stick calling me dago and darkie

i would have left immediately but i liked the church for its buildings and rites
god and the other world filled my imagination as i knelt before the altar
mary the mother of god reached out with silent compassion filling me with hope

and her miracle happened the 20th of february 1954 when i took the regis test
if you conquered you got a free jesuit educatuon on 84th street and park avenue
regis high school had a classical palace a beaux arts theatre and a marble chapel

this is for me i thought climbing up the heavy slate steps to the third floor
we wrote an iq test and an essay on the meaning of the marian year and i got in

47.11

regis stood atop the new york roman catholic male pyramid of school distinction
each catholic school sent five eighth grade boys with the highest marks to test
that made two thousand boys from greater new york and regis took a hundred eighty

everyone was smart and most were poor ambitious healthy and willing
they competed for grades and they competed for mastery at the lunch table
sister alice patricia approached me at eighth grade graduation

you got into regis she said and i smiled
no one from their school had ever gotten in before and i knew that
you didn't deserve it she said and you'll never graduate

regis was famous for throwing people out when they didn't do their work
the sisters never wavered in their original belief that i could not be good
so i went to regis determined to graduate and prove her wrong

i graduated regis and proved her wrong but i kept calling myself unworthy
the nuns helped me hate myself body mind and soul

47.11–47.12

47.12

the woman i married twenty two years later had been a josephite nun herself
we discovered comfort sharing exploits we had had trying to escape the system
but then inevitably i found myself hiding behind my big raymond body again

sometimes i lost weight and got athletic
even then i thought it mattered enormously that i projected force and power
these were not qualities exactly but hard leather extrusions i wore to work

belts buckles norfolk jackets black shoes boots pens cases hats gloves i bore
unbuttoning the cashmere overcoat i slipped my scarf off me and onto a hanger
my children my wife my house surrounded me at all times like a circle of mountains

we find heavy fragments of a colossal buffalo hide mask armed with bronze
parts of my body i have not felt in a long time as pieces come loose i now feel
sometimes the big raymond body was not mine but hers

now that i no longer am using so much heavy armor things are changing
my history includes victories and defeats but mostly undecided battles

48. in this poem i have followed a wide ellipse as a form of self study

48.1

my old idea went through the rituals as forms of salvation
the rituals enact and express sickness finding healing
it took me a long time to discover what i needed to heal in myself

at last i see my sickness was that my body and i did not live together peaceably
inner conflict made me so uncomfortable i kept seeking larger areas of territory
my hunger loped restless as a caged tiger across the front of the classroom

the dilemma slips into the banal but it produces continual dysfunction strings
though not all strings have the names of diseases all of them give discomfort
string strains can constrict vessels while self hatred can cause pain storms

how does one live in one's body out of one's body through one's body
compassion compassion compassion heals others where they live within the self
when the inner others are healed they themselves give less pain

now when pains come i let them pass through like lightning storms
the winds howl but sometimes i see clearly anyway

48.1–48.2

48.2

i looked back at the statue of liberty mostly bones in the snow
people were still climbing icy stairs carrying children on their shoulders
now it was only a scaffolding with bronze drapery fragments a nose and a crown

i remembered it a place where my father would not hurt me
i was so afraid of him the rest of the time partly through my mother's eyes
when i looked out the statue's eyes i was looking through her eyes

i hid in the mother colossus because there my father treated me protectively
he actually carried me on his shoulders i could hardly believe it
now i have taken down the colossus because sheets of thin bronze were not my body

sitting on the ellis island esplanade i lay down a piece of my armor
my students examined it and said where did you get this
they had never seen a piece quite like it so i told them

my story begins in the french renaissance
i am a figment leonardo sent to paris

48.3

in america everyone has an assigned role to play
a black boy wanting to wear a colossus could be bigger thomas and scare people
irish boys in that case chose prizefighters policemen or parish priests

my colossus was the bronze woman
i wore her whenever i liked which confused people because i was a competent boy
imagine a bank president who occasionally does a carmen miranda song at a meeting

people may think he is stoned but he is only putting bananas on his head as armor
altar boy looks up from studying bible greek to ask why do priests wear dresses
gets ninety ninth percentile on college boards but dances with rose in his teeth

i put on the french immortal bronze italian colossal woman
my grandmother can kill you i would say because i saw her order a chicken killed
people do not fool with an italian wearing a murderous grandparent mask

indeed once you put on one of these the usa accepts you as an italian american
it's just as tricky as a bunch of bananas and it does break up a lot of meetings

48.3–48.4

48.4

my uncle patsy's colossus was the desoto he rolled out of the garage every sunday
he polished its fenders as if he were rubbing hair oil into his own black hair
patsy was dark and mostly bald on top but the hair he had gave off a deep blue shine

the desoto was black and rolled on white sidewalls he mended with white shoepolish
he had a dazzling smile and a saxophone and the desoto had a hundred chrome teeth
the car had the grin of a saber tooth tiger

on the hood a silver woman colossus pointed her firm silver breasts at the wind
her hair streamed out behind her in the chrome sunshine as patsy polished her
her arms streamed straight behind her as she gleamed there a statue of the wind

she signified how patsy shot through air in a silver black white colossus desoto
its large red chrome bound tail lights set off the broad brake light bound in chrome
its back was moulded like the neck of a great sea creature black and gleaming

as the desoto rolled down the long shady hill the women screamed with pleasure
when patsy died all the machines on long island stopped for a moment

ellis island

48.5

every italy requires a colossus i happily chirped the family tune
meanwhile in actual italy they were hiding in dungeons
after the fall of mussolini the germans and italians fell out

in my cousins' town covered wells hid men days and weeks
the germans lined up an entire clan of thirteen on a staircase and shot them down
in the nights and mornings american bombers rained down the end of the world

saint benedict founded monte cassino in the sixth century
fourteen centuries monks built this first convento of europe into its greatest
it sat on the brow where latium and the holy see look south into campania felix

it sent wines and manuscripts and a thick philosophical culture all over italy
in the italian system every city was like the organ of a great body
monte cassino worked at the head of the spinal cord of italy

the americans bombed it to a powder
when you visit now it is all rebuilt and there is nothing to do but stand there

48.5-48.6

48.6

what they later did in vietnam the americans had first done in italy
my grandfather cried every night over his cousins and his mother
he used to dream of running guns into italy on a boat like garibaldi

when i removed the great spiked brow of my colossus i cried for italy
the americans destroyed the old italy
today it looks like disneyland

they try hard to polish the seams of the reconstruction but it fools no one
all these so called medieval cities are now stops on an interstate highway system
what used to be railroad hotels in the nineteenth century are now whole provinces

tuscany the veneto lazio campania sicily lombardy liguria are each a tourist zone
regional juntas have the job of producing visitors as a way of promoting exports
if tourists sleep there three nights they will buy the local produce for years after

no matter how far away they live the italian global distribution system reaches them
mussolini dreamed an empire and the postwar made it into a mail order catalogue

48.7

italian doctors specified some cities for liver others heart others nerves
it had to do with the water the altitude and the willingness of the personnel
italy was a country rich in microclimates doctors had studied since antiquity

looking carefully you can see traces of this medical paradise here and there
but mostly the invading machine world armies have destroyed all the old climates
the famous spas still renew you but require much more in the way of nerve tonics

postwar peoples live pharmaceutically including those in what used to be italy
now i have to say i always suspected this slow poisoning would take over
my grandfather said war had killed italy and he was usually right about things

in those days though you didn't talk out loud about how bad you felt for italy
italians had tangled italy up in fascism so it was hard to be italian in the usa
once the dust of fascism cleared italy was lying in heaps needing a new start

the new italy has some charming corners of the old which we all love to visit
when prices rise in a place people content themselves with smaller helpings

48.7–48.8

48.8

in postwar the americans made everything american including the italian people
new italians cut highways through domains that had been untouched for millennia
some old guys still say it is international capital that drives highways

it has finally opened a tunnel under the channel that makes england an island
consuming this border has proven to be an indigestible meal to financiers
but if brokers and ministers fall the chunnel will still flow money a long time

under these conditions italy became the object of intensest magic everywhere
my grandfather placed hands on my head asking me to bear seeds of a new italy
he was actually my step grandfather but he loved the land where ancestors died

these serious people walked the hills and climbed mountains of campania singing
they sang the praises of the mother of jesus till they arrived at the fountain
as they knelt on the stones someone called out that the madonna filled the sun

i saw them seeing this in 1987 and so i said it has lived here anyway alleluia
i later returned with my grandfather's ghost and showed him italy alive again

48.9

in this month i achieved a small victory in the battle for the humanities
my proposed new wolfe institute for the humanities won an endowment grant
now the trouble of maintaining my own personal bronze monument grew too great

in my heart i had begun to give it up when i was sick in 47.11 in february 1989
now i continued the work of defining italian from a more deeply secured position
this far in we no longer need monuments as the mountains are themselves monuments

every crevasse has a name and strategic history on file in military archives
postwar cybernetic map proliferation has made every point infinitely specifiable
we secure the humanities because they capacitate the revival of insurance

every world crisis means a crisis of faith that the humanities can often heal
if a nation tribe clan family or couple is sick the humanities can help heal it
healing these elements the humanities can heal the world

the humanities now teach what we can remember of the arts of human dignity
after hiroshima and nagasaki that isn't much

48.10

nineties nineties now or never nagged the tom toms of forever
it was now january 1990 and i resolved an incipit vita nova
from this moment forward i devoted myself to an epic of self esteem

to begin with total humiliation i started writing what i called a self help novel
the hero is someone with a classical education but a working class soul
his life is in tilt and he can't seem to get it to go as it should

none of the rituals of high international scholarship helps him or heals him
instead all these transatlantic flights set him down amid a permanent confusion
i called it adventures of a codependent later changed to hell a self help novel

humanities mends wounded souls at the end of this catastrophic millennium it says
o humanity you claimed equality with god made yourself a god that destroys you
my novel's hero is a postwar soul for whom every street is a cold war nightmare

after she broke his heart in 18.9 december 10 1960 he imagined an atom bomb fell
only the two survive and he thinks the world well lost in exchange for her

48.11

he started thinking now is the time to assemble my essays on italian america
not that they are really ready but how will they ever get there unless i try
he started to think about applying for a grant to assemble the essays

his self help novel was dealing with his encrusted shit fear of being a writer
every morning he drank a gallon of hot coffee and carted away tons of crap
holy shit he cried before flushing looking down at a turd shaped like the louvre

he was full of culture the way a napoleon is full of custard
it oozed out everywhere leaving unpleasant stains on things but what could he do
fortunately many americans appreciated italian culture better than he did

governarsi italianamente seemed to imply impluvia and we implore thee o jesus
so what was one to do miltonics did no more harm than hair tonics
nonetheless this going to the toilet in armor is awful even with oiled hinges

was he responsible for this accumulation or could he call himself a witness
things began growing wearisome on top of wearisome

48.11–48.12

48.12

now i am an ellis island professor at brookyn college
a professor of ellis island gives examinations concerning migratory themes
such a professor may teach students how to follow a line of migration backwards

sometimes we write catalogues of all the possible ellis island narratives
surveyors who have studied euclid understand triangles circles and squares
all these figures categorize narrative plots as do the great ellipticals

in this poem i have followed a wide ellipse as a form of self study
my desire to become a great writer drove a great two hearted ellipse
my father wanted to be an artist which i reframed as desire to write

i don't want you to have to dirty your hands his heart ordered me thus into orbit
reaching my heart of the ellipse i was afraid to complete the tour
this fear made my return itself elliptical in the sense of incomplete expression

still a journey finds its perfection reaching the goal and embracing its desire
style may enhance interest power and speed but purpose in the end secures arrival

49. i did not want to hang on a cross anymore but slipping off it is not easy

49.1

i wish i could write this poem without killing myself for the privilege
it knocks me down and has done so many times this poetry writing
in april of 1990 i decided to face up to it and applied for a grant

since that time i have been more and more the writer and less and less hidden
now for the most part this has worked out pretty well
a publisher found me and i saw through the publication of my first long poem book

another publisher took astoria and i saw that one through publication too
the work of the grant has proved hard to finish even now five years later
it seemed nearly done as the grant began and it went forward rapidly but stopped

i started to write this poem which is an answer to 4.12 about carrying crosses
carrying 4.12 i went downstairs to share it with someone and slipped and fell
i held myself with the baluster so i didn't really get hurt but did make thunder

all night long i will be able to discuss death with pains in my back and arms
i did not want to hang on a cross anymore but slipping off it is not easy

49.2

i was walking on ocean parkway singing lascatemi cantare con la chitarra in mano
two days later along lac léman lausanne lasciatemi cantare sono l'italiano
i had travelled thirty five hundred miles carrying the same tape in the walkman

i had now given up every theme but one
i cared about italy and i cared about poetry and i was putting them together
it endowed me with a sexual liberation that to this day i scarcely enjoy

a sexual repression punishment chain tripped my legs going down stairs just now
oklahoma tornadoes of agonized terror cross my body after such episodes for days
today is my anniverary of losing jane in 1960 and of finding my poem in 1969

every year december 10 have come many strong things such as my poem which i loved
i thought all of them came in compensation for jane who flirted with my friends
i had crucified myself for her but she was indifferent and on this day i saw it

seeing it gave me great strength and here i feel a new excellent freedom
falling on the stairs i broke the brace that held the pogo stick cross to my back

49.3

we were thinking of forming ourselves into an organization
theresa aiello gerber had a meeting in her apartment on the upper west side
peter carravetta and i were there but the chemistry with the others was not

now this organization was about to become yet another large commission in my life
i already had the expanded institute and the italian phd crusade to service
these jobs need a steady flow of written communication

i approach writing as a professional and find it difficult to sign things
steady flow the forms publicity business letters applications and recommendations
paper cargo fills my sicilian cart and painted on its sides you see me writing

i carry poems computers reports bibliographies up and down escalators and jets
my service is to the sacrificed writers and to the sacrificed italians
qualis artifex pereo nero cried out what an artist i die when he was about to go

we all feel that way sometimes washing the dishes or paying the bills
perhaps this whole grand opera of the crucified executive poet is due for review

49.3–49.4

49.4

in accepting the grant i placed myself on the road to a different depth of joy
now my life would present a steady series of opportunities to speak to the world
i expected the world not to listen yet there was a good chance of a good surprise

worrying about fame amounted to nothing more than the usual strangulation anxiety
you were born famous bobby they used to show you from windows prince of brains
walking encyclopedia bobby take us through the wonderland of knowledge tonight

we leaned on the loading curb john optiz roach paste factory corrugated iron door
steve congelosi told the epic of the loaf of bread with black nipples like tits
johnny pepsi piccola told the story of the baby that was born a fat mozzarella

the tale claims girls carve themselves long firm mozzarellas to masturbate with
in another story nuns give birth to balls of wax thanks to hot friendly candles
all these avenues of knowledge we explored smelling our way through summer nights

we talked as people did in italy but faster because of all the translating
i now plunged into these language vines that come up from under the sidewalk

49.5

the new text erased the old so it began upon a surface peculiarly prepared
when the inspector asked who you were you said i am a mohawk brave
my father was born dockside among sacks of cereals along the mohawk river

but what were these canal dreams of italy you were singing
in mohawk italy we dance all night and sing to the wolf the wind and the moon
tomorrow we come out of the woods to record the italian american story in beads

once upon a time a tribe of people lived with the god of a mountain to guide them
we have always lived here old women would sing carrying water jugs on their heads
they did not touch the jugs with their hands but the mountain guided them

the priest said the mass and gave the eucharist which renewed us at eastertime
beato roberto a monk who advised celestino not to be pope is buried on the mountain
more than seven hundred years ago he encouraged celestino to abdicate the papacy

dante sent celestino to hell and the popes left roberto in the mountains
he is more catholic than the pope and more italian than the king says the song

49.6

more catholic than the pope and more italian than the king
nevertheless as you can guess he's paid to sweep and not to sing
beato roberto says i have been a sturdy advocate but i am not that kind of god

i only accept such divinity as divinity divides and passes through my hands
we cannot always translate these ancient stories so easily he reminds me
it is true word systems have homologies and exploring these can help a translator

but meanings of words in use interact with words themselves in muscular ways
disentangling them is next to impossible and translating them near inconceivable
for things do inhere deeply where they grow as they do in how they grow there

thus taught beato roberto and this i have in my own life repeated in brooklyn
though i grew up in queens i was born in brooklyn and have lived here since 1969
brooklyn gave me my first earnest of poetic vocation twenty six years ago today

when i returned to brooklyn walt whitman met me in prospect park as the mud grass
brooklyn college treated me as a son in all seasons good bad and ordinary too

49.7

many glories i wanted to claim but few brought i home from the fair
all the troubles of the world began melting and boxes tumbled down the stairs
you know she said i have never met anyone who seemed to respond as you do

you maybe yes responded she oil of salamander no but we can try something simple
as the stratoliner turns the corner the rockies come into full view of your seat
return to the compartment tonight she said and we can try again you keep thinking

now we felt the the train's chug over the flat plains as time pitilessly passing
maybe these mountains can last forever you thought lying down in her compartment
i love the way you flex she said hard and tight against you up and down

should you tell a story or should you just go to the movies in a stupor
every occasion has its own logic but it helps if you find a cradle song for two
this is what they mean by an easy song that it leads to a love song

o i'll tell you the truth if you want to hear i have no use for lies
a promising youth with an accurate ear is actually a prize

49.7–49.8

49.8

i have been working out seating arrangements
tables of four should be grouped in fours and these sixteens in sixteens
two hundred fifty six per quadrant of two hundred fifty six quadrants per city

arrange the world in sixty five thousand five hundred thirty six cities
each has as ideal population sixty five thousand five hundred thirty six citizens
four billion two hundred ninety four million nine hundred sixty seven thousand

and two hundred ninety six persons is a current idealized world population frame
we begin our broadcasting careers in smaller groups so a city looks for tribes
when you get to the nation it is either a city nation like france or a world city

a city nation usually costs a lot of money to run but is a show taxpayers love
world cities put up hotels that specialize in city nation embassies
new york london rome istanbul delhi beijing charge for promulgating ideals

know the audience and characters before you start to write the play
then construct a plot that lets them see their specific capacities in action

ellis island

49.9

in the clan they tell the story of the brother who married a white girl
she wasted his money and gave herself airs and was lousy in bed
in the tribe they tell of the clan where all the cousins married whiter or up

sometimes they go to bed hungry horny and hopeless the tribe whispers
many of them win prizes for lawn maintenance or for excellence in sonnet writing
in the nation they tell the story of the tribe that went to college

all these people live on casters coasters christmases and easters together
no one knows where they are but their families of origin lost in space and time
the world court is considering cases of whole nations declaring themselves white

as usual out of town priests crowd the temple porch selling explanation booklets
but the central mysteries celebrated inside elude them as does how they work
entire populations enter and later emerge mysteriously colorless forever

the world judge says try not to go on too much about things of the moment
concentrate instead upon the things that stay with you through ten thousand lives

49.9–49.10

49.10

when a person dies the moisture continues to moisten but elsewhere
you cannot see that from here
where does the rushing flower of existence dissipate you ask

as it has been doing under your own observation time twists in winds and waters
these turn and return as they do in your stories and songs
water and land large as they are flex with the breathing of larger lives

the planet lives as planets live largely uninterrupted harmony balance and flow
i turn the pedals and the axle turns the spokes the wheel the rushing rubber tire
a roll of toilet paper unravels rolling down the steep lawn

you hear the tape grinding squeaking as part of any music it records and plays
you multiply this effect if you record it playing its own recording of itself
our moments our shared dangers wept aeneas over his drowned steersman palinurus

we are rolling through existence each of us like a storm from the horizon
oh yes the old ones say once i was a thundercloud in the alleghenies

49.11

in deciding to make the best of things we continually revise the story
they came wanting to push you out and you asked them for help redecorating
in not wanting to do things they made life easier for you you told them

no longer did you have to accommodate their working needs when they did not work
slowly the empire sank into the mud and you kept saying how peaceful it is
the failure to do things seemed to create a wild panic in you

when you failed to do things you laid it off on other people
they realized this and simply replied listen buster that is your problem
such representations have no special privileges inborn

now the great gate swings open and the walled city becomes a public highway
life was not so secure any more in places like these we discovered
and we had to start thinking like executives this is what we need to do he said

every success seemed to send me running back to infancy for cover
perhaps a less drastic retreat would suffice i thought

49.11–49.12

49.12

the first meeting of the italian american writers group takes place march 23 1991
at theresa aiello gerber's new apartment in the village thirty people show up
this time we have carefully invited only people who have published books

they have crossed the first field where writers struggle and they have prevailed
we begin by sharing the strengths that have brought us to this first meeting
then we complain about how much the italian american glass ceiling weighs us down

each of us mostly knows nothing about everyone else's work
we decide to get to know one another as writers and we begin reading and talking
after many sessions of that we decide to separate reading from conversation

we turn our monthly meeting into an open list amateur performance
everyone gets five minutes and many take ten when the moderator allows it
after years of this we are finally learning how to pay attention to one another

aiello gerber is a psychoanalyst and it makes sense that we started in her rooms
our group needed to cultivate a compassionate ear and where better to begin

50. italian american freedom still shows marks of three thousand years of slavery

50.1

on the day a man is fifty he must sit down for half an hour and do nothing
for many years now he has scarcely paused because he is afraid and guilty
who knows what to make of him but he floats over them like a blimp full of water

oh well he thinks sentencing himself to die for the ten millionth time
you do not deserve to live you monster you made me do everything wrong
you yourself do not do things perfectly so why do you expect that of me

well we used to do it to you at christmas they said with wired lights
each light butter yellow rosebud red baffin island sky blue means an alarm
this means every time something bothers you all alarms shine bright at once

people come to watch you perform in your cage at the university
afterwards though if you leave these things on you you had better go home alone
you can replace them with other sets that respond to and express other stimuli

your inborn equipment has ideas of its own but these emerge through interaction
no idea can be pure but many feelings can be mutual

50.1–50.2

50.2

today we are going to discuss the writings of the italian americans
i have personally read the works of hundreds of italian american writers
it would be easy to tell you they are all the same but are they

some of them seem the same because they write in similar voices about same things
mamma the sauce the grandpa the table the neighborhood girls the cars the aunts
what joey and frances did in the back bedroom while the grownups were eating
downstairs

the powerful procession of the saint stepping together down the hill all torches
how they carried the great leader home in a black satin casket wearing black
all these shells of transformation lie about on the many surfaces in my study

i always thought that once i could take off my armor i wouldn't need it any more
that is not true but it is true that now i arm selectively for each encounter
when i retire i remove the entire equipment of the day

living in private requires armor too but something much lighter
even with no clothes on an italian american is never entirely naked

50.3

how i would love to care for my books and my papers properly
they lie about me in ungainly heaps and i don't know how to manage them
i need to spend some money on bookcases and on some sort of assistance

so now it is time to plan that job for the coming season
all these systems reflect one another
if you decide to go to california that is one thing if venice that is another

in california you will engage in complex interaction with the local economy
professors bookstores graduate students radio audiences colleges will hear you
in venice you will be planting the seeds of a major revolution

the italians will not be an easy audience to crack
they do not think well of italian americans and they never have
the only way to reach them is through fashion

alta cultura in the prose means haute couture in the body
speak to them of the italian american mandarin

50.3–50.4

50.4

thinking of why i could not change i felt heavy weights on my whole body
as i sat still in my arm chair i could feel how metal plates cloaked every limb
i said to myself all right i will just breathe and let the feeling run its course

i lived my whole paralysis of all these years wanting but not being able to move
even now it lay across me large enough to keep rearranging its pressure
i did not try to stop it or run away from it but i let myself feel it intensify

i closed my eyes and it seemed i was far under the water
a large circular stone about eight feet across moved away leaving a large opening
the water now could flow freely under a sort of natural bridge that had closed

old faithful and the natural bridge for me signified inborn social roles
someone was behind the stone swimming silently pushing it away
was it me swimming or was it the action of a process that involves so many others

yellow fish green ferns red flowers move at the rhythm of the atmosphere here
inside it caresses and fills me as outside it caresses and supports

50.5

so now i see the italians are in a boat that they threw us out of
they don't want us back they say anyway you have america
and we say wait a minute we thought italy was part of america now

no now you've got another think coming so we were divided
some keep trying to recover italy and some have decided to forget it
others think wait until we are so rich we can buy italy but that will take long

in italy world time is the same as world time everywhere
italian local time is older than many going back to the founding of rome
italy began imagining itself then in a shape we can recognize

imagination only became a national sovereignty in 1861
by that time everyone had grown used to the idea so the country was born old
all of it is imaginary and a new imaginary can alter things gradually

when the united states separated from britain at first things did not change
later on they realized they had been new longer than anyone else

50.5–50.6

50.6

italian american independence day dawned early for the immigrants
lives names wives games names not all at once but at definitive moments changed
leaving passing through ellis island lonely meeting someone getting a first job

plenty went back to italy but plenty had burned their bridges and could not
the extra wife and children were waiting back there or there was no job
hardly anyone made enough money to go back and live like a gentleman

their children worked hard to fulfill their dreams but did not satisfy them
avenging themselves the immigrants taught their grandchildren to be gentlemen
this produced much strife in families where everyone worked for a living

freedom from slave labor was my father's big theme at supper time
he washed his hands but they never got clean because he was a mechanic
he wanted to be an artist but grew dispirited and accepted this lesser destiny

i don't want you to get your hands dirty he would say to me
he later had to carry the burden of a son he had himself trained to be genteel

50.7

one of the main things about freedom is it's hard to enjoy without money
money has many parts of which spending money is only one
knowing how to spend it is itself a form of money as is your last name

your gender and your color are forms of money as is the place you worship
money you win as a prize is good but inherited money is better
with inherited money comes the construction of the dominant character

words ideas rituals interactions build pedestals for people in high positions
around the pedestals we place rows of doric columns
pediments carry off the rain associating the powerful with the sky gods

italian american freedom still shows marks of three thousand years of slavery
you inherit slave words ideas rituals interactions like other forms of money
money dominates so it includes a sadomasochistic element in every transaction

words ideas rituals interactions prepare the slaves for their daily crucifixion
in roman christian slave temples blood of the poor runs down gutters like rain

50.7–50.8

50.8

now we have entered the vale of impatience where sinners tap their feet
you must have an awful lot of this clear so what are you waiting for they ask
one million impeccably sorted uniforms do not make an army you answer

respect what clarity of purpose you possess and build from there
of lessons i have found this the most valuable if often most difficult
so my clarifications always grow from my clarity of purpose is that what you mean

your clarifications come from investigating your clarity of purpose
in you hate lives with love humility with pride low position with high
you can have thoughts without acting on them

if you watch a show and then change the channel where does the show go
do you mean there is a two way transaction between me and the transmitter
you bet there is and if you don't see it that's because they'd rather confuse us

a million years from now children will read that line carved in stone
the three apostrophes will stand out and legends will attach to them

50.9

marco polo came to a lodge in the mountains where monks contemplate the silence
from it you might see ten countries but thick rivers of mist shroud every direction
a shift in the wind may reveal a snowy peak or sudden green crevasse

we practice nonviolence the monk told marco suggesting an allegory of mist
marco polo remained a long time with these monks and returned to italy with silk
silk became the basis of new italian mercantile empires

venezia lombardia liguria toscana lazio puglia have all been known for silks
the byzantine hand slides its satins across polished tables all over europe
no cargo cults have ever practiced more successfully than these chinese italians

in monasteries the italians had already been cultivating silence a long time
in the silent lombard rice paddies the silk worms made their small intense music
the italians brought this silence to market as the new opulence

in silk bound with gold fillets the venetian ambassador approached the queen
as a gift he brings the carpet he says where the princess scheherezade slept

50.10

whitman compared himself with the grass and planned to return to the grass
who can say why brooklyn has flourished with grass since whitman's time
but other poets resemble magnolia trees elms sycamores oleander bushes

i have given a great deal of thought to these trees as allegories of the family
when you say a great deal does that mean you just thought of it now
here is how to trace a family tree of transformation patterns across generations

you have to work backwards through the arithmetic of couplings
sometimes you will have astonishing revelations
you did not know that your family ran with the blood of the antonines

i have been living inside a family tree my whole life
my window as a small boy and my window as a man have opened on a tree
the faultlines of history slide down the sky as lightning bolts

the steeple of st raphael's went up in flames during the thunderstorm
as the scaffold went up the pastor explained the name raphael means god heals

50.11

with all the things that i have had to learn
how amethyst the eyes of certain cats
how deep the keel how dangerous the turn

how flagrant and perpetual the rats
i nonetheless already scratch my balls
while secretly i practice swinging bats

i sought america in shopping malls
but everywhere i looked i met more eyes
their gazes made for subtle prison walls

the map by now of course has shrunk in size
we think of it as strategy not place
our art can teach you how to see through lies

i furl my sails and look you in the face
the wind is down but this is not a race

50.11–50.12

50.12

you cannot exaggerate the subtlety of human interactions
no amount of finesse can ever be too much in dealing with others
finesse need not always use a light touch but must go swiftly when using force

paranoid epics whether in dreams or conversations always suggest rigidity
a stiffly responding person has good reason to be terrified of his or her shadow
finesse subsumes steady practical daily flexibility breath transmuting gymnastics

at ellis island we learn the arts of self dissolution and self reconstitution
we contemplate ancestral elliptical journeys and those our descendants will make
our own ellipses caress the backs of our necks like soft boomerangs that return

so this is india i always think leaving the boat we have arrived here at last
many europeans have failed to understand the divinity of this floating continent
but others see it still dripping with the ocean from which it so recently emerged

sometimes you will see things plainly that no one has ever seen before
afterwards you will search diligently for others who will see them as well

ellis island

51. after dinner grandpa sat me on his knee and told me how dante invented italy

51.1

travel into one's own distant past worlds requires ever greater speeds
below the age of three the distances between things become interstellar
this is what the guidebook says and as usual it is out of touch

what happens at this point in the investigation is that you fly by instruments
you know the coordinates and you have a lot of aerial surveillance photographs
every now and then you find things big enough to land on

sitting in the crook of your grandfather's arm you look a hundred years old
your head is bigger than your body and you look right through the picture
i remember smells of driving rain and sounds of manhattan air raids a mile west

when you go into a factory the roar of transformation obliterates everything else
ellis island the elliptical gateway opened onto the factory floor
hundred ton die presses slam down thirty times a minute bang bang bang bang bang

you are screaming all night afterwards remembering the soda bottle neon sign
huge and green it hung in the air outside the factory window leering at the poor

51.1–51.2

51.2

ellis island is one focus of an elliptical journey whose other is naples or rome
in rome all paths radiate elliptically so that rome includes ellis island
curving along viale libia or corso trieste you explore one model imperial cortex

giolitti lighting a flame at the foot of via del corso made an elliptical gesture
the altare della patria altar of the fatherland gleamed in the 1911 sunlight
italians thirty years had been streaming over the parapets and into the world

they entered new york harbor a river of light following an ocean current
the flow of italian light supposed it came from india and returned to india
birds encouraged them as they came creaking and rocking across the breaking ocean

they sang the hymns for the end of the world begging mercy from the mother of god
on wet decks they lay down in spasms of empty nausea and waves washed over them
oh jesus women cried as if they had been flung onto the deep lashed to logs

where one ellipsis crosses another you find the restaurant
everyone looks both ways before sitting down

51.3

when it comes time to plan a concert all the swans are always in the pond
so you have tuned untuned retuned but without the help of a proper piano
your consequent art of perfecting and discarding daily selves confuses people

they think you mean what you publish as if it expressed not a signature but you
you answer sometimes i recur in forms i occupied before but others replace them
but the master narratives of money will empower you if you let them

my problem is i have not taken ownership of my own difficulties
i needed to face them more simply and plainly than i was doing
swim every morning in the river of money six days a week and get the feel of it

turn your bills and letters daily and you begin working as the world works
doing so requires strength that you may not know you have but you have it
anger and desperation sometimes can lead you to a solid standing place

although changes are continual the forms of change also change
the signature simplifies itself in the act of transmitting power

51.3–51.4

51.4

how can you stand so much uncertainty
good question
my only guess is less is more

does that imply the obverse and does it mean that more uncertainty is less
when we consider this conundrum the relativity of relative terms stands forth
a large culture grows the way a slime combines sunshine with lake producing life

an uncertainty combines voice positions to make money
continual doubt reenacts the original construction of currency
wait a minute you said give me back my duck this is nothing but a piece of paper

only many guarantees can suffice to sustain the good faith that supports money
without good faith as we know money turns to nothing much
the guarantors who guarantee good faith include the gods minerva and mars

in her temple mint the goddess of good management keeps the money standard
the god of war keeps troops in the forum to keep the poor down and the rich up

51.5

when you take off your clothes winter disappears and your body exfoliates heat
leave on just one long stocking and one long glove then slowly draw them off
in these moments you play with the fullness of your being that was lost to you

in the moment of becoming money your body ceased being your body and became naked
naked is a relative term useful in gauging the civility of peoples
if others call them naked but they do not call themselves naked they are gentle

if they call others naked who do not call themselves naked they are cruel
cruel european admirals and priests certified the tainos naked
we can only wonder at the degree of civility such nakedness requires for survival

it was europeans who felt naked and so armed their bodies with leather and bronze
europeans carried across the ocean this compacted terror of fabric and metal
returning to ellis island i found myself suddenly free to begin removing layers

people debate what should be done with the many ellis island buildings not in use
let people bring their old clothes here and burn them on altars in the buildings

51.6

there's no way of knowing there's no way of showing
the thing you supposed that you came for
there's no water flowing and no flower snowing

some petal we haven't a name for
there's nothing of seeing and none of agreeing
on what you are taking the blame for

i end up not seeing you simply not being
the sign you are feeling the shame of
a pooing and peeing and kissing and fleeing

a love you are seeking the aim of
as shallow and slowing as mud that is growing
a swamp you have followed the fame of

i am undergoing a maximum mowing
and learning and teaching the game of

51.7

san clemente got you down or san francisco got you up
i'm proud to say that you're my buttercup
go santa mama cause were really gonna rock tonite

the vines slid along the lanai caressing the glass table under her wet scotch
mark antony lay for an hour with his head investigating a famous person's crotch
they kissing together consulted his wedding rolex watch

nothing rhymes like money honey nothing rhymes like cash
they fuck you for fucking with your mother they fuck you for giving them a rash
go santa mama cause we're greasing up the chimney tonite

i saw the harbor begin to glimmer along the edge like a lace of luminous insects
as mark antony and the famous person play it each alternately accepts and rejects
people who drink this scotch are known for their huge intellects

the fear of communication subsides and a large silence begins vibrating
all things have voices

51.7-51.8

51.8

after driving hours through snow we come to a famous bay where ice floes collect
they bob downriver collide and jam within the embrace of two long capes
the dark cape south glints sunlit cliffs the cape north runs grassy through hills

from this huge mouth ships sail forth for china the guide reads from the plaque
the inner self begins to express normal understandings that run deep
murderers slipped into the bodies of people living in your mother's head

she said we'll sit in the window seat and i'll sing bobby shaftoe's gone to sea
silver buckles on his knee he'll come back and marry me pretty bobby shaftoe
this stayed inside because if someone outside called you pretty you had to fight

when she suddenly got angry she would smack you shoulder back or fanny
where we sat the family tree pressed a thick forest of leaves against the window
my thickest armor still protects me from these surprise changes in the weather

every day i woke up asking if it had snowed because i wanted a new world
when the blizzard came everything would die and change form coming back to life

ellis island

51.9

the path of the winter doctor winds through the purple woodland midnight
trees bend over him screaming as his mare snorts flame coming through the door
she beats her hooves on my chest and i can scarcely breathe

ruthie i cry i want ruthie which my aunt says to my mother sounds how cute
at age two you feel the connectedness of things tearing away from you daily
tissue veils of amniosis fall from your skin till it begins to feel yearning

i only saw ruthie from the window now that we had entered our third year of life
sexual danger begins there said the old sicilians and ruthie now stayed indoors
christmas i was sick i threw a candy down to the sidewalk when i saw her braids

my name is queenie and i live in queens with my husband quincy
my name is ruthie and i live in rumania with my husband robert
she could bounce a spaldeen crossover rhyming direct faster than any other girl

her father sang solo in the pentecostal church choir
his name was bob too

51.10

sunday twelve of the family sat in the parlor and grandpa said silenzio
then he sang an aria to the whole family and turned to me and said bobby
what is that song about and i said it was about wanting and not having

grandpa held up his index finger and said to them all see
then he sang another and asked and i said it was about going to war on a horse
another was about chasing robbers down an alley another was about rowing a boat

after dinner grandpa sat me on his knee and told me how dante invented italy
as far as i could tell it had to do with singing and rhyming for a long time
first he made the language then he wrote the poem then he made italy grandpa said

to get to my grandpa's factory in the cellar you had to pass the coal bin
we watched the driver adjust the chute then went downstairs to watch it come in
a roaring black sweet lava filled the air inviting you to play in its heap

these things come from deep inside the earth where dante went my grandpa said
he forked coal into the furnace mouth where flaming tongues swallowed it down

51.11

i went into the park with lina when i was thirteen next to ps 199
this part of the park used to have on it a garage my grandfather owned
when they built the school he had to sell the land to the city

his reach extended far in space and into time so that i felt easy with lina
she knew what she wanted and she knew what i wanted
in choosing a style for an epic i had to deal with the question of opera

my grandfather owned the six family house the factory the garage
every clan on the block had a woman who worked at the factory where he was boss
the opera spoke the boss's voice out of the victrola

the problem with lina was i liked marietta who didn't know what to make of me
things that come to you on the opera stage have a stagey feel to them
my other grandfather swept the streets and lived in a rented apartment

the poor grandfather lived splendidly feasts every weekend and rivers of wine
the opera grandfather found the machines more absorbing than sausages and ravioli

51.11–51.12

51.12

when you sleep with the old world you see its body young as any new world's body
jefferson and franklin designed a united states model europe can never reproduce
rectangular with malice it anticipates disturbances discounting them in advance

europe has dignity but the united states has these mammoth turbine lifter rockets
this is the empire of alienable metaphors said jefferson buying louisiana cheaply
nineteenth century americans built exploitation machines on insect prototypes

one million pounds press railroad ties as the train transmits its stress curves
what they tell you about native americans also characterizes many native italians
they live close to the sky and speak plainly with animals as sentient beings

my mother's aunt in italy did not see why we wanted a car to climb a kilometer
we thought it too hot to walk and insisted only to find the car made her seasick
if a car is an animal is it a steel hornet sucking essences out of native bodies

in that dry mountain air you see how people might live as long as certain turtles
they darken with age but blind you with more light in every word they say

52. see how things change places

52.1

now i think of it as albert ellis island
i was reading his book how to live with a neurotic and i was changing my mind
let a equal the event that bothers you and let b equal your belief about a

if b is a mistaken belief proceed to c which is a statement that disputes b
if at a an act of prejudice upsets you then b believes that prejudice harms you
c says ok prejudice poses obstacles but finesse can turn obstacles to advantages

some say ellis is too simple or too complex but i had begun to try his method
in the reasonings of this poem ellis island you will find traces of it
my trouble or a was i was always feeling that things kept me from doing things

i believed a formal obligation required me to stay where i did not want to be
unpacking the matter this obligation used the threat of extinction
if i left i would die was my belief and this b required to be disputed

at c i disputed if i go away that will pose obstacles but i can use finesse
the water is the water but it is only the water

52.1–52.2

52.2

see how things change places
astronomer stirs tea with long firm chocolate biscuit
organ grinder turns handle while monkey dances

each transformation pattern has a park laid thick with granite slabs
my father taught me everything there is to know about thinking big
he subscribed to popular science and popular mechanics and i too read them

every month we would discuss space colonies or cars that swim fly and fold up
we considered the power of inventions that allow fishermen to read trout trails
the aswan dam went up every night on the floor in front of the philco television

ellis island's great hall looks like a french renaissance revival roman bath
but popular science let me see it as a broken seam in the space time continuum
we pull them out of mountains and wash them through an ocean of churning action

by the time they walk in here they have lost many layers of self definition
all around the island these selves hover seeking people who will never come back

52.3

i had the dark moment again he said
you must have had something wonderful happen to you she said
how did you know he rejoined

you always think you will have to suffer for your good fortune
yes mommy i thought noticing that her intelligent remarks annoyed me
point b irrational belief your wife is your mommy

point c if you make women into mommies think of it as a worn out habit
i kept conflict vivid to distract me from dark moments coming up as the poem grew
point b irrational belief said poetic ambitions cause dark moments

point c you can use your poetry to enclose decorate package and mail dark moments
to some they will taste like hazelnut truffles made of three tone chocolate
practiced italian finesse turns poor women's sorrows into spaghetti alla chitarra

distractions grow threadbare so dispute the importance of things that go wrong
venerate what matters to you and that will strengthen your faith

52.3–52.4

52.4

my cousin judy viscusi alzmann fyler listened to every poem in ellis island
for each one i read she told me a story many of them about her father patsy
my friend theresa cerasuola listened to the whole poem as i wrote it

she told me long island stories about her father and frank and sal and her aunt
pietro di donato richard gambino angela danzi and many others were in the stories
my sister linda viscusi lentini is always exploring territories not far away

i read a poem about marco polo and she says i was just thinking of marco polo
or she says i was thinking of mommy and i say i just wrote a poem about mommy
my sister carole viscusi presti my first tutor knew what she had taught me

when i started writing poems she used to say how did you get this out of that
my father joe viscusi taught me how to articulate a vision as an artist does
mark the relative proportions in things he said the master science is mathematics

this poem uses elliptical topology so things are not always where you expect them
every poem has another heart it answers and every other heart can find a poem

52.5

in dark moments i sometimes saw stumbling heroes and distracted empresses
life is already wonderful they murmur it may not be so easy to make it more so
despite our sorrows we have decided to erect this marble platform on a high hill

we cut one layer of mountain stone into rectangles and lay it upon another
when they interlock firmly we set in place bases columns capitals and architraves
then we raise the pedimented roof and crown it with pedestals and pinnacles

proud ornaments tell us we touch the gods and teach us to despise troubles
mr presti inscribed mausoleums and inscriptions along strict ancient patterns
your writing will outlast mine i would say to him and he would laugh denying it

he could afford to make light of it as he clearly saw i had spoken the truth
his hand had laid out the letters for two cardinals' tombs in saint patrick's
sacred bits of written stone survive as long as the planet's crust keeps cooling

all creatures have secrets god allows them to take
birds fly the world without maps poets make things change without touching them

52.5-52.6

52.6

why is a poet like a priest of money
poets make us believe in the unbelievable
when poets put on ties they become philosophers

when philosophers put on boots they become police
later taking off our steel teeth and heartvalves we start again eating leaves
after a million years one of us writes another poem

poems show how you change one thing for another
under the doric portico bankers taking refuge from the sun trade news and worry
is changing one thing for another unbelievable you ask but that is not the point

the defect a poem cures lies not in the object of belief but in the organ thereof
atop the sunset boat back from ellis island we watched wall street turn colors
a poem need not teach belief in lies but belief in even a tiny change of chances

revolutions begin as discoveries of what matters to us
i connect mine with yours and the energy begins to charge the field of changes

52.7

i wanted to get everything clear so i could leave the island behind
don't worry about these other papers now but is your passport in order they asked
two per cent of those who arrived had to turn and go back where they came from

these migrants the doctors judged too sick for american medicine to deal with
but thanks to medical arrogance they admitted millions who turned out incurable
gradually their homeless illness has spread across the whole continent like water

the usa pays geologists to repeat daily how the grand canyon is a wide tidelands
americans give fossil encyclopedias for christmas as if they were family albums
their interminably breaking wave raises its jade tunnel before them rich in light

elsewhere unmoored from mountaintop anchors we drift and thrive in warming brine
we are the ones who did become americans and now live with the freedom of sharks
we bullet across the continent making waves that break windows on farmhouses

it's another ocean out here the amiable salmon replied to the lobster
as he turned to go back in the house the lobster grumbled happy halloween

52.7–52.8

52.8

chickasaw santee pueblo and navajo return this time as artists of change
they used to fight by trojan war rules till capital flattened them with factories
capital planted norwalk and bridgeport with ironmonger generator methane mills

now new casinos let them in behind the armor to where capital itself accumulates
you knew they were there but you did not find them where you looked for them
often they began taking shape for an instant just before a thing collapsed

people who understand the world do not let other people's neuroses torture them
rather they concentrate on their purposes and practice kindness
they learn to accept new frames for their own ideas not only when it makes sense

those from the east occasionally recognize the power their ideas have for others
open the side door of the space ship and come down to live on the pampas with us
you think these beads and ribbons do not matter but they have things to tell you

even the most solid principles you have found have come to you by chance
imagining things is only one way of discovery not imagining them also works well

ellis island

52.9

i have always loved stories because they keep things where you can follow them
when it came time to remove another master narrative i started to shiver
here is one that explains coming to america as if arriving resembled leaving

at the head of the harbor ships turn before beginning their major entry
they lowered us into a boat off sandy hook with our crates of napoleon brandy
a boat came for the cargo so we boarded the next ship out never touching land

flying in one night from london we found almost all new york city under water
the citicorp tower rose from a glazed cityscape one saw from the helicopter
every street in long island city had turned brown under the eddying tide

in general we try to run the whole mobile stage through all its movements daily
at radio city music hall our motto is maintain the machinery
most of the spectacular vaudeville stages are gone but this one continues to work

you can do a lot with lights and the organ but the orchestra makes the show
not only is it a story but all these voices are telling it at the same time

52.10

every accordion calls to mind tango parlors where we danced throughout long youth
this boat that carries us howls in storms and whimpers through the summer nights
on brilliant winter solstice noon snow we prayed healing for all hearts and minds

as july leads on to january the bay changes its texture but not its brilliance
from a million miles away liquid water may seem to differ only in theory from ice
a different difference separates sleep from waking death from life gods from dogs

the old idea that you could make one thing more important than another is gone
i doubt you can even know where one thing ends and another thing begins
after a blizzard the blue sky funnels into an oak tree laced with ice

light slides down its fluid shell of prismatic water
lovers sing an old goodbye boogie as they dissolve into two different dimensions
the story of healing begins with a light in the east thinks the tree

i knuckle out glittering along the ground under my own longest shadow of the year
at dawn i am a diamond drinking brightness the sun pours into the elemental cold

52.11

i used to hover over the air in certain places like a miasma
people did not say jesus you stink but they felt it and acted it anyway
i wished i could have blamed them but i did not hope to feel that i could do so

intensity of course has this price
too much of it is really too much
i tried to dilute it in the ocean but life curls around its own squishy tentacles

the rushing currents both ice you and enwomb you among the brightly colored lives
they exhilarate you but you keep acquiring new kinds of firm grip on things
when you were a cloud you were the kind that looks like a thing that eats things

you are a message that repeats itself perfectly a finite number of times
from certain points of view no such notion as a finite number can even be thought
and in your repetition the rhythms of self difference themselves recur variously

all these numbers with their extravagant perfections are an architecture of foam
life returns as a wall of water that weighs as much as the world

52.11–52.12

52.12

this is a poem about decisions and how we make them although we know nothing
it is not exactly that it does not matter what we decide
as we all know it matters a great deal in some ways and not at all in many others

in the fullness of time we start to realize how deeply we choose each thing
if god put all the troubles in a pile and everyone could pick my grandma sang
we would all pick our own as everyone knows it says but would we you wonder

if you listen to river water slapping between the rocks you hear the voice of god
they used to tell me that on my first birthday i had a convulsion and turned blue
point b it scared me as my mother's dying on my forty third birthday reminded me

point c stories about the past always have a lot of someone's wish in them
do not be scared if some one you know may wish you bad things at some points
wishes flow in and out on the tides

i used to be afraid to think of loving anyone as if love could do us great harm
talk about changing the subject

afterwords

ellis island

thirty extra hours make a year*

you go to ellis island to see something
is it your ancestors and who they were
or you and what are you

i went for the first reason as people do
eating old valises full of ribbons and pictures
opening crates of plates real food and real estate files

the frozen doctor putting a hook in your eye
coal smoke steamers pouring out rivers of people
website with mother's name and grandma's on the ship europa

an earthquake door squealed shut on the rust
opening my wallet i found identity papers of the dead
flakes of red ambition scraps of love notes filled with lies

the second reason lay before me
examining the who they were the who i was came into focus
the unsparing sky lit up my faint still visible tattoos

i'd thought i would be proud to be ashamed of them
but after a while i hardly noticed any figure as i could see no frame
was this america or was it a fragment of something else

at every corner In the city they were selling flags
irish female white italian jewish bengali moroccan
i pledge allegiance to the bank

write a letter to your lover's now impossible politics
i picked my covering all to pieces
inside it was just me so far as i could tell

i found a lock of hair in my pocket
glued it to some bones i had wired together
loved it but left it on a bench in the boat

did you love your country before it disappeared
are you always losing your way in the water or the sky
do you sit near a tree because it refuses to move

------

*Ellis Island is composed of fifty-two books of twelve fourteen-line sonnets each. That is the same number of
lines as there are hours in fifty-two weeks. To make a full year, a little more time is required. "thirty extra hours
make a year" refers to the actual length of a terrestrial circuit of the sun, roughly 365.25 days. Ordinary years have
365 days. The .25 is taken up every four years to make a leap year of 366 days. The hours in the present thirty-
line poem are "extra," constituting a supplement that pretends to explain the 8,376 lines of Ellis Island itself. These
thirty lines are not included in ellisislandpoem.com's Random Sonnet Generator.

A Letter to the New York City Landmarks Preservation Commission

July 2, 2012

I am sorry not to have written sooner. Stanley Aronowitz gave my name to a member of the New York City Landmarks Preservation Commission in late winter 1993. Within a few days, the chairperson called to ask if I would testify about the proposed redevelopment of the abandoned hospital buildings at Ellis Island. Scarcely thinking, I said yes. And, though I did testify, a little anyway, I have always expected to provide a more comprehensive response. Everything takes longer than you think.

Delay 1

I had never been to Ellis Island. The main building had been restored and made into a museum in the late nineteen-eighties by the Statue of Liberty/Ellis Island Foundation. It had become a big attraction. My aunt Margaret had paid to have the names of her parents engraved on the Memorial Wall of Honor. I had stayed away, claiming that it was too blatant an appeal to the ethnic politics of those days — not to say too sentimental and cemeterial to be of any living interest. So why did I say yes to the Landmarks Preservation Commission?

The Commission's request touched me in a sore spot. I knew about those hospital buildings. In 1919, my grandmother, then twenty-six years old, and my mother not quite four, had been detained there for weeks. In my family, *Ellis Island* had never been the name of a museum. Instead, it was what we called any institution — from a jailhouse to a madhouse — where a person might be held against her will. It was right up there with *Sing Sing* (New York State maximum security prison at Ossining) and *Creedmoor* (New York State Psychiatric Hospital in Queens Village, which held 6000 patients in 1950), names for hell on earth, places we would drive past in the car but only look at out of the corners of our eyes. When I was a boy of three, my father took my big sister Carole and me to the Statue of Liberty. When we sailed past Ellis Island, we turned away from it altogether, as if the very sight of the place might make us dizzy, might plunge us into the swirling waters. We could be sucked under, right there, under those broken windows and crumbling lintels, those haunted ruins still vivid in the minds of millions — at least vivid in the mind of our mother, who chose not to come with us to the Statue of Liberty. Young as she had been on Ellis Island, she had taken away a permanent sensation of fear and loathing.

What did I think about these derelict buildings as a civic project? Almost fifty years had passed since my childhood trip to the Statue of Liberty, and now the Landmarks Preservation Commission wanted to know. Did I think they'd make a good Holiday Inn or a convention center? Did I even care? I answered the Commission's request with a request of my own: "Could I wait till I've had a chance to visit?" "Yes, but not too long," they told me. The hearing would be in May.[1]

---

[1] The New York City Landmarks Preservation Commission's report, *Ellis Island Historic District,* November 16, 1993, p. 6, says that a hearing was held on November 10, 1992. My recollection was of a hearing in the spring of 1993, but the report does not mention any such hearing. In any event, what I had to say was entirely out of the spirit of the proceedings. I am writing to the Commission now for the sake of fulfilling my intention. In these affairs, it is hard to know what really matters. According to the *New York Times,* November 17, 1993, "Officials of the National Park Service, which operates the island as a national landmark, said the city's designation was largely honorific and that its Federal designation was enough to preserve it. But Laurie Beckelman, the commission's chairman, contended that the designation was significant, giving the city an important advisory role in the preservation of the island."

First Visit, Delay 2

A week later, on a raw March Sunday afternoon, my 14-year-old son Robert and I took the boat for Ellis Island. There weren't very many visitors, but already I felt myself entering the chambers of bad memory. More than half the passengers on the boat got off at the Statue of Liberty. They were the lucky ones, I thought, the Americans. The rest of us huddled against the icy breeze as the boat churned away from Liberty Island, out into the bay, and then nuzzled back in along the quay at Ellis Island. We filed down the gangplank and set foot on this magic island where the emigrants of other nations became immigrants to the United States. A large red brick building with limestone facings, framed in green ornamental copper, waited to greet arriving passengers. It stood far enough from the mainland that anyone trying to swim the distance would surely drown among the many swimming rats, or else be plucked out, not gently, by the police who cruised the green tides of the deep-water harbor.

Walking into the building under the twisted-copper-canopies with their fin-de-siècle frosted glass, like a station of the Métro, I found it easy to imagine that we were descending into an underground, joining the dead march of the numb and numberless millions filing in, sick with the sea and weary with the stench of steerage, to meet the cold gaze of the immigration doctors, who were to choose the lucky ones who could enter, and to separate them from the others: the unacceptable, who would have to get back on ships and go home in defeat; or the questionable, like my grandmother and her little daughter, whose heads would be shaved to prepare them for weeks or even months of waiting, until the doctors should finally decide to fold them into the file marked *Cured* or the file marked *Hopeless*.

We did not immediately go towards the hospital buildings. We were following the immigrants. We climbed the stairs to the Great Hall. They had sat there in rows that were practically caged. They had come wrapped in wool and perspiration, dragging huge bundles of their things along with them. But now, this place, scene of so much apprehension and dismay, had been restored to spotless good cheer. The barrel-vaults and the high Diocletian windows produced an abundance of light and air, exactly the effect the architects must have had in mind. The walls were fresh-painted, the Guastavino tiles gleaming on the lofty ceilings, the woodwork polished, the window frames impeccably clad in darkened copper. There was no stink of suffering here. The rest of the building was rich in edification. Room after room exhibited the fetishes of the poor as if they were jewels in shop-windows, rather than the hand-made comforts of hard lives. Intricate embroideries spoke of women who had sat long days in kitchens or outside the doorways of tiny houses, their hands ever busy. Holy pictures and figurines of saints, prayer books, mezuzahs. There were photographs of life in the Russian fields and life on Eldredge Street in the Lower East Side. Valleys of laundry hanging between tenement buildings. Big-eyed children sitting on curbstones. Everything was beautifully set forth, as if singers were about to appear in Menotti's opera *The Saint of Bleecker Street*.[2] It was informative, entertaining, surprising. On the ground floor, one encountered a sizable globe, all silver like a satellite, with little lines tracing migration routes. Some led from the Mediterranean to New York. Others from Africa to South America. Indonesia to the South Sea Islands. It was a spherical version of the famous subway maps of Paris. If you pressed buttons next to your point of origin and your point of arrival, your trajectory would light up in tiny red or green or purple

---

[2]Gian Carlo Menotti, music and lyrics, *The Saint of Bleecker Street: Musical Drama in Three Acts* (New York: G. Schirmer, 1955).

bulbs. This object gave the entire establishment an address in the Universe, as if Ellis Island were the name of an exhibit at Cape Kennedy. I enjoyed showing it to my son. This was not the Isle of Tears. This was an Exploratorium.

Nonetheless, I was not fooled. It was waiting there, the other Ellis Island, the one I had come to look at. But all these displays were holding me back. Their formidable charm expanded the meaning of this monumental destination. It was not just my family here. It was not just my clan, my tribe, my nation. It was many families and tribes, many nations. It was the teeming surface of the terrestrial globe. This realization seemed, at least for the moment, to lighten the burden of fear and sorrow. We lingered long in these galleries, explaining to each other what we were seeing.

The gray afternoon was going, and the sky was taking on the weight of steel plates. It was time to visit the south side of the island. You could not actually go there. You could only stop at the southernmost edge of the restored buildings, and look through the corridors that led into the sealed chambers of the sick and the insane that stood there, still rotted, not very far away. You could look across a narrow channel of water and see into the windows: broken beams, rusted bedsteads. My grandmother and my mother had long since passed away. They had lived full, rich American lives without ever forgetting the time they had spent in this lockup, but mostly they had not wanted to talk about it.

The sealed asylum gave me no clear idea what to say to the Landmarks Preservation Commissioners. My son agreed that its odd assortment of buildings clearly would not make much of a hotel. "Maybe you could turn it into a college," I said. "Yeah," he replied, "everyone wants to go to college on a maximum-security island." If you transformed it into another museum, what would you put in it? Crutches, bandages, old medicines, syringes big enough for horses? Would you clean it up and hire exhibition directors to make it a soft-spoken introduction into the gospel of American success? "These people were sick and crazy. Then they became powerful and rich." I gave it up. We boarded Miss Liberty and crossed the windy bay back to Battery Park. A couple of months later, I shared my doubts with members of the Commission. It was a duty, and they were polite, but they could see I had nothing useful to offer. Those old buildings had shut me down. As I left the hearing, I made a private resolve, promising silently that I'd have something more to offer, and soon.

Second Visit, Delay 3
That same summer, I was teaching a group of honors students at the CUNY Graduate Center, members of what the University called the Diamond Undergraduate Minority Fellowship Program Humanities Institute. I had ten students, selected from the CUNY senior campuses, students we thought might go to graduate school in the humanities. I was introducing them to method in the humanities. That included two things: the art of making a good case in prose, and the art of investigating the traces of the past. Each student examined traces of his or her own choosing — usually manuscripts, sometimes other artifacts. But I also wanted some traces we could all look at together. I decided to take them to Ellis Island.

This was not an obvious choice. These students were African Americans, Latino Americans, Asian Americans. None of them was aware of any personal ancestors who had passed through Ellis Island. But I was drawn by that globe with the lighted pathways. My students, like everyone else in America, had a lot of traveling behind them. We went on a clear hot morning, July

2, 1993. I led them into the building and then, for the most part, followed them around, listening to their comments and answering their questions as best I could, mostly by referring them to the lucid explanations posted on the walls next to the exhibits. They were drawn to the idea that Ellis Island was not the cemetery of European immigrants but a location in the universal vortex of human displacement. I was thinking, as a teacher does, more about their feelings than my own. Maybe that was why I was taken by surprise by what happened next.

At lunchtime, we bought food in the cafeteria and took it outside onto the wide stone terrace that had been made spectacular as part of the restoration. We sat at tables under the high noontime sun of midsummer. The stone pavement was white. There was light in all the air — it came straight down from the sky and it reflected from that pavement and from the water all around us — so much light that nothing seemed entirely solid. In the blinding glare, I thought I saw a sort of palpable form. It was not a person or a building or a ghost ship. It was a thickness of feelings and memories that hovered around me in the air. I couldn't compare it to anything. I couldn't tell anyone about it. It lingered as long as we stayed.

This experience was puzzling. When I got home that night, I started to write about it. At first there were just a few poems that, one way and another, addressed what had happened that morning. But soon the subject of the poems became another Ellis Island altogether. This Ellis Island wasn't just what befell my mother and my grandmother. It was the world I had been living in my whole life. A new world, not the one of the Pilgrims or the Founding Fathers.

I was getting used to the idea of needing to take my time. Clearly, I was looking at a world that began with a plain displacement, sudden as an earthquake, followed by a long awakening into something entirely unexpected, a change that needed to be examined and studied with a straightforward eye.

Delay 4

This turned out to be an impossible task. I was patient. I sat at my desk and listened for voices that would help. I heard them, too, usually after long silences. The first poems that I wrote were not very much about ships and doctors. They were about changing one's destiny in America. Sometimes they were witty, sometimes surprising. But there was nonetheless an insistent murmur, occasionally a whine, that never let up. The trouble with these voices was that they wanted you to trust them, and you wanted to comply. That was dangerous for a writer: "That inspiration which consists in blind obedience to every impulse is in reality a sort of slavery," according to Raymond Queneau.[3] *Slavery* is a strong word here. It only makes sense if you think that writing must be a Jacobin form of self-liberation. On this view, anything of the past that you repeat implies involuntary submission. This view does not consider that you might sometimes actually choose to repeat what you had heard. And it is worth thinking about what you would get from examining what you had accepted in that way.

With a little tempering, nonetheless, Queneau's observation seemed like a good guide for writing about Ellis Island, which has everything to do with leaving the past behind, or at least with considering the idea of leaving it behind. Queneau, one of the founders of the *Ouvroir*

---

[3] Cited by Marcel Bénabou, in "Rule and Constraint," *Oulipo: A Primer of Potential Literature,* ed. Warren Motte (Champaign: Dalkey Archive Press, 1988) 41.

de littérature potentielle, like its other members, invented mathematical and logical constraints as aids to composition. It was his view that only formal, preferably mathematical, constraints in composition can free the writer from involuntary submission to the self-reporting and self-repeating past.

Following Queneau's practice, I invented constraints for the poems I was writing. My first constraint came from Edgar Allan Poe. "I hold that a long poem does not exist. I maintain that a long poem is simply a contradiction in terms." The small poems in my long poem needed to be small indeed. I used the Italianate sonnet form that Shelley adopted in his "Ode to the West Wind," where the largest unit is three lines. Thinking about this, oddly enough, I realized that *Ellis Island,* in spite of its apparent length, could still be a poem on Poe's terms, since it was made up of tiny poems, the way the buildings on Ellis Island were made of bricks.

Delay 5
I still needed more constraints. I needed to formalize the theme of Ellis Island, which is the theme of *rupture.* While I respected Poe's taste for short poems, I had come to understand a superseding theorem of Raymond Queneau's: "Every sentence includes an infinity of words, the others being in the infinite or being imaginary."[4] And this became, as you might guess, the source of a major interruption.

For I realized that I could compose *Ellis Island* in such a way that the entire long poem intervened between any two sonnets in it. This method is an ancient arrangement called *chiasmus.*[5] In my epic the chiasmus is built with sonnets. Between the first sonnet of book one and the last sonnet of book fifty-two, the whole epic intervenes. And yet the last sonnet answers the first sonnet. The next-to-last sonnet in book fifty-two answers the second sonnet in book one. All the sonnets are paired in this way, and whole epic is included on either side of any two such sonnets.[6] Around them always lies the total number of sonnets in the long poem. And each one of these sonnets belongs to a pair massively surrounded on either side. "Every sentence includes an infinity of words, the others being in the infinite or being imaginary." Admittedly, Queneau's sentence is enigmatic, but that allowed me to make of it what I needed.

Delay 6
Even as I was plotting the construction of my chiasmus, I realized that no matter how symmetrically a book might be built on paper, it was still likely to live more on the Web than anywhere else. And there, the stable classical symmetry might not mean much or last long. The Web was new then, but people had been watching it grow on the horizon for some time already. In 1990, Guy Debord had written, in his *Comments on the Society of the Spectacle,* concerning issues that were going to arise when the whole archive sank into the ocean of the internet. Debord was particularly acute on the coming disappearance of historical truth:

---

[4]Cited in Jacques Roubaud, "Mathematics in the Method of Raymond Queneau," Motte 92.
[5]This scheme of composition is at least as old as Homer. See R. Viscusi, *Max Beerbohm, or the Dandy Dante: Rereading with Mirrors* (Baltimore: Johns Hopkins UP, 1986) 159–94, and 254n8, for a review of the topic.
[6]For any sonnet, you can find the answering sonnet by subtracting its number from the total number of sonnets. This is an easy trick to do. There are fifty-two books, each book containing twelve sonnets. But the total number is not 52.12. The total number begins with book 1, sonnet 1. So the total number is 53.13. With this in hand, it's easy to apply find the answering sonnet to any given sonnet. You can check this out with the book in your hand. Subtract 22.8 from 53.13, and you get 31.5. You will find that sonnets 22.8 and 31.5 have a lot to say to one other

Nothing remains of the relatively independent judgement of those who once made up the world of learning; of those, for example, who used to base their self-respect on their ability to verify, to come close to an impartial history of facts, or at least to believe that such a history deserved to be known. There is no longer even any incontestable bibliographical truth, and the computerized catalogues of national libraries are well-equipped to remove any residual traces.[7]

At the end of April, 1993, the National Center for Super Computing Applications at the University of Illinois Urbana-Champaign had released the Mosaic browser. This application made the internet easy for everyone to use and sealed its hegemony over the collective archive.

Thus, by the time I had begun writing, it had already become evident that things on the internet were not going ever to be dependable in the same way that a printed book could be dependable. You found a site on Tuesday. When you went to look for it on Thursday, it was no longer there. The whole archive had become liquid.

We had entered a moment of rupture much like the moment signified by Ellis Island itself. I decided that this meant I had to publish my poem on paper, and to do it in such a way that not only the sonnets, but every single line would have a clear numerical address. Each line would be referable to the whole numerical system of the poem. The lines would have a good chance of staying put where I had put them.

But I decided, too, to seize the moment and to publish the whole long poem on the Web in such a way that you would never find anything where it had been the last time you saw it. I projected an aleatory machine that would pick 14 lines at random and make them into a sonnet. After you refreshed the screen, this sonnet would disappear into the ocean of possibilities from which it had emerged. A fresh random sonnet, equally evanescent, would appear.

Like an immigrant, the poem *Ellis Island* belongs to two epochs. The old epoch poem has exactly 8,376 lines, all in order every time you open this book. The new epoch poem is always different. Every time you click on the Random Sonnet Generator at ***ellisislandpoem.com*** you get a different sonnet. The number of possible sonnets is more than a duodecillion — virtually infinite. You certainly could never read a tithe of them, no matter how long you lived. The actual number is 624^{14}, an unimaginably huge number of sonnets (the number is printed on the cover of this book).

Delay 624^{14}

All of this took a long time to do. And then I had two poems. The one was a Gutenberg-era epic, written on a computer that was the last word in moveable type. Everything had been moved around and was now settled into a single order of words and lines and sonnets and books. The other was a Berners-Lee-Andreesen-era electronic file whose lines had started moving again, this time in ways you really couldn't control, a book whose ligaments had been dissolved in the aleatory fluid of the world wide web, where books go to die and be reborn as something slightly different every time you refresh the page. Any line can appear anywhere. They are all wanderers, as if they were heavenly bodies.

For ten years, I doubted my plan. I loved it, mind you, but that was no reason to believe it was

[7]Guy Debord, *Comments on the Society of the Spectacle,* trans. Malcolm Imrie ([1990] London: Verso, 1988) 19–20.

any good. For ten years I woke up every day resolved to publish the work, for all the world like someone who had announced at bedtime that he would quit smoking or drinking in the morning, only to waken at dawn, walk into the kitchen, and decide to wait until tomorrow. Obviously, this was the period where the number of delays reached astronomical scale. It grew in logarithms while I was asleep. The better I liked my plan, the more compelling appeared the choice to avoid putting it in into action.

Finally, I began to move. Slowly. My very moves were themselves forms of postponement. The first thing I did was to spend a couple of years going over the fifty-two books of the poem, first to see if I still liked it (six months) and then to go through the whole thing line-by-line and fix all the little things I had found that needed improvement. I went through the poem making these little fixes from beginning to end twice (two and a half years more).

I had long talks with Scott Dexter, a forward-thinking computer scientist at Brooklyn College, asking his advice about how to put up a site and a Random Sonnet Generator. He got really interested in the project, which made it move faster. Soon, another colleague, Wythe Marschall, had designed the site, and Scott Dexter had made the algorithm, and I put up *ellisislandpoem.com* in spring of 2008.

Delays began to fall away. I had taken the decisive step of letting other people into my project. My colleague Peter Taubman would ask me, So what about *Ellis Island*? Against all my hesitations, he scheduled me to read from it at "The Day of the Poet," an annual event at Brooklyn College. The poet Nora Almeida came to work at the Wolfe Institute. She knew how to make books. She kept enthusiastically showing me books that she had made or that her friends had made. It looked so easy, so unthreatening. I asked her would she consider working on such a book for *Ellis Island*. Nora Almeida produced a beautiful handmade edition of the first four books in 2009.

Now my palace of delay had really collapsed. Some people read this handmade edition. They asked me to give readings. Letizia Airos and Ottorino Cappelli had a great idea for putting the poem on their i-italy Website. One person they involved in the planning was the brilliant videographer Luca Fantini. He read some of the poems in Nora's edition, and showed them to his wife Veronica Diaferia. She showed it to her aunt Ombretta Diaferia, an enterprising publisher of poetry in Varese (city north of Milan). Ombretta loved the book. She called me when she was in New York. Soon her publishing house abrigliasciolta editore had published Sandro Sardella's translation of those first four books in an Italian bilingual edition in 2009 and the next four in 2010. In 2011, Anthony Tamburri offered to publish the whole book with Bordighera Press. The last delay was writing this report.

My Report to the Landmarks Preservation Commission
Every island in a bay reminds me of Venice. Civic virtue and Italian ingenuity are working nonstop to keep that sandbar city above the surface, but every so often, the Venetians must deal with what they call *acqualta,* high water, and they must walk through the streets wearing big boots. The paving stones look as if they lie under plate glass windows. While this situation endures, occasionally for days and days, the Venetians practice a garrison humor you might have encountered on the ramparts of Troy after the death of Hector, when Trojans knew their city's days were numbered.

The fate of Venice will one day claim Ellis Island too. And this was clear to me, right from the start. No one thinks about this. City planning concentrates its attention upon a short time line. Buildings and bridges go up with an expected usable life of fifty or at most a hundred years. This allows for the optimism necessary for effective management. Like all noble planners, the New York City Landmarks Preservation Commission is full of spirit and good intentions. Perhaps it can transform this sanatorium into a colony for writers and sculptors and landscape architects, an American Academy of Ellis Island. While I would like that, I really have nothing useful to say on the subject. The only future I can see for Ellis Island is in the halls of memory.

For me, the place and its people have the two great epic qualifications.

Troy, Carthage, Machu Picchu. Ellis Island, you say, is still there. No. For me, the fragility of the place and the frailty of its people are already accomplished facts.

Second, in an epic specific people meet with history in a specific place. The whole North American experiment was waiting for the immigrants in that Great Hall. That meeting reverberates, one way and another, in every line of this poem. The encounter will be worth remembering even after the walls of Ellis Island, like the marble steps on the library of Saint Mark, have returned to the deep.

So, in the end, my delays were a silent confession of my disqualification. I await with good cheer the announcement of your latest plans.

Sincerely yours,
Robert Viscusi

ellis island

Acknowledgements

The students who came to Ellis Island with me on July 2, 1993 asked me questions I couldn't answer. We saw a large globe there showing paths of migration that lit up when you asked about countries they connected. That opened a lot of other questions.

My late cousin Judy Viscusi Alzmann Fyler listened to every word of the poem during the 30 months it took to write the first draft. Many friends encouraged me: Vittoria repetto, Maria Gillan, Peter Carravetta, Bill Astwood, Gloria Salerno, Theresa Cerasuola, Peter Taubman, James Periconi, Michael Graves, George Guida, Evelyn Rossetti, Stefano Albertini, Matthew Frye Jacobson, William Boelhower, EllenTremper, Julie Agoos. Anthony Tamburri, Fred Gardaphè, and Paolo Giordano have supported my work since we met decades ago. Antonio D'Alfonso, Francesco Durante, Martino Marazzi, Bill Boelhower have all been brilliant readers and staunch supporters, as have my sisters Linda Lentini and Carole Presti.

Nora Almeida designed and published a handmade edition of the first four books of *Ellis Island.* This beautiful edition inspired Ombretta Diaferia of abrigliasciolta editore in Varese to publish a bilingual edition of those books, with Italian translations by Sandro Sardella, and to continue with further volumes of this project, a project which is still going forward. Letizia Airos and Ottorino Capelli have worked on a web presence for the poem. The videographer Luca Fantini has begun recording performances of the poem. The cover of the present edition was designed by Nora Almeida and Deborah Starewich. The photo on the back cover is Nora Almeida's, and Deborah Starewich has designed the book itself. The website ellisislandpoem.com was designed by Wythe Marschall. I described the Random Sonnet Generator to my colleague Scott Dexter. How long will it take to do this? I asked him. He said, Is Monday soon enough?

Parts of this poem have appeared in print: *From the Margin: Writings in Italian Americana,* 2nd edition, includes an earlier version of Book 5. *Poesia* (Italia) published a large selection from the first four books, both in English and Italian. Individual sonnets have been published in *Brooklyn Review, Italian Americana, The Phoenix.*

Everyone I knew when I was a boy was either an immigrant or the child or grandchild or greatgrandchild of immigrants. All of these people appear in this poem, not as themselves but as names, or else as gestures or feelings or single words that have stayed in my memory waiting to be used. My wife Nancy and our children Robert and Victoria endured experiments in bicultural living. We invented our own ways of being American and Italian at the same time.

Jesuits taught me to study the epic verse of Homer and Vergil. *Ellis Island* is nothing like what they hoped a student might make of that study, but the bad surprise is always a chance that teachers have to take. There are many other poetic debts I need to record, and you can find good deal about them on ellisislandpoem.com under "Two Kinds of Text." Three generations of scholars have taught me innumerable things about the contingencies that we refer to when we say "the mass migration" — everything from its economics and its naval architecture to its aspirations and sorrows. I have recorded my debts to these scholars in the "Acknowledgements" to *Buried Caesars, and Other Secrets of Italian American Writing.*

The poem itself is the voice of one struggling to overcome a chronic condition. It never stops talking about getting better. It has been good company nonetheless, and I owe it more than I have been able to give.

Robert Viscusi is a poet, essayist, and novelist who teaches English and directs the Wolfe Institute for the Humanities at Brooklyn College. His published works include the mathematical poem "Dodecahedron" (0 to 9, 1966), a critical study *Max Beerbohm, or the Dandy Dante: Rereading with Mirrors* (Johns Hopkins UP, 1986), the long poem *An Oration upon the Most Recent Death of Christopher Columbus* (Bordighera, 1993), *Astoria: A Novel* (Guernica, 1995), a book of poems *A New Geography of Time* (Guernica, 2004), a literary history *Buried Caesars, and Other Secrets of Italian American Writing* (SUNY P, 2006), and many essays on topics of literary and cultural interest. *Ellis Island* is being published in a bilingual edition by abrigliasciolta editore (Varese), with Italian translations by the poet Sandro Sardella. His awards include a National Endowment for the Humanities Fellowship, a Calandra Institute Fellowship, an American Book Award, the Gladiatore D'Oro of Benevento, the Fante/DiDonato Award of the New York State Sons of Italy, and the Premio Giuseepe Acerbi of the Fondazione Giusepe Acerbi, Castelgoffredo. He is a member of OpLePo (Opificio di Letteratura Potenziale [Napoli]), a union of scholars of poetry and mathematics, inspired by the OuLiPo (Ouvroir de Littérature Potentielle [Paris]).

A kaleidoscopic autopsy on the Italian American soul. A centrifuge of consciousness. "*deep in my eyes you see via appia antica run backwards to the sea*" Viscusi lines hyperspace from tender concrete detail to the sage metaphysical. "*like cards in a deck being thumbed universes fan out so fast you can't see them.*" These sonnets contain parables and allegories filled with surrealismo philosophy of space and time dimension. "*there is more dark matter than anything else but you can't see it*" "*close your eyes and think about that for fifteen minutes*" Viscusi is Marco Polo to our Italian American psyche. His lines pierce as stage directions for the reader's life at this exact moment. "*keep asking but you can best tune the instrument you actually play*" There are thousands of fortune cookies in here. "*a good night's sleep under an artful quilt can soften your wounded heart.*" The ocean is Viscusi's online random sonnet generator, churning out an infinite number of sonnets like a one-armed bandit. Let it give you what it will. The book you hold in your hands is the island the ocean charges into. Read it through. Then read it front and back toward the middle. After reading this book I am left with the realization that I am a poet because it is the only way to struggle as much as my grandparents did on the barren *mezzogiornese* fields that turned their back on them for political reasons. Any other life would be too easy. Any cubicle. Any bay. You will sing this book like a rock song. "*i am looking for the freedom I have had all along*"

— Annie Lanzillotto, poet and playwright,
author of *Confessions of a Bronxtomboy* and
How To Wake Up a Marine in a Foxhole

[Robert Viscusi's ELLIS ISLAND is a remarkable project, and there is a lot of remarkable poetry to be found here.] In the half-mad tradition of the Italian Futurists (Marinetti et al.) Ted Berrigan, and the brilliant scribblers of OULIPO, Robert Viscusi has concocted a wonderful machine for generating sonnets, an effort that reproduces the equally demented project of Ellis Island itself as a venue for the introduction of myriad peoples into the vastness of this unknown, perhaps unknowable land. Not particularly optimistic in its tenor, Viscusi's rotating island is nevertheless cheerful, brave-hearted and irrepressibly adventurous: 22/8 begins *If you do what you want to do will you burn in hell for it,* and ends 13 lines later in: *like cards in a deck being thumbed universes fan out so fast you can't see them. . . .* What better way, both as indictment on and doxology, can one imagine apropos of These States as they emerged into what they are now?

—Mac Wellman, poet and playwright,
author of *Murder of Crows* and
Description Beggared or the Allegory of WHITENESS

Robert Viscusi's *Ellis Island* is an American epic; it is both a personal and universal exploration of journeys. It speaks of immigrants and the children of immigrants; it speaks of America and American dreams and the way that those dreams both came true and failed. It is the story of one man and his family and it is the story of all of us. It speaks of interior and exterior journeys. It speaks of place and home. It is written as a series of interconnected sonnets, each of which can stand alone. It is brilliant, witty, sardonic, moving, intelligent insightful. In this book Viscusi proves himself to be the Alexander Pope of Italian American poetry. *Ellis Island* is truly an American masterpiece.

— Maria Mazziotti Gillan, poet, author of
What We Pass On: Collected Poems 1980–2009;
Barnes & Noble Writers for Writers Award, 2011

Viscusi gives us fifty-two books of lost grandeur, homelessness, haunting and sadness, resilience, humor, fitful protest, wise comfort, and, not least, appalling beauty. You don't have to be Italian; you have only to be among the multitudes "too changed to go home." This is a philosophical, even metaphysical epic, yet it springs directly from the craggy earth, trellised in sturdy truths, rough-hewn and hard-won. *Ellis Island* speaks eloquently to any individual, any people, any nation possessed of — and dispossessed by — a history that is proud and unjust.

— Matthew Frye Jacobson, author of
Special Sorrows and *Barbarian Virtues*

More than two years in the making, Robert Viscusi's *Ellis Island* is a *tour de force* of history, language, memory, allegory, generosity and wonder. Let's start with generosity: Viscusi gives us several Ellis Islands. There is the stable, printed text of *Ellis Island,* a long poem of 624 sonnets which you, the reader, can hold in your hands. Then there is the constantly shifting Web-based text that exists digitally, and can be rearranged by you, the reader, using the random sonnet generator feature. Book and site, then, join with the geographically located place to form an allegory: an imaginary space of history, language, memory, and wonder. Whether you hold this *magnum opus* in your hands or view it on a screen, you participate, over and over, in that wonder.

— Sharon Mesmer, poet, author of
Half Angel, Half Lunch and *The Virgin Formica*

VIA FOLIOS

A refereed book series dedicated to the culture of Italian Americans in North America.

ELENA GIANINI BELOTTI, *The Bitter Taste of Strangers Bread,* Vol. 73, Fiction, $24

PINO APRILE, *Terroni,* Vol. 72, Ethnic/Cultural Studies, $20

EMANUEL DI PASQUALE, *Harvest,* Vol. 71, Poetry, $10

ROBERT ZWEIG, *Return to Naples,* Vol. 70, Memoir, $16

LETIZIA AIROS AND OTTORINO CAPELLI, eds., *Guido,* Vol. 69, Italian American Studies, $12

FRED GARDAPHÉ, *Moustache Pete Is Dead! Long Live Moustache Pete!*Vol. 67,
     Literature/Oral History, $12

PAOLO RUFFILI, *Camera oscura,* Vol. 66, Poetry, $10

HELEN BAROLINI, *Crossing the Alps,* Vol. 65, Fiction, $14

COSMO FERRARA, *Profiles of Italian Americans,* Vol. 64, Italian American Studies, $16

GIL FAGIANI, *Chianti in Connecticut,* Vol. 63, Poetry, $10

PIERO BASSETTI AND NICCOLÓ D'AQUINO, *Italic Lessons,* Vol. 62, Ital. Amer. Studies, $10

CAVALIERI & PASCARELLI, eds. *The Poet's Cookbook,* Vol. 61, Recipes/Poetry, $12

EMANUEL DI PASQUALE, *Siciliana,* Vol. 60, Poetry, $8

NATALIA COSTA-ZALESSOW, ED., *Bufalini,* Vol. 59, Poetry, $18

RICHARD VETERE, *Baroque,* Vol. 58, Fiction, $18

LEWIS TURCO, *La Famiglia/The Family,* Vol. 57, Memoir, $15

NICK JAMES MILETI, *The Unscrupulous,* Vol. 56, Humanities, $20

BASSETTI, ACCOLLA, D'AQUINO, *Italici: An Encounter with Piero Bassetti,* Vol. 55, Ital. Studies, $8

GIOSE RIMANELLI, *The Three-legged One,* Vol. 54, Fiction, $15

CHARLES KLOPP, *Bele Antiche Stòrie,* Vol. 53, Criticism, $25

JOSEPH RICAPITO, *Second Wave,* Vol. 52, Poetry, $12

GARY MORMINO, *Italians in Florida,* Vol. 51, History, $15

GIANFRANCO ANGELUCCI, *Federico F.,* Vol. 50, Fiction, $15

ANTHONY VALERIO, *The Little Sailor,* Vol. 49, Memoir, $9

ROSS TALARICO, *The Reptilian Interludes,* Vol. 48, Poetry, $15

RACHEL GUDIO DEVRIES, *Teeny Tiny Tino's Fishing Story,* Vol. 47, Children's Lit., $6

EMANUEL DI PASQUALE, *Writing Anew,* Vol. 46, Poetry, $15

MARIA FAMÀ, *Looking for Cover,* Vol. 45, Poetry, $12

ANTHONY VALERIO, *Toni Cade Bambara's One Sicilian Night,* Vol. 44, Poetry, $10

EMANUEL CARNEVALI, Dennis Barone, ed., *Furnished Rooms,* Vol. 43, Poetry, $14

BRENT ADKINS, ET AL., EDS. *Shifting Borders, Negotiating Places,* Vol. 42, Proceedings, $18

GEORGE GUIDA, *Low Italian,* Vol. 41, Poetry, $11

GARDAPHÉ, GIORDANO, TAMBURRI, *Introducing Italian Americana,* Vol. 40, Ital. Amer. Studies, $10

DANIELA GIOSEFFI, *Blood Autumn/Autunno di sangue,* Vol. 39, Poetry, $15/$25

FRED MISURELLA, *Lies to Live by,* Vol. 38, Stories, $15

STEVEN BELLUSCIO, *Constructing a Bibliography,* Vol. 37, Italian Americana, $15

ANTHONY J. TAMBURRI, ED., *Italian Cultural Studies 2002,* Vol. 36, Essays, $18

BEA TUSIANI, *con amore,* Vol. 35, Memoir, $19

FLAVIA BRIZIO-SKOV, ED., *Reconstructing Societies in the Aftermath of War,* Vol. 34, History, $30

TAMBURRI, ET AL., EDS., *Italian Cultural Studies 2001,* Vol. 33, Essays, $18

ELIZABETH G. MESSINA, ED., *In Our Own Voices,* Vol. 32, Ital. Amer. Studies, $25

STANISLAO G. PUGLIESE, *Desperate Inscriptions,* Vol. 31, History, $12

HOSTERT AND TAMBURRI, EDS., *Screening Ethnicity,* Vol. 30, Italian American Culture, $25

PARATI AND LAWTON, EDS., *Italian Cultural Studies,* Vol. 29, Essays, $18

HELEN BAROLINI, *More Italian Hours,* Vol. 28, Fiction, $16

FRANCO NASI, ED., *Intorno alla Via Emilia,* Vol. 27, Culture, $16

ARTHUR L. CLEMENTS, *The Book of Madness & Love,* Vol. 26, Poetry, $10

JOHN CASEY, ET AL., *Imagining Humanity,* Vol. 25, Interdisciplinary Studies, $18

ROBERT LIMA, *Sardinia/Sardegna,* Vol. 24, Poetry, $10

DANIELA GIOSEFFI, *Going On,* Vol. 23, Poetry, $10

ROSS TALARICO, *The Journey Home,* Vol. 22, Poetry, $12

EMANUEL DI PASQUALE, *The Silver Lake Love Poems,* Vol. 21, Poetry, $7

Joseph Tusiani, *Ethnicity,* Vol. 20, Poetry, $12

Jennifer Lagier, *Second-Class Citizen,* Vol. 19, Poetry, $8

Felix Stefanile, *The Country of Absence,* Vol. 18, Poetry, $9

Philip Cannistraro, *Blackshirts,* Vol. 17, History, $12

Luigi Rustichelli, ed., *Seminario sul racconto,* Vol. 16, Narrative, $10

Lewis Turco, *Shaking the Family Tree,* Vol. 15, Memoirs, $9

Luigi Rustichelli, ed., *Seminario sulla drammaturgia,* Vol. 14, Theater/Essays, $10

Fred Gardaphè, *Moustache Pete Is Dead! Long Live Moustache Pete!,* Vol. 13, Oral Lit., $10

Jone Gaillard Corsi, *Il libretto d'autore, 1860–1930,* Vol. 12, Criticism, $17

Helen Barolini, *Chiaroscuro: Essays of Identity,* Vol. 11, Essays, $15

Picarazzi and Feinstein, eds., *An African Harlequin in Milan,* Vol. 10, Theater/Essays, $15

Joseph Ricapito, *Florentine Streets & Other Poems,* Vol. 9, Poetry, $9

Fred Misurella, *Short Time,* Vol. 8, Novella, $7

Ned Condini, *Quartettsatz,* Vol. 7, Poetry, $7

Anthony J. Tamburri, ed., *Fuori: Essays by Italian/American Lesbians and Gays,* Vol. 6, Essays, $10

Antonio Gramsci, P. Verdicchio, Trans. & Introd., *The Southern Question,* Vol. 5, Soc. Crit., $5

Daniela Gioseffi, *Word Wounds & Water Flowers,* Vol. 4, Poetry, $8

Wiley Feinstein, *Humility's Deceit: Calvino Reading Ariosto Reading Calvino,* Vol. 3, Criticism, $10

Paolo A. Giordano, ed., *Joseph Tusiani: Poet, Translator, Humanist,* Vol. 2, Criticism, $25

Robert Viscusi, *Oration Upon the Most Recent Death of Christopher Columbus,* Vol. 1, Poetry, $3

Bordighera Press is an imprint of Bordighera, Incorporated, an independently owned not-for-profit scholarly organization that has no legal affiliation with the University of Central Florida or with The John D. Calandra Italian American Institute, Queens College/CUNY.

CPSIA information can be obtained at www.ICGtesting.com
Printed in the USA
BVOW051503090413

317718BV00003B/5/P

9 781599 540337